WOMEN IN ENGLISH RELIGION
1700 - 1925

WOMEN IN ENGLISH RELIGION
1700 - 1925

Dale A. Johnson

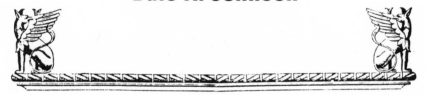

Studies in Women and Religion

Volume 10

The Edwin Mellen Press
New York and Toronto

Library of Congress Cataloging in Publication Data

Main entry under title:

Women in English religion, 1700-1925.

    (Studies in women and religion ; v. 10)
    Bibliography: p.
    Includes index.
    1. Women in Christianity--England--History--Sources.
2. Women--England--Religious life--Sources. 3. Women
clergy--England--History--Sources. 4. England--Church
history. I. Johnson, Dale A., 1936-   . II. Series.
BR758.W65 1983   280'.088042   83-12124
ISBN 0-88946-539-8

Studies in Women and Religion   ISBN 0-88946-549-5

    The Edwin Mellen Press
    P.O. Box 450
    Lewiston, New York 14092

Permission has been granted to reprint portions of *The Letters of John Wesley*, edited by John Telford (London: The Epworth Press, 1931) and Maude Petre, *My Way of Faith* (London: J.M. Dent & Sons, Ltd., 1937).

Printed in the United States of America

In a year of special anniversaries,
to my mother and father
and to Norma

PREFACE

Each person will have his or her own stories of raised consciousness with respect to issues relating to women. Some of mine had to do with language. While working on another topic a few years ago I found an early twentieth-century study entitled *Men of Fire, and Consecrated Women Also.* If the author had a problem with the title, he did at least want to acknowledge the contributions of women to the beginnings of Primitive Methodism! From this encounter and others it was no longer possible to accept the notion that the word "man" is generic or that the language question is unimportant. Other developments followed, frequently spurred by the documents included in this book.

No historical research could be done without the assistance and support of libraries and librarians. I am particularly grateful for the use of materials and the work of individuals at the Vanderbilt University Library; the Bodleian Library of Oxford University; the Oxford libraries of Manchester College, Mansfield College, and Pusey House; the British Library; and the Fawcett Library, London. I owe much to the students in the initial seminar which used the documents, especially for their interest and their lively engagement with the issues that emerged from the sources. Tracey Harris DeVol performed valuable research assistance, read drafts of the materials, and offered helpful criticism. Once again John Walsh gave advice and suggestions on several dimensions of the topic. The Vanderbilt Research Council provided financial support for the project. Bill Hook very generously introduced me to the mysteries of word-processing. Finally, my thanks to the editor of this series, Elizabeth Clark, and to Herbert Richardson for the encouragement they gave to a very preliminary idea.

Dale A. Johnson
Nashville, TN
February, 1983

CONTENTS

WOMEN IN ENGLISH RELIGION
1700 - 1925

INTRODUCTION

Investigations into the activities of women and perceptions of womanhood in various historical contexts increased dramatically in the past decade. Religious dimensions of these topics have been included along with political and social history, but American themes and issues have received more attention than, for example, the English or continental European. Much more research is needed to explore this neglected area. This effort at a documentary history aims both to introduce readers to the issues of one particular period and encourage further reflection on topics within it.

In English religious history, as in much other, it has been relatively common to construct a narrative without much regard for women. With the ministry, religious leadership, and academic theological work almost exclusively a male enterprise, this is not surprising. But if the perspective is shifted slightly, a very different picture emerges. Similarly, if one looks for direct engagements by church bodies or congregations on the question of roles of women in church and society, not much will be found, and some of that will be misleading. But if one seeks to discover the ways in which religion has influenced perceptions of womanhood, the understandings of woman's "proper" role, and the like, shaping views that have been prevalent to the present day, a much wider and more significant set of materials is opened.

Limiting dates for this study are approximate, but provide reasonable boundaries for such an investigation. The beginning date puts us beyond the English Civil War and its aftermath, the decline of radical movements, and the first generation of Quakers, in which significant roles were played by women but which, save for the Quakers, did not continue in a major way into the eighteenth century.[1] The *terminus ad quem* enables us to consider the climax of the suffrage movement and the impact it had on such questions as the involvement of women in the governance of the church and ordination of women to the ministry. Within this period an "ideal of womanhood" developed which depended greatly upon a religious foundation. Feminist critique of the ideal from within and outside of the churches was not widely heard, but the debate as it was engaged provides insight into the historical context of ideas.

Additional interesting though frequently obscured topics become visible in such a study. Under the broad theme of relationships between religion and society one can consider diverse issues as the nature of the family and its religious underpinnings or the involvement of women in social reform movements. Within the churches themselves there are developments concerning the character of a "female piety" or affinity for religion, possibilities of female preaching, the participation of women in new religious movements, and support for as well as opposition to the ordination of women. On all these questions there was considerable discussion, although it was clearly not a case of unrelenting progress toward equality.

Two particular benefits from this study can be noted. One has been called "contribution history," which seeks to enlarge horizons by exploring the life and work of people whose efforts had a certain importance in their lifetimes but have been lost from view in later study of the period.[2] In situations where church histories have been written without respect to women, "contribution history" is a necessary activity. To place in history the work of such individuals as Mary Astell, Mary Bosanquet Fletcher, Joanna Southcott, Elizabeth Fry, Catherine Booth, Frances Power Cobbe, Mother Lydia Sellon, Mary Sumner, and Maude Royden, to name just a few, not only gives neglected people their due and enriches the fabric of understanding, but provides insights into the problems and possibilities faced by women. Later generations can find their work and their struggles instructive. One can learn, for example, not only about Elizabeth Fry and her society for the visitation of prisoners, but also what she experienced in doing the work—opposition from home and religious community, hostility from magistrates and prison wardens, and personal anguish in being a woman involved in a public issue. And one can learn about Florence Nightingale's frustrations over the lack of opportunities for exercising her religious vocation as well as about her accomplishments in the profession of nursing.

But "contribution history" takes one only so far. Concentrating on the work of some individual women can skew the larger picture—of those who filled the pews and taught the Sunday School classes, who participated in the charitable and reform work of nineteenth-century voluntary societies, or who by virtue of class or social position did not have the opportunities others had. Further, in the church, one wants to know what people heard from the pulpit or read in religious books and tracts, what models of Christian existence were held out for women, and what views on womanhood were discussed in the congregations in any particular period. Part of the larger picture, then, are the issues and the contexts of discussion that bequeath to us the burdens of the past.

Where, for example, does the "separate spheres" notion have its grounding? In God's law, biological nature, or culture? It affects perceptions of appropriate work, education, and worth. Although present much earlier, of course, its full flowering occurred in our period. We want to know not only what went into such views and what the impact was, but also why so many who devoted themselves to the women's cause also held pieces of the "separate spheres" understanding.

More particularly, concerning religion, how did it come about that women were regarded as more moral and more religious than men, and what are the implications of this widely held view? If women were the majority of the congregations, as they were said to be from the eighteenth century, why were they kept from leadership roles? More than simply the Pauline injunctions against female leadership, is it, as some have argued, that the collapse of the church's public significance gave women too much control over religion already?[3]

Several monumental developments beginning at the end of the seventeenth century and continuing over the next two centuries overlapped and affected one another. One can point to a diminished role of the church in society and an increased attention to the personal dimensions of faith; the corresponding rise of a secular spirit, giving more value to the things of this world and fostering even a sacred/secular split in certain segments of society; and the gradual movement from an agricultural to an industrial or business economy. In the face of all this, what happened to religion? One answer is that it was given to the women, as well as to the clergy. That is to say, women are the religious persons in the family; they do not have to fight in the marketplace for a living or confront evil and corruption at every turn. They can provide solace and comfort for the husband, nurture for the children in the faith, and a refuge from the onslaughts of the secular spirit which society desperately needed. Thus, women are more moral and more religious than men. Thus also, the strongest point to be made about the woman's place being in the home is that it is a religious argument.

The following chapters provide contexts for viewing the contributions of women to and within English religion as well as the burdens they experienced which have become part of the legacy of the past to the present. More of the documents represent ideas rather than action. Some inferences concerning action or impact can be drawn from the lives of the authors or from the popularity of a particular work, but less is known as to how widely these views influenced readers or hearers. Research on several dimensions of the topic is needed. It is obvious that religious views confirmed social understandings of relations between men and women, perhaps even shaped them. That connection certainly retarded revision of the ideal and change in the patterns of relationship; the influence of the past on present understandings of this matter is broad and deep. But one of the uses of historical study is to make clear at what points and to what extent one will not be content with the legacy of the past. Another is to be able to locate the core of the problem. Confronting the arguments, both positive and negative, that contributed to the subjection of women can help to free one from them. Understanding their implications can heighten one's sensitivity to present issues. To these ends, as well as to the more traditional ends of historical investigation, this volume is offered.

CHAPTER 1

PATTERNS AND PERSPECTIVES, 1700 - 1815

Is it war? One can hardly be surprised if many thought so, given some of the arguments offered during the eighteenth century on two closely related topics, the nature of womanhood and the relation of women to religion. In this introduction we will explore one dimension of each topic and then consider some implications of their association, allowing the several documents to extend the discussion further.

From Mary Astell and before to John Bowdler and after, the issue of education for women was prominent in the discussion of woman's nature. Too often, however, contention, satire, and fear of change set the tone; certainly more questions were raised than answered in the reflection. What kind of education? How much? What possible uses or implications for society did it portend? More bluntly, and related to the basic issue, what would happen if women advance? Quite simply, it could damage or destroy the precarious but finely-tuned, eternally grounded pattern of relationships that all the world (or so it was thought) knew! God's will, social order, and control of sexuality were all involved in any small shift in the condition of woman, who was ruled but also reigned, as Samuel Wesley, Jr. implied in the poem he entitled "The Battle of the Sexes."[1]

What would happen if women advance? Male writers were quick with answers. They will assert authority over men, leave husbands and children, foster heresy, and upset society's balance in seeking the impossible. Worse, they will become unsexed; that is, they will cast off their feminine virtues and seek to become like men.[2] From such a view suggestions on education for women were very cautious, indeed. In addition to assaults as these came satires on women for being frivolous, occupied with trivialities, and only interested in such entertainments as music and dance. John Stuart Mill later aptly commented, "Men thought it a clever thing to insult women for what men made them."[3] He could have added that many of these same men compounded the problem by ridiculing attempts to alter what they themselves had criticised. That approach to the question put women in a no-win situation, damned for living up to society's expectations and damned for trying to change them.

Before our period, of course, some notable women had received a substantial education in their homes or educated themselves, making a mark in the social or literary world. But from the late seventeenth century more women took up this particular issue than ever before.[4] The attacks thus received replies, and language escalated on both sides. Against charges of insufficient intelligence, excessive credulity, or other accusations of defective nature, critics were told that the condition of women had been determined by historical limitation, social exclusion, and inadequate education. Men were responsible for this, and it could be changed. The interest in education as the most important solution shared in the century's increased confidence in human capacities. Of many replies, Mary Wollstonecraft's was the most thorough; the causes of women's degraded position, she argued, "all spring from want of understanding." Her opponents assumed that intelligence and virtue were correlated to one's sex, but neglected how these were determined by social expectations and oppression. Wollstonecraft agreed that women may have different duties than men; "but they are *human* duties," she added, "and the principles that should regulate the discharge of them . . .   must be the same." Two things must therefore change before woman could truly be a "helpmeet" to man; men had to understand the reasons for women's condition, and women had to receive an education commensurate with their "human" condition.[5]

Fundamental questions require answers based on fundamentals, and thus the question of woman's nature led inevitably, for that time, to the religious framework for an answer. When one can discover at least three different creation motifs in the literature, one sees that even the eternally grounded pattern of relationships was a disputed item! Because of this plurality biblical imagery itself became part of the weapons of warfare.

The most widespread motif made the subordination of women part of "the nature of things" established in creation and thus not subject to change. It is perhaps best stated by John Milton in *Paradise Lost*:

Two of far nobler shape, erect and tall,
God-like erect, with native honour clad,
In naked majesty seemed lords of all,
And worthy seemed; for in their looks divine
The image of their glorious Maker shone,
Truth, wisdom, sanctitude severe and pure—
Severe, but in true filial freedom placed,
Whence true authority in men; though both
Not equal, as their sex not equal seemed:
For contemplation he and valour formed,
For softness she and sweet attractive grace;
He for God only, she for God in him.[6]

Milton here described life in Eden before the temptation and fall. Man and woman each possessed the image of God; thus, the argument went, subordination did not imply inferiority. But they were not equal, for sex differences determined both character and task; and they related to God differently. Elaborations sought support in the creation story of Genesis 2. There, by taking a mere rib from man to make woman, God demonstrated both the priority of man and the weakness of woman. As one writer put it, God "left it frail and full of foibles, as he first found it when he riddled Adam's noble composition of it."[7] Genesis 3, the fall, only confirmed what had been determined in creation.

Implicit in this motif was a hierarchical model of society. With God above all creation, the king represented this authority in the nation and the husband/father in the home. The minister did the same in the church. If Milton had his personal difficulties with royal and ecclesiastical authority, he had none with respect to the domestic scene. Eve's statement to Adam affirmed both the hierarchy and the theological priority of man:

> God is thy law, thou mine; to know no more
> Is woman's happiest knowledge and her praise.[8]

If others were less explicitly theological in their understanding of the hierarchies, they were no less aware of the theological connections to their argument that without such controls there would be social chaos. Thus any claim to altered status or greater opportunities by women could be and often was taken as a challenge to the entire social system. For example, Lucifer's rebellion against God was made analogous to the rebellion of women "against the natural Lords, to whom God made them subject here on earth."[9]

Two other understandings stood in sharp opposition to this view of creation and its implications for men and women. One was offered by the Quakers and involved the entire process of salvation, not just creation. At creation man and woman were equal, intended by God to share the responsibilities for life. The basis for this was the narrative of Genesis 1. George Fox declared, "God said to them 'have dominion;' he did not say to them 'do thou have dominion without thy wife,' but he said to *them* 'have dominion,' to *them* 'be fruitful,' etc., and to them all was blessed and good and they good also. Here was a blessed concord and unity. Man was blessed and so was woman, and all things was blessed unto them."[10] But the fall destroyed this condition of blessedness, and God's punishment for human sin included expulsion from the garden and the subordination of woman to man. This state of existence continued until "the seed of the woman," namely Jesus Christ, came to break the power of the serpent and restore man and woman to equality and blessedness in the image of God. Once again they are able to be "meet helps" to each other. This is confirmed in the event of the resurrection, where women were the first to report it: "when they came into the belief of it, male and female believed; so both are one in Christ Jesus, and all can praise God together."[11]

Some women writers in opposing the male-dominant view presented a third creation motif, arguing for the equality, even the superiority, of woman to man. They appealed to Genesis 1 and even used St. Paul against St. Paul (e.g., that I Cor. 11 counters I Cor. 14, showing both sexes to be mutually dependent and equally subject to God). But the argument took a new twist, in that the chronology of Genesis 2 was used to prove the latter creation (woman) more complete than the former: "how much more natural it is to conjecture that man being form'd a mere rough draught of that finished creature woman, God snatch'd from the lumpish thing the few graces and perfections he found in it, to add them to the many he design'd to enrich her with." If, then, man is held to be superior to the rest of creation because he was not created until they were ready for him, it must equally follow that "man was made for the woman's use and not she for his."[12]

Religious people in the century very largely embraced the first creation motif, with its attendant implications for relations between men and women. Some tried to work within the general framework of this view, while at the same time criticising certain dimensions of it. The more radical third view was not heard in the churches. Its implications for social transformation were even more sharply rejected in the fears sparked by the French Revolution (thus Wollstonecraft's inability to receive a hearing). Models held out for women in the churches stressed obedience, sacrificial devotion, and private philanthropies. Female preaching was limited to the Quakers and dismissed by the rest as contrary to scripture or simply peculiar.[13] The great majority of people accepted the Pauline injunctions against women speaking in churches and assuming authority over men (I Cor. 14 and I Tim. 2). No doubt the distant memories of radical women preachers in the 1640s had an impact as well,[14] linking concern over education, attention to religious foundations, and fears of societal disruption into one dominant point of view.

Women's place on the fringes of Protestantism, without an opportunity for service in a religious order, had an additional rationale. Again, Genesis was used to argue that woman had been the one more easily tempted, the more likely to be in league with the devil, the one who bore the burden and blame for sexual sin. From *Malleus Maleficarum* (1484) to the persecutions and trials of the sixteenth and seventeenth centuries, women were thought much more likely than men to be witches.[15] Although witchcraft ceased to be regarded as a threat in the eighteenth century, association of the phenomenon with women continued among the common people, emerging only occasionally, as in the case of Joanna Southcott at the end of the century, to public view.

Despite the continuation of the suspicions, prohibitions, and war of words, a gradual transformation took place over the century on the questions of the nature of womanhood and the relation of women to religion which was both subtle and profound. Even on the question of the biblical sanctions small openings were made. John Locke was one early biblical critic who determined that I Cor. 11 put I Cor. 14 in a clearer context: women did prophesy and pray in the assemblies, but they did so while retaining a mark of their subordination. Thus, he said, the prohibitions of I Cor. 14 applied "only to reasoning and purely voluntary discourse," and women were free to speak "where they had an immediate impulse and revelation from the spirit of God."[16] Locke thus modified the framework of the first creation motif without overturning it. Later writers appealed to his authority as well as to his distinction between having an extraordinary call or commission from God and not having one,[17] and the argument also became important for John Wesley (see chapter 2).

This transformation is more easily seen in the growing number of claims to a special relation between women and religion. It was a far cry from the medieval and early modern suspicions. But now Christianity was on the defensive, having suffered political setbacks resulting in a gradual disengagement of government's support for the Church of England, criticism from deists, and increasing casualness in the society at large with respect to matters of faith. In this context women became central to the very continuation of Christianity. Their character as persons of the heart, motivated by love, seemed to fit the subject. The question of their intelligence, or their deficiency here, seemed not to matter. In fact, many argued that it was impossible to imagine a woman as an unbeliever; not so for men.

So over the course of the century women came to be regarded as preservers of religion in the home (traditionally the father's role) and urged to be visible models of faithfulness and piety. The contributions of William Law, James Fordyce, Hannah More, and others made the connection real in the minds of church people, as the frequent reprinting of their works testifies. Yet this positive reconstruction, even though significant, was only a subtle modification of the first creation motif. There, women were subordinate in a religious framework. Later, when they were made guardians of religious faith, religion itself had lost its prominence within culture— to business or to reason. And men were given charge over these. Thus, the shift for women did not alter their own subordinate status in relation to men, even though they could be honored as their equals, even their superiors, in religious faith. An additional wall had been built in the "separate sphere" for women, which because of its religious foundation was particularly hard to tear down.

1. [Mary Astell], *The Christian Religion, as Profess'd by a Daughter of the Church of England* (London, 1705), pp. 6-7, 36-40, 102-04, 292-93, 295-97. (Capitalizations and spellings modified according to current usage.)

In the latter half of the seventeenth century a number of women achieved some measure of notoriety by arguing for women's right to greater education. Mary Astell (1666-1731) was one of them.[18] Their argument went as follows: if women are not naturally defective in relation to men in soul or body, one must look elsewhere to explain woman's subordinate position and limited accomplishments. That explanation is found in the fact that women have been industriously kept in ignorance by men, thus creating a subjection which neither nature nor God had intended.[19] "Were the men as much neglected, and as little care taken to cultivate and improve them," claimed Astell, "perhaps they would be so far from surpassing those whom they now despise, that they themselves would sink into the greatest stupidity and brutality."[20] The solution was wider opportunities for education, to the end that women might make greater contributions to church and society and not be distracted by frivolities from their more serious duties. Astell proposed to establish a "monastery," which had the double purpose of freeing women for a time from the temptations of the world and enabling them to concentrate on learning. The idea was not pursued by her or others, but it did become the basis of one line of reflection over the next century concerning the source of women's difficulties and appropriate ways of addressing them.

Astell's proposals had a strong religious dimension. She believed that education in the Christian faith would keep women from being susceptible to doubt or error. Besides, women are needed for the current defense of the faith, and they can do that without losing their distinctive qualities. In *The Christian Religion* she contended that such new opportunities would not lead to any rejection of existing church authority or any attempt to change the church's God-given structure. But within this essentially conservative stance emerged a rather bold claim: that since men have an active life engaged with the world and women seem more suited to a life of contemplation, it is women who more appropriately could be the church's theologians.

If God had not intended that women should use their reason, he would not have given them any, for he does nothing in vain. If they are to use their reason, certainly it ought to be employed about the noblest objects, and in business of the greatest consequence, therefore in religion. That our godfathers and godmothers answered for us at the font, was an act of charity in them, and will be a great benefit to us if we make a right use of it; but it will be our condemnation if we are Christians merely upon this account, for that only can be imputed to a free agent which is done with understanding and choice. A Christian woman therefore must not be a child in understanding; she must serve God with understanding as well as with affection, must love him with all her mind and soul, as well as with all her heart and strength; in a word, must perform a reasonable service if she means to be acceptable to her maker.

I am a Christian then, and a member of the Church of England, not because I was born in England, and educated by conforming parents, but because I have, according to the best of my understanding, and with some application and industry, examined the doctrine and precepts of Christianity, the reasons and authority on which it is built. I say authority, because, though reason will never permit me to submit to any mere human authority, yet there is not anything more reasonable than to submit entirely to that authority, which I find upon a strict enquiry, has all the evidences that reason can ask, to prove that it is divine. Reason is that light which God himself has set up in my mind to lead me to him, I will therefore follow it so far as it can conduct me. And as for further illumination, as it would be the height of folly and a great injury to myself to reject it, so it would be the utmost ingratitude to Almighty God not to be thankful for it. Let me see then how far reason can carry me, and next what further light God has been pleased to afford.

. . .   most of, if not all, the follies and vices that women are subject to, (for I meddle not with the men) are owing to our paying too great a deference to other people's judgments, and too little to our own, in suffering others to judge for us, when God has not only allowed, but required us to judge for ourselves.

How those who have made themselves our governors, may like our withdrawing from their yoke I know not; but I am certain that this principle of judging for ourselves in all cases wherein God has left us this liberty, will introduce no disorder into the world or disobedience to our lawful governors. Rather, it will teach us to be as tractable and submissive to just authority, as we are careful to judge rightly for ourselves, in such matters wherein God has not appointed any to judge for us. The insinuations of those who have no right to be our directors, but who have only usurped an empire over our understandings, being one of the principal causes of our disobedience to lawful authority. Both by their rendering us disaffected to our proper governors, as is their usual practice, that so they themselves may entirely command us: and also because sooner or later we shall be convinced of the dishonour and damage of being any one's property, and thence grow suspicious of, and uneasy at the just commands of those who have a right to prescribe in some cases. . . .

But how much soever I am, and I am as much as anyone can be, against private doctors and directors, who are often but corrupt and muddy streams which withdraw us from that well of life that is freely offered to all who will apply themselves to it; false lights who lead us into by-paths and turn our eyes from that Sun of Righteousness, which enlightens everyone who humbly and reverently looks up to him; and am of opinion that guides, though when prudently chosen they may be of excellent use to men, can never unless upon an extraordinary occasion, and under great caution, be proper for women because of scandal; yet none can pay a greater deference to the church universal, or to that particular national church, by whose charity through the blessing of God, I am a member of the Catholic or Universal Church, the body of Christ. Who has been pleased to constitute a Church, and had ordained an order of men to admit into this society and to shut out of it, to govern and direct, and to minister to all its wants, as it is a spiritual community; as the scripture teaches us, and as is also evident from the reason of things. For there must of necessity be an established government, where there is a formed society; nor can it be imagined that the God of order, the wisdom of the Father, by whose commission temporal governments are settled for the good of mankind, should leave his church, whom he so dearly loves, in anarchy and confusion, and not constitute divers orders in it, for the work of the ministry, for the edifying of the body in love. And therefore let the men that execute this office be what they may, the order and the authority is God's, and as such I reverence it, considering him who sent them.

So that if through the sublimity of the subject, my ignorance of the sacred languages, of ecclesiastical history, and the ancient usage of the church, any point in controversy be too difficult for me, and that after all my diligence I can't clear up the matter with evidence and certainty, but that all I can attain to is probabilities on both sides: if it is a matter in which a final decision is not necessary, I will suspend my judgment in hopes of further information; but if there is a necessity to determine, I will with all humility submit to God's authority in his church. Not to the man whom I may fancy or choose, for this were to follow my own way and not God's; but to him or them who shall have lawful authority over me. For though they should happen to lead me into error, yet in this case they, and not I, must answer for it; as for me, I am safer in my obedience, than I could have been even with truth in a disorderly way. I will consult the bishop of the diocese in which I live, if it be a matter of great concern; but upon less occasions, the parish priest, to whom he has committed the cure of souls. For it is not because a man talks finely in a pulpit, or has an agreeable way in private conversation, that I depend on him; or because I think he is a man of learning; or which is better, of good sense; or which is best of all, of great integrity of mind, and of an holy and unblemished conversation; but in pure obedience to God, who has commanded me to obey them who have the rule over me, and who watch, or at least ought to watch, for my soul: and in this way because it is his own, I may humbly, yet confidently expect his blessing. . . .

To be a Christian is a greater thing, and a more honourable character than most of us imagine; but as all real honour is attended with difficulty and dangers, so they must not expect to be exempt from combats who engage in the Christian warfare, and list themselves under the banner of a crucified savior. . . . Your ladyship sees I have pursued a warlike metaphor, which we frequently meet with in holy writ. But "the weapons of our warfare are not carnal" (II Cor. 10:4), they enable us indeed to conquer the world, and which is more, ourselves, but all this without doing violence to any person. A woman may "put on the whole armor of God" without degenerating into a masculine temper; she may "take the shield of faith, the sword of the spirit, the helmet of salvation, and the breastplate of righteousness" without any offence to the men, and they become her as well as they do the greatest hero. I could never understand why we are bred cowards; sure it can never be because our masters are afraid we should rebel, for courage would enable us to endure their injuries, to forgive and to despise them! It is indeed so necessary a virtue that we can't be good Christians without it; for till we are got above the fear of death, 'tis in anybody's power to make us renounce our hopes of heaven. And it can't be supposed that men envy us our portion there; since however desirous they are to engross this world they do not seem so covetous of the other. . . .

But to what study shall we apply our selves? Some men say that heraldry is a pretty study for a woman, for this reason, I suppose, that she may know how to blazon her lord and master's great achievements! They allow us poetry, plays, and romances, to divert us and themselves; and when they would express a particular esteem for a woman's sense, they recommend history; though with submission, history can only serve us for amusement and a subject of discourse. For though it may be of use to the men who govern affairs, to know how their forefathers acted, yet what is this to us, who have nothing to do with such business? Some good examples indeed are to be found in history, though generally the bad are ten for one; but how will this help our conduct, or excite in us a generous emulation? since the men being the historians, they seldom condescend to record the great and good actions of women; and when they take notice of them, 'tis with this wise remark, that such women *acted above their sex.* By which one must suppose they would have their readers understand, that they were not women who did those great actions, but that they were men in petticoats!

Speculation is one of the most refined and delicious pleasures, but it is not to be followed only as a pleasure, but as an exercise and duty. There is as great variety in understandings as in faces, they have not all the same beauties nor the same defects, but every genius has its particular turn, and therefore the same course of study is not equally fit for everyone. The business is, to learn the weakness and strength of our minds; to form our judgments, and to render them always just; to know how to discover false reasonings, and to disentangle truth from those mazes of error into which men have hunted her; and whatever method tends to this end ought to be pursued. . . .

It is the misery of our depraved nature to be too fast tied to sensible things, to be strongly, and in a manner wholly affected with them; and whatever loosens this tie and weans us from them, does us a very considerable service. But we are not apt to think so, and have ways to frustrate the advantage might be reapt by speculation. Most men are so sensualized, that they take nothing to be real but what they can hear and see, or which is some way or other the object of their senses. Others who would seem the most refined make sensation the fund of their ideas, carrying their contemplations no farther than these, and the reflections they make upon the operations of their minds when thus employed. Men speculate what will be of use to human life, what will get them a name in the world, and raise them to the posts they covet. But the contemplation of immaterial beings and abstracted truths, which are the noblest objects of the mind, is looked on as chimerical and a sort of madness; and to study to come up to the pure morals of the gospel, is in their account visionary.

Except in the duties of our Christian calling, and the little economies of a house, women's lives are not active, consequently they ought to be contemplative; for I hope our Christian brethren are not of the Turks' opinion, that women have no souls; I heartily wish indeed, that we made more use of them. And since it is allowed on all hands, that the men's business is without doors, and that their's is an active life; women who ought to be retired, are for this reason designed by providence for speculation: providence, which allots every one an employment, and never intended that any one should give themselves up to idleness and unprofitable amusements. . . .

However, not to contest whether learning be their prerogative or our privilege; not to deny their self-evident principle, and therefore what they do not attempt to prove, *that women's understandings are inferior to men's*, though my blind soul can't discern it: since the duties of a Christian are as much our business as theirs, all I shall contend for, is only that we may be suffered to improve our minds so far as this may influence our duty. And had I any interest with my sex, I would humbly entreat them to learn the measures of their duty from the word of God and right reason, not by hearsay.

2. *Woman Triumphant; or, The Excellency of the Female Sex.* By a Lady of Quality (London, 1721), pp. xiv-xv.

Why are women inferior? Those men in the seventeenth and eighteenth centuries who asked the question tended to settle on a biological argument, claiming that women were too delicate, too fine, and too soft to withstand the rigors of scholarship and speculation.[21] The threat that the proposals for the education of women by Mary Astell and others might alter social conventions and take them out of expected roles in marriage and family played a significant part in the development of the biological argument, which was linked with the scriptural argument for female subordination. One response by a few women was a direct counterattack, namely, that women are not only not inferior to men but are in fact superior. It is a mark of the times that most of these claims were made anonymously.

One part of the argument appealed to a social analysis of women's subjugation. Astell had not found history to be instructive because the histories had been written by men and therefore had distorted or ignored the contributions of women.   The fable in *Woman Triumphant* argued more broadly that society's perception of male superiority had been created by the simple fact that men controlled the pen. Another part appealed to biology, arguing from the greater beauty of women "Can we suppose that women have souls any thing inferior to men," the writer asked, "when as I have proved, their bodies are of a more refin'd nature? Or that man who is made of grosser Earth, should be endow'd with a soul superior?" Thus, "it is reasonable to suppose, that women are more penetrating in their judgment, quicker in thought, in reasoning more subtle and cunning, in disputes more warm and vigorous, seeing their spirits are not loaded with such dull and lumpish matter as the men's."[22] One strident claim to counter another! It was not widely heard, even though, as another writer noted, at its root was simply an appeal for greater opportunities to take a more rightful place in society. "I only mean to show my sex," she declared, "that they are not so despicable as the men wou'd have them believe themselves, and that we are as capable of as much greatness of soul as the best of that haughty sex."[23]

For shame ye snarling criticks all forbear,
With envious satyrs to attack the fair;
Scrible no more your doggerel wit to shew,
But give what's justly to our virtue due;
With high encomiums you your own sex praise,
Whilst we who merit are deny'd the bays.
Would you each sex in equal ballance weigh,
Woman's superior worth must gain the day.
But give me leave a fable to relate,

Which will the case between us rightly state.

A lyon ranging in a forrest great,
Happen'd one day a traveller to meet;
Long time there has contention been says he,
'Twixt men and lyons, who the strongest be,
Now we are met let us the cause decide;
The man affrighted, trembling thus reply'd;
Why should we two, for such a triffle strive,
Come, go with me, and e'er that we arrive
Unto the city, I will plainly show,
Man's strength superior; let it then be so,
Answer'd the lyon; and far they had not gone,
Before they saw a figure carv'd in stone;
A man, beneath whose feet a lyon lay:
The traveller crys what have you now to say?
You see a lyon here o'ercome in fight,
Which proves that man is of superior might.

Reply'd the lyon,
Could lyons carve in stone you then should see,
At bottom man, at top the lyon be.

So let our sex be unto learning bred,
Like you in liberal sciences be read;
In one short age the press from our keen wit,
Should out-shine all that men have ever writ.

As women now, so men should truckle then,
Beneath the lashes of each female pen.

3. William Law, *A Serious Call to a Devout and Holy Life* (1728); in *The Works of the Rev. William Law*, 9 vols. (London, 1762), IV: chapters VII-IX, XIX.

The ascetic ideal of the Christian life developed by William Law (1686-1761) depended greatly on female role models. A Cambridge graduate and a nonjuror (he refused to abjure the Stuarts and to swear allegiance to George I), he was first a college fellow and then private tutor to the Edward Gibbon family. While in this latter service he was ordained as priest in the Church of England, wrote *A Treatise upon Christian Perfection* and *A Serious Call*, and founded a school for girls in his native village, to which he returned around 1740. Within three years he was joined by two women, Hester Gibbon and Mrs. Archibald Hutcheson, and the three formed a small community, intending to put into practice the religious life laid out in *A Serious Call*. It was a call to personal holiness, set in contrast to the frivolities and worldliness of contemporary life. The model was proposed for both men and women, but Law implied that this life could only be achieved by withdrawing from the distractions of the world, something more possible for women. Law was also interested in the education of girls, but from a different vantage point than Mary Astell had been. The images of womanhood represented in attention to beauty, dress, and social skills concerned him; not only did they prevent the development of true piety, but they also encouraged society to regard women as "of little and vain minds." This critique of female education would be continued by others; it did not envision greater opportunities for women, but it contributed to the growing recognition that traditional expectations did not take women very seriously.

Chapter VII.

Flavia and Miranda are two maiden sisters, that have each of them two hundred pounds a year. They buried their parents, twenty years ago, and have since that time spent their estate as they pleased.

Flavia has been the wonder of all her friends, for her excellent management, in making so surprising a figure in so moderate a fortune. Several ladies that have twice her fortune, are not able to be always so genteel, and so constant at all places of pleasure and expense. She has everything that is in the fashion, and is in every place where there is any diversion. Flavia is very orthodox, she talks warmly against heretics and schismatics, is generally at church, and often at the sacrament. She once commended a sermon that was against the pride and vanity of dress, and thought it was very just against Lucinda, whom she takes to be a great deal finer than she need to be. If anyone asks Flavia to do something in charity, if she likes the person who makes the proposal, or happens to be in a right temper, she will toss him half-a-crown or a crown, and tell him, if he knew what a long milliner's bill she had just received, he would think it a great deal for her to give. A quarter of a year after this, she hears a sermon upon the necessity of charity; she thinks the man preaches well, that it is a very proper subject, that people want much to be put in mind of it; but she applies nothing to herself, because she remembers that she gave a crown some time ago, when she could so ill spare it.

As for poor people themselves, she will admit of no complaints from them; she is very positive they are all cheats and liars; and will say anything to get relief, and therefore it must be a sin to encourage them in their evil ways. . . .

Flavia would be a miracle of piety, if she were but half so careful of her soul, as she is of her body, The rising of a pimple in her face, the sting of a gnat, will make her keep her room two or three days, and she thinks they are very rash people that do not take care of things in time. This makes her so over-careful of her health, that she never thinks she is well enough; and so over-indulgent, that she never can be really well. So that it costs her a great deal in sleeping-draughts and waking-draughts, in spirits for the head, in drops for the nerves, in cordials for the stomach, and in saffron for her tea.

If you visit Flavia on the Sunday, you will always meet good company, you will know what is doing in the world, you will hear the last lampoon, be told who wrote it, and who is meant by every name that is in it. You will hear what plays were acted that week, which is the finest song in the opera, who was intolerable at the last assembly, and what games are most in fashion. Flavia thinks they are atheists that play at cards on the Sunday, but she will tell you the nicety of all the games, what cards she held, how she played them, and the history of all that happened at play, as soon as she comes from church. If you would know who is rude and ill-natured, who is vain and foppish, who lives too high, and who is in debt: If you would know what is the quarrel at a certain house, or who and who are in love: If you would know how late Belinda comes home at night, what clothes she has bought, how she loves compliments, and what a long story she told at such a place: If you would know how cross Lucius is to his wife, what ill-natured things he says to her when nobody hears him; if you would know how they hate one another in their hearts, though they appear so kind in public; you must visit Flavia on the Sunday. But still she has so great a regard for the holiness of the Sunday, that she has turned a poor old widow out of her house, as a profane wretch, for having been found once mending her clothes on the Sunday night.

Thus lives Flavia; and if she lives ten years longer, she will have spent about fifteen hundred and sixty Sundays after this manner. She will have worn about two hundred different suits of clothes. Out of this thirty years of her life, fifteen of them will have been disposed of in bed; and of the remaining fifteen, about fourteen of them will have been consumed in eating, drinking, dressing, visiting, conversation, reading and hearing plays and romances, at operas, assemblies, balls and diversions. For you may reckon all the time that she is up, thus spent, except about an hour and half, that is disposed of at church, most Sundays in the year. With great management, and under mighty rules of economy, she will have spent sixty hundred pounds upon herself, bating only some shillings, crowns, or half-crowns, that have gone from her in accidental charities.

I shall not take upon me to say, that it is impossible for Flavia to be saved; but thus much must be said, that she has no grounds from Scripture to think she is in the way of salvation. For her whole life is in direct opposition to all those tempers and practices, which the Gospel has made necessary to salvation.

Chapter VIII.

.   .   .   The two things which of all others, most want to be under a strict rule, and which are the greatest blessings both to ourselves and others, when they are rightly used, are our time, and our money. Those talents are continual means and opportunities of doing good.

He that is piously strict, and exact in the wise management of either of these, cannot be long ignorant of the right use of the other. And he that is happy in the religious care and disposal of them both, has already ascended several steps upon the ladder of Christian perfection.

Miranda (the sister of Flavia) is a sober, reasonable Christian; as soon as she was mistress of her time and fortune, it was her first thought, how she might best fulfill everything that God required of her in the use of them, and how she might make the best and happiest use of this short life. She depends upon the truth of what our blessed Lord hath said, that there is but one thing needful, and therefore makes her whole life but one continual labour after it. She has but one reason for doing, or not doing, for liking, or not liking anything, and that is, the will of God. She is not so weak as to pretend to add, what is called the fine lady, to the true Christian; Miranda thinks too well, to be taken with the sound of such silly words; she has renounced the world to follow Christ in the exercise of humility, charity, devotion, abstinence, and heavenly affections; and that is Miranda's fine breeding. . . .

Miranda does not divide her duty between God, her neighbour, and herself; but she considers all as due to God and so does everything in his name, and for his sake. This makes her consider her fortune, as the gift of God, that is to be used as everything is, that belongs to God, for the wise and reasonable ends of a Christian and holy life. Her fortune therefore is divided betwixt herself, and several other poor people, and she has only her part of relief from it. She thinks it the same folly to indulge herself in needless, vain expenses, as to give to other people to spend in the same way. Therefore she will not give a poor man money to go see a puppet show, neither will she allow herself any to spend in the same manner; thinking it very proper to be as wise herself, as she expects poor men should be. For is it a folly and a crime in a poor man, says Miranda, to waste what is given him in foolish trifles, whilst he wants meat, drink, and clothes? And is it less folly, or a less crime in me, to spend that money in silly diversions, which might be so much better spent in imitation of the divine goodness, in works of kindness and charity towards my fellow-creatures, and fellow-Christians? If a poor man's own necessities are a reason why he should not waste any of his money idly, surely the necessities of the poor, the excellency of charity, which is received as done to Christ himself, is a much greater reason why no one should ever waste any of his money. . . .

Excepting her victuals, she never spent ten pounds a year upon herself. If you were to see her, you would wonder what poor body it was, that was so surprisingly neat and clean. She has but one rule that she observes in her dress, to be always clean and in the cheapest things. Everything about her resembles the purity of her soul, and she is always clean without, because she is always pure within.

Every morning sees her early at her prayers, she rejoices in the beginning of every day, because it begins all her pious rules of holy living, and brings the fresh pleasure of repeating them. She seems to be as a guardian angel to those that dwell about her, with her watchings and prayers blessing the place where she dwells, and making intercession with God for those that are asleep. . . .

When you see her at work, you see the same wisdom that governs all her other actions, she is either doing something that is necessary for herself, or necessary for others, who want to be assisted. There is scarcely a poor family in the neighbourhood, but wears something or other that has had the labour of her hands. Her wise and pious mind neither wants the amusement, nor can bear with the folly of idle and impertinent work. She can admit of no such folly as this in the day, because she is to answer for all her actions at night. When there is no wisdom to be observed in the employment of her hands, when there is no useful or charitable work to be done, Miranda will work no more. At her table she lives strictly by this rule of holy Scripture, "Whether ye eat, or drink, or whatsoever ye do, do all to the glory of

God." . . .

She thinks, that the trying of herself every day by the doctrines of Scripture, is the only possible way to be ready for her trial at the last day. She is sometimes afraid that she lays out too much money in books, because she cannot forbear buying all practical books of any note; especially such as enter into the heart of religion, and describe the inward holiness of the Christian life. But of all human writings, the lives of pious persons, and eminent saints, are her greatest delight. In these she searches as for hidden treasure, hoping to find some secret of holy living, some uncommon degree of piety, which she may make her own. By this means Miranda has her head and her heart, so stored with all the principles of wisdom and holiness, she is so full of the one main business of life, that she finds it difficult to converse upon any other subject; and if you are in her company, when she thinks it proper to talk, you must be made wiser and better, whether you will or no.

To relate her charity, would be to relate the history of every day for twenty years; for so long has all her fortune been spent that way. She has set up nearly twenty poor tradesmen that had failed in their business, and saved as many from failing. She has educated several poor children, that were picked up in the streets, and put them in a way of an honest employment. As soon as any labourer is confined at home with sickness, she sends him, till he recovers, twice the value of his wages, that he may have one part to give to his family, as usual, and the other to provide things convenient for his sickness. . . .

This is the spirit, and this is the life of the devout Miranda; and if she lives ten years longer, she will have spent fifty hundred pounds in charity, for that which she allows herself, may fairly be reckoned amongst her alms.

When she dies, she must shine amongst apostles, and saints, and martyrs; she must stand amongst the first servants of God, and be glorious amongst those that have fought the good fight, and finished their course with joy.

Chapter IX.

. . . If you would be a good Christian, there is but one way, you must live wholly unto God; and if you would live wholly unto God, you must live according to the wisdom that comes from God; you must act according to right judgments of the nature and value of things; you must live in the exercise of holy and heavenly affections, and use all the gifts of God to his praise and glory.

Some persons perhaps, who admire the purity and perfection of this life of Miranda, may say, How can it be proposed as a common example? How can we who are married, or we who are under the direction of our parents, imitate such a life?

It is answered, Just as you may imitate the life of our blessed Saviour and his apostles. The circumstances of our Savior's life, and the state and condition of his apostles, were more different from yours, than that of Miranda's is; and yet their life, the purity and perfection of their behaviour, is the common example that is proposed to all Christians.

It is their spirit therefore, their piety, their love of God, that you are to imitate, and not the particular form of their life. . . .

Do not think therefore, that you cannot, or need not be like Miranda, because you are not in her state of life; for as the same spirit and temper would have made Miranda a saint, though she had been forced to labour for a maintenance, so if you will but aspire after her spirit and temper, every form and condition of life, will furnish you with sufficient means of employing it.

Miranda is what she is, because she does everything in the name, and with regard to her duty to God; and when you do the same, you will be exactly like her, though you are never so different from her in the outward state of your life. . . .

If . . . persons, of either sex, moved with the life of Miranda, and desirous of perfection, should unite themselves into little societies, professing voluntary poverty, virginity, retirement and devotion, living upon bare necessaries, that some might be relieved by their charities, and all be blessed with their prayers, and benefited by their example: Or if for want of this, they should practise the same manner of life, in as high a degree as they could by themselves; such persons would be so far from being chargeable with any superstition, or blind devotion, that they might be justly said to restore that piety, which was the boast and glory of the church, when its greatest saints were alive. . . . .

Chapter XIX.

That turn of mind which is taught and encouraged in the education of daughters, makes it exceeding difficult for them to enter into such a sense and practice of humility, as the spirit of Christianity requires.

The right education of this sex, is of the utmost importance to human life. There is nothing that is more desirable for the common good of all the world. For though women do not carry on the trade and business of the world, yet as they are mothers, and mistresses of families, that have for some time the care of the education of their children of both sorts, they are entrusted with that which is of the greatest consequence to human life. For this reason, good or bad women are likely to do as much good or harm in the world, as good or bad men in the greatest business of life. . . . .

It is therefore much to be lamented, that this sex, on whom so much depends, who have the first forming both of our bodies and our minds, are not only educated in pride, but in the silliest and most contemptible part of it.

They are not indeed suffered to dispute with us the proud prizes of arts and sciences, of learning and eloquence, in which I have much suspicion they would often prove our superiors; but we turn them over to the study of beauty and dress, and the whole world conspires to make them think of nothing else.

Fathers and mothers, friends, and relations, seem to have no other wish towards the little girl, but that she may have a fair skin, a fine shape, dress well, and dance to admiration.

Now if a fondness for our persons, a desire of beauty, a love of dress, be a part of pride (as surely it is a most contemptible part of it) the first step towards a woman's humility, seems to require a repentance of her education.

For it must be owned, that, generally speaking, good parents are never more fond of their daughters, than when they see them too fond of themselves, and dressed in such a manner, as is a great reproach to the gravity and sobriety of the Christian life.

And what makes this matter still more to be lamented, is this, That women are not only spoiled by this education, but we spoil that part of the world, which would otherwise furnish most instances of an eminent and exalted piety.

For I believe it may be affirmed, that for the most part there is a finer sense, a clearer mind, a readier apprehension, and gentler dispositions in that sex, than in the other.

All which tempers, if they were truly improved by proper studies, and sober methods of education, would in all probability carry them to greater heights of piety, than are to be found amongst the generality of men.

4. George Whitefield, "Christ the best Husband: Or an earnest Invitation to Young Women to come and see Christ," in *The Works of the Rev. George Whitefield*, 6 vols. (London: Edward and Charles Dilly, 1772), V: 65-66, 69-73. Text: Psalm 45:10-11.

The greatest preacher of the eighteenth century, George Whitefield (1714-70) was a leader of the Evangelical Revival on both sides of the Atlantic. It was he who began the Revival in England and who invited John Wesley to preach in Bristol in 1739 and to take a leading role there while he travelled to the American colonies. A split between Whitefield and Wesley in 1740 over the doctrine of predestination caused them to go in separate ways in the organization of their work, even though cordial personal relationships were soon restored. Whitefield eventually became associated with the

Countess of Huntingdon as one of her preachers (see chapter 2).

What would men preach to an audience of women? One common theme was the particular service that women could perform for the church. This sermon of Whitefield's, however, first published in 1740, addressed women as sexual beings and in so doing suggested that this was the best way to promote their commitment to Christ. Speaking to his audience in language that could not be used with men, Whitefield encouraged them to eschew coyness and modesty and embrace Christ in a conjugal bond. Contrasting the attractions of Christ with those of other men, he declared, "Some marry in haste, and repent at leisure; but if you were once espoused unto Jesus Christ, you would never repent; nothing would grieve you, but that you were not joined to him sooner." One can hardly resist the judgment that this was taking unfair advantage of the emotions of young women.

This psalm is called the song of loves, the most pure and spiritual, the most dear and delightful loves; namely, those which are between Christ the beloved, and his church, which is his spouse; wherein is set forth, first, the Lord Jesus Christ in regard of his majesty, power, and divinity, his truth, meekness and equity: And then the spouse is set forth, in regard of her ornaments, companions, attendants and posterity; and both in regard of their comeliness and beauty. After the description of Christ, an invitation to his espousals, is given the children of men, called by the name of daughter; and therefore, particularly applicable unto you, my dear sisters, as being the daughters of men, yet not so as excluding the sons of men.

I shall now, therefore, consider the words, as spoken to you in particular, and containing this doctrine; That the Lord Jesus Christ doth invite the daughters of men to be his spouse; and is exceeding desirous of their beauty; who, forgetting their people and father's house do hearken, consider and incline to his invitation, and join themselves to him in this relation. . . .

Such of you, my dear sisters, as are espoused to the Lord Jesus Christ are very beautiful. I do not mean in respect of your bodies; you may have less of external comeliness than others, in respect of your bodies, but as to your souls you will exceed in beauty, not so much in the eyes of man as in the eyes of God; such have the most beautiful image of God stamped upon them; none in the world, beside them, have the least spark of spiritual beauty. Such as are not married to Christ, are unregenerated, they are not born again, nor brought from sin unto God, which must be done before you be espoused to Christ.

And the Lord Jesus Christ desireth to see this beauty in his spouse, for he cries out, "O my dove, thou art in the clefts of the rock, in the secret places of the stairs, let me see thy countenance, let me hear thy voice, for sweet is thy voice, and thy countenance is comely." He calleth his spouse his love, being the dear object of his love; and he admireth her loveliness; he repeats it twice in one verse, "Behold thou art fair, my love, behold thou art fair." Thus you see he describes their beauty. And then, my sisters, we have a wonderful expression of Christ to his spouse, "Thou hast ravished my heart, my sister, my spouse, thou hast ravished my heart with one of thine eyes, with one chain of thy neck." Thus you see how pleased the Lord Jesus Christ is with his spouse; and will not you, therefore, be espoused unto the Lord Jesus? I offer Jesus Christ to all of you; if you have been never so notorious for sin, if you have been as great a harlot as Mary Magdalen was, when once you are espoused to Christ, you shall be forgiven. Therefore be not discouraged, at whatever slights and contempts the world may pass upon you, but come and join yourselves to the Lord Jesus Christ, and all your sins shall be washed away in his blood; and when once you are espoused to Jesus, you are disjoined from sin, you are born again. You are now, as it were, espoused unto sin; sin is your husband, and you are too fond of it, but when once you are married to Christ, when you are born again, then you may be said to die unto sin; but till then, sin liveth in your affections; therefore, my sisters, give sin its death-wound in your hearts; you have been called by the word time after time, and it has had no effect upon you; but when you are espoused unto the Lord Jesus Christ, then you will be brought to him by his Spirit: You will then lay hold on him by faith, his Spirit will draw you unto himself, he will make you to be willing in the day of his power; he will give you faith in him. Faith is the hand of the soul which layeth hold on Christ; therefore, do not rest contented till you have this grace of faith wrought in you with power; do not be contented till you have received the Lord Jesus Christ.

Embrace Christ in the arms of your dearest love; then you love the Lord Jesus Christ with sincerity, when you love and esteem him before father, mother, or all the delights and pleasures of this life; but if you do delight in any thing that this world can produce, more than in the Lord Jesus Christ, you have no true love to him.

If you are espoused to Christ, you have acquaintance and converse with him; you will endeavour to promote his interest, and advance his name in the world; when others are going to the polite and fashionable diversions of life, you will be labouring to bring honour to the Lord Jesus Christ; you will commend your beloved above all other beloveds, and endeavour to bring others into love to him. Can you, my dear sisters, who are now assembled to worship God, shew such evidence of your espousals unto the Lord Jesus Christ? O! how joyful, how comfortable an estate is this! Surely this is a marriage worth seeking after; this is the only desirable marriage, and the Lord Jesus Christ is the only lover that is worth seeking after. . . .

It is your glory that you are espoused unto the Lord Jesus; and therefore glory in your espousal; glory not in yourselves, but in the Lord who hath thus freely and graciously bestowed these favours upon you. It is your safety to be espoused unto the Lord Jesus Christ, he will protect and defend you even from sin and satan, and eternal ruin; and therefore thus far you are safe; he hath a regard for you in times of danger from men, and these times of danger seem to be hastening; it is now arising as a black cloud no bigger than a man's hand, and by and by it will overspread the heavens, and when it is full it will burst; but if you are espoused to Christ you are safe. . . .

Be not coy, as some of you possibly are in other loves: modesty and the virgin blush may very well become you, when proposals of another kind are made unto you; but here coyness is folly, and backwardness to accept of this motion, is shame: you have ten thousand times more reason to blush at the refusal of Christ for your beloved, than at the acceptance; when otherwise the devil and sin would ravish your virgin affections. Never had you a better motion made to you; never was such a match proffered to you as this of being matched and espoused unto the Lord Jesus Christ.

Consider who the Lord Jesus is, whom you are invited to espouse yourselves unto; he is the best husband; there is none comparable to Jesus Christ.

Do you desire one that is great? He is of the highest dignity, he is the glory of heaven, the darling of eternity, admired by angels, dreaded by devils, and adored by saints. For you to be espoused to so great a king, what honour will you have by this espousal?

Do you desire one that is rich? None is comparable to Christ, the fulness of the earth belongs to him. If you be espoused to Christ, you shall share in his unsearchable riches; you shall receive of his fulness, even grace for grace here, and you shall hereafter be admitted to glory, and shall live with this Jesus to all eternity.

Do you desire one that is wise? There is none comparable to Christ for wisdom. His knowledge is infinite, and his wisdom is correspondent thereto. And if you are espoused to Christ, he will guide and counsel you, and make you wise unto salvation.

Do you desire one that is potent, who may defend you against your enemies, and all the insults and reproaches of the Pharisees of this generation? There is none that can equal Christ in power; for the Lord Jesus Christ hath all power.

Do you desire one that is good? There is none like unto Christ in this regard;

others may have some goodness, but it is imperfect; Christ's goodness is complete and perfect, he is full of goodness, and in him dwelleth no evil.

Do you desire one that is beautiful? His eyes are most sparkling, his looks and glances of love are ravishing, his smiles are most delightful and refreshing unto the soul; Christ is the most lovely person of all others in the world.

Do you desire one that can love you? None can love you like Christ: His love, my dear sisters, is incomprehensible; his love passeth all other loves: The love of the Lord Jesus is first, without beginning; his love is free without any motive; his love is great without any measure; his love is constant without any change, and his love is everlasting.

5. James Fordyce, *Sermons to Young Women*, 2 vols., 3rd ed. (London, 1766), I:271-73; II:117-21.

Several volumes of advice to young women were written in the eighteenth century by men. Chief among them were James Fordyce's *Sermons to Young Women*, John Gregory's *A Father's Legacy to His Daughters* (1774), and Thomas Gisbourne's *An Enquiry into the Duties of the Female Sex* (1797). Each author emphasized the differences between the sexes in terms of abilities, temperament, and sensibilities, exalting the perceived weakness of the female sex into a strength that must be maintained at all costs. "I will take it for granted, that the sons of Reason should converse only with the daughters of Virtue," wrote Fordyce (1720-96), a Presbyterian minister, this time to an audience of men, implying by the distinction that each sex had a greater interest in that particular characteristic.[24] Women were not intended to pursue rigorous intellectual activity, not only because of their relative incapacity, but because it did not sit well with men. Gregory advised his readers, "If you happen to have any learning, keep it a profound secret, especially from the men, who generally look with a jealous and malignant eye on a woman of great parts, and a cultivated understanding."[25] Religion and morality, on the other hand, were particularly spheres for female activity. Women have a "Propensity to devotion," Fordyce declared, and they are commonly said to represent by far the greater number of worshippers. The supports of religion seemed

particularly designed for women, thought Gregory: "Your whole life is often a life of
suffering. You cannot plunge into business, or dissipate yourselves in pleasure and riot,
as men too often do, when under the pressures of misfortunes. You must bear your
sorrows in silence, unknown and unpitied. . . .   Then your only resource is in the
consolations of religion. It is chiefly owing to these that you bear domestic misfortunes
better than we do." Again, religion is more a matter of sentiment than of reasoning for
these authors, and thus it is peculiarly suited to women.[26] It was such thoughts that
led Mary Wollstonecraft to single out Fordyce and Gregory for special criticism, asking,
"If women be ever allowed to walk without leading-strings, why must they be cajoled
into virtue by artful flattery and sexual compliments? Speak to them the language of
truth and soberness, and away with the lullaby strains of condescending endearment!"
She went on to argue that "this desire of being always women, is the very consciousness
that degrades the sex."[27]

Despite Wollstonecraft's strictures, Fordyce saw himself somewhat as a reformer,
especially in terms of the eighteenth-century image of the gentlewoman as vain and
frivolous. He opposed the frequent disparagement of women, argued for a single standard of morality, and encouraged the criticism of social standards that prevented a
greater appreciation of religion—to the point that he was attacked for trying to destroy
fashion and make women into Quakers.[28] Of course, Fordyce was objecting to those
perceptions of women which undercut the ideal, not to the ideal itself.

The degree of those Intellectual Accomplishments which your sex should aim
at, I pretend not to determine. That must depend on the capacities, opportunities,
and encouragements, which you severally enjoy. With regard to all these however,
this may be said in general, that they are better, and more than many of you seem
solicitous to improve.

As to the first indeed, I scruple not to declare my opinion, that Nature appears
to have formed the faculties of your sex for the most part with less vigour than those
of ours; observing the same distinction here, as in the more delicate frame of your
bodies. Exceptions we readily admit, and such as do the individuals great honour

in those particular walks of excellence, wherein they have been distinguished. But you yourselves, I think, will allow that war, commerce, politics, exercises of strength and dexterity, abstract philosophy, and all the abstruser sciences, are most properly the province of men. I am sure those masculine women, that would plead for your sharing any part of this province equally with us, do not understand your true interests. There is an influence, there is an empire which belongs to you, and which I wish you ever to possess: I mean that which has the heart for its object, and is secured by meekness and modesty, by soft attraction and virtuous love.

But now I must add, that your power in this way will receive a large accession from the culture of your minds, in the more elegant and polished branches of knowledge. When I say so, I would by no means insinuate, that you are not capable of the judicious and the solid, in such proportion as is suited to your destination in life. This, I apprehend, does not require reasoning or accuracy, so much as observation and discernment. Your business chiefly is to read Men, in order to make yourselves agreeable and useful. It is not the argumentative but the sentimental talents, which give you that insight and those openings into the human heart, that lead to your principal ends as Women. . . .

Nothing can be more plain, than that Providence has placed you most commonly in circumstances peculiarly advantageous for the exercises of devotion, and for the preservation of that virtue, without which every profession of godliness must be regarded as an impudent pretence. The situation of men lays them open to a variety of temptations, that lie out of your road. The bustle of life, in which they are generally engaged, leaves them often but little leisure for holy offices. Their passions are daily subject to be heated by the ferment of business; and how hard is it for them to avoid being importuned to excess, while sometimes a present interest, frequently a pressing appetite, and yet more frequently the fear of ridicule, stimulates them to comply! . . .   In the case of our sex, do we not often see ranked on the side of licentiousness that reputation which ought to attend on sobriety alone? Is not the last openly laughed at by those, to whose opinion giddy young men will pay most respect, their own companions? Is not its contrary cried up as a mark of spirit? And if, in their unrestrained conversation amongst a diversity of humours, they meet with affronts, are they not constantly told, that the maxims of honour require them to take revenge? Is not all this extremely unfavourable to the religious life, of which so great a part consists in purity and prayer, in regularity and coolness, in self-command and mild affections? But from such snares your sex are happily exempted.

In many instances men are attacked by folly, before they surrender; whereas women must generally invite it by art, or rather indeed take it by violence, ere they can possess themselves of its guilty pleasures. So far the Almighty, in consideration of their debility, and from a regard to their innocence, has raised a kind of fence about them, to prevent those wilder excursions into which the other sex are frequently carried, with a freedom unchecked by fear, and favoured by custom.

Corrupt as the world is, it certainly does expect from young women a strict decorum; nor, as we have seen before, does it easily forgive them the least deviation. Add that, while you remain without families of your own, few of you are necessarily so engaged, as not to have a large portion of time with daily opportunities for recollection, if you be inclined to improve them. I go farther and subjoin, that your improving them by a piety the most regular and avowed, if withal unaffected and liberal, will be no sort of objection to the men, but much the reverse.

A bigoted woman every man of sense will carefully shun, as a most disagreeable, and even dangerous companion. But the secret reverence, which that majestic form Religion imprints on the hearts of all, is such, that even they who will not submit to its dictates themselves, do yet wish it to be regarded by those with whom they are connected in the nearest relations. The veriest infidel of them all, I am apt to believe, would be sorry to find his sister, daughter, or wife, under no restraint from religious principle. Thus it is, that even the greatest libertines are forced to pay, at the same instant, a kind of implicit respect to the two main objects of their profligate satire, Piety and Women; while they consider these as formed for each other, and tacitly acknowledge that the first is the only effectual means of ensuring the good behaviour of the last. Let them talk as long, and as contemptuously as they will, about that easy credulity, and those superstitious terrors, which they pretend to be the foundation of your religion; something within will always give them the lie, so long as they perceive that your religion renders you more steadily virtuous, and more truly lovely.

6. Quaker Accounts: (A) *Some Account of the Life and Religious Exercises of Mary Neale, Formerly Mary Peisley* (Dublin, 1795), pp. 41-43, 54-55; (B) *Letters, etc., of Sarah (Lynes) Grubb* (London: A. W. Bennett, 1865), pp. 4-9.

From the beginnings of the Quaker movement, women had a prominent place in its activities and proclamation. Relative to the orthodox Christian viewpoint of the mid-seventeenth century, this was little short of revolutionary. The theological foundations articulated by George Fox were followed by a ministerial corollary, that the Spirit of Christ, not any human agency, set people apart to the ministry. Robert Barclay noted, "This is not monopolized by a certain kind of man, as the clergy . . . and the rest to be despised as laicks; but it is left to the *free gift of God* to choose any whom he sees meet thereunto, whether rich or poor, servant or master, young or old, yea, male or female."[29]

But the character and form of women's activities in the movement was hotly debated for many years. Fox's support of separate Women's Meetings was opposed by some who wanted men and women to meet together and by others who feared that the authority of women would increase through separate organization. Despite the opposition regular Women's Meetings were established on a local and regional level from 1671, although a full Women's Yearly Meeting was not created in England until 1784. Their work within the Society concentrated on preparation of people for marriage, visitation, and poor relief; they were not allowed to participate with men in considering matters of discipline.

By the eighteenth century the early informality of worship and organization had been gradually replaced by official meeting houses, the seating of women and men on opposite sides for worship, and a greater division between members and ministers. The Toleration Act of 1689 permitted greater openness than before, and some of the changes may have come about through accommodation to practices of other churches. But opportunities for women ministers continued, enhanced in some respects by the separate women's meetings. Sarah Tuke Grubb, for example, noted in her diary for 1781 that after a particularly difficult meeting, it was as if she heard a voice saying, "Visit the men and women when separated, for they require different food."[30]

Since there was no training or remuneration, any person who felt called to the ministry needed only the official support of his or her Monthly Meeting and a letter of introduction to other Meetings, which were expected to provide local hospitality in one's travels. Some women ministers travelled widely, at times with husbands who were also ministers, often with other women. Mary Peisley (1717-57) entered into the ministry in 1744 and travelled in Ireland and England; she also made an extensive trip to America from 1753 to 1756. Shortly after her return to England she married, but died suddenly just a few days later. Sarah Lynes Grubb (1773-1842) became a minister at the age of eighteen, left an eight-month-old baby to travel for five months among the Meetings in the United Kingdom, and spoke frequently in the open air to general audiences. Their personal reflections provide a few glimpses into the private and public concerns of Quaker women ministers of the eighteenth century.

(A)   I take kind thy seasonable warning to watchfulness, which I surely stand in need of, in this time, that drowsiness and spiritual lethargy have generally infected mankind. Thou wilt, perhaps, like to hear an account of my spiritual progress, and travel Zion-wards, and of the states of the churches here, so far as my sight can reach, and I may say, it has been a real grief and affliction to my mind, to see the desolation, darkness and insensibility that generally prevail; having been made to go mourning on my way, with this language in my soul, Lord, to whom hast thou sent me? where shall I find thy flock and family upon earth? for I see very few who like even to hear or speak of thee, and surely if thy love had the pre-eminence, out of the abundance of the heart, the mouth would speak, or, at least, the soul love to wait in silence for thy divine appearance. But alas! many seem to have nothing further to enquire about, than whence we came? whither we go? our names, or if we be married? to which I often answer, I hope I have been honourably espoused to one husband, but they are quite ignorant of him whom my soul loveth, and of my meaning. Yet altho' it be thus, there is a living remnant in this part of the world, but under great suffering and oppression; with which I have been made deeply to sympathize, and have greatly admired the Lord's goodness and condescending love; his forbearance and suffering to a disobedient and gainsaying people, not willing that they should perish.

As to my own particular, I find the truth of that saying, that "they who preach the gospel, live by it," in a spiritual sense; and tho' the Lord has been pleased at times to cause his candle to shine upon my head, and clothe me with his royal robes, yet I often witness, a being entirely emptied, stripped and destitute almost of daily bread, and have had as Mordecai, to go down and sit at the king's gate, all which I see is for my good; . . .   therefore I strive to learn that great lesson, of being content in all states, and may say to the praise and honour of my kind master, that he hath (since I have given up the same to serve him) caused his peace to flow in my soul as a river: whose current is not long to be controlled by all the impediments which can be laid in its way. Blessed for ever be his holy name, he has afforded me strength to discharge myself faithfully wherever my lot has been cast, both publickly and privately; so that I have no condemnation on that account, nor have I repented leaving all to answer his holy requirings, but humbly thank him, that he enabled me so to do; and, were crowns and diadems laid at my feet, I would not give his approbation for them.

. . . Oh! may my soul fear always, lest I, or any of my dear brethren and sisters in the truth, should fall short of an admittance in the great and notable day that draws near apace. When I consider the very few bright shining examples that this age affords, who have disinterestedly devoted themselves to the service of truth, and been kept unspotted of the world, having on the white linen which is the righteousness of saints; my fears are augmented, and my cries to the God of my life increased, not only for my own preservation, but that of his heritage in general. In a peculiar manner, am I concerned for those whom he hath called to the weighty work of the ministry, that the eyes of our souls may be kept so single to the honour of God, as that we may minister suitably, from the divine spirit, to the states and conditions of the people, without partiality, or respect to persons, for in this case (as saith the apostle) if we have respect for persons, we commit sin. In order to avoid this heinous, dangerous crime, we had need to take notice of the wise caution frequently mentioned in the writings of our worthy elders and faithful ministers, in the morning of this latter day; not to be taken by the affectionate part with any, lest it should prevent seeing rightly the situation of the lowly seed of immortal life, and hinder ministering suitably to it, but minister life and strength to that which should be slain, famished and brought to the death of the cross. Oh! may we fulfil our ministry so as to be pure from the blood of all men, in the tremendous day of account, studying to shew ourselves approved unto God, as labourers that need not be ashamed, rightly dividing the word of truth.

(B)   I was then [1791] eighteen years old; had come forth as a minister, yet discovered great need of further refinement, both for my own acceptance with the Lord, and that I might be fit for the Lord's use. Truly I had to abide the fiery furnace.

With respect to my first appearances as one called to speak in the high and holy name of the Lord, they were in great fear, and under a feeling that my natural inclination would not lead me into such exposure, for I shrunk from it exceedingly; and often have I hesitated, and felt such a reluctance to it, that I have suffered the meeting to break up without my having made the sacrifice: yea, when the word of life, in a few words, was like a fire within me. Great has been my mourning through these omissions of duty, although but seventeen years old when I first gave utterance publicly to a sentence or two; and I had opened my mouth in private many months previously, under the constraining influence of the Spirit of truth; being without the shadow of a doubt that it was indeed required of me, poor child as I was. I had sweet consolation in coming into obedience; and after a while was surprised to find, that although I stood up in meetings expecting only to utter a *little* matter, more passed through me, I scarcely knew how.

Thus the gift grew, and much baptism and suffering was my portion from time to time; the great work of my salvation and sanctification going on, while I was occasionally induced to invite others to the needful acquaintance with Him who came to redeem us from all iniquity. I have never known an easier way to favour with the Lord of life and glory, than that of passive submission to all His holy will concerning me, even under dispensations most annoying and mortifying to the fleshly mind.

I lived nearly ten years in the family to which I went from school, viz., that of Sarah Grubb, of Anner Mills, near Clonmel, Ireland. Never, all that time, could I see my way to change my situation; for, through all the difficulty that lay in my way of fulfilling my religious duty, I believed that the Great Master had some good end which He designed to answer, in permitting me to be as it were cramped in the gift dispensed to me as a minister of Christ; and my faith was at times renewed and confirmed, that if I would patiently endure to the end, my reward would be sure. Thus I was mercifully enabled to "wait all the days of my appointed time until my change came;" until, in the clear openings of truth, I was led back to my native land, to my near relatives, and sent forth *largely* to publish the glad tidings of the Gospel. I had been some journeys in Ireland, but now a very wide field of labour opened before me; and, with the consent of my Monthly Meeting, I travelled much, up and down in England, both among Friends and others, for some successive years; and many blessed and powerful meetings we had, to the praise of His excellent Name, without whom we can do nothing, and are nothing. For some considerable time I was joined by my beloved friend Ann Baker. . . . We passed through tribulation together, which, as well as experiencing some rejoicings, had a strong tendency to unite us in true sisterly love and friendship; and in it we were preserved to the end of her course, which was finished with holy triumph many years since. Neither hath death itself dissolved the heavenly bond by which our spirits were united; even in that which outlives all probation.

It pleased the Lord to call me into a path much untrodden, in my early travels as a messenger of the Gospel; having to go into markets, and to declare the truth in the streets. This sore exercise began in Cork, Ireland; but it was only in one instance required of me in that nation: in England, however, many, very many such sacrifices I had to make in pursuit of peace; and in pure obedience to the will of my Heavenly Father I gave up. No one knows the depth of my sufferings, and the mortifying, yea, crucifying of my own will, which I had to endure in this service; yet I have to acknowledge to the sufficiency of Divine grace herein. Many times I had brave opportunities on these occasions, to invite the people to the Lord Jesus Christ, who manifests Himself in the conscience as a light, and who would discover the evil of covetousness and of all unrighteousness; leading and teaching "to do justly, to love mercy, and to walk humbly with God." Hundreds, possibly thousands, who would not, even though requested, come to meet us in a house, or place of worship, have thus felt the power of the living God, in hearing tell that He rewardeth every man according to his ways, and according to the fruit of his doings. In some instances we were rudely treated. Once in a great town (Leicester), while I was speaking in the market, there came two men who looked really furious. They said the mayor ordered me down; coming toward me through the crowd that stood round, evidently intending to pull me down from where I stood; but I observed them, and looking at them, their countenances fell, and they appeared to have no power to touch me: however, as they came with an order from the mayor of the town, I told the people how it was, and commended them to their inward Teacher—Christ. When we obeyed the order, and were leaving the place, some said, had it been a mountebank who stood in my place, he would have been suffered to proceed; but that which drew their attention to God was prohibited. Others who were light and wicked, reviled us. I had, as usual, some dear and tender friends among the brethren, who accompanied and stood by me in such great exercise. These partook of the insults offered—the people throwing at them; indeed somebody was unfeeling enough to bring hot melted lead and cast at us; some of which was found on some part of the clothing of one dear friend. I retired to my chamber at a friend's house, after this bustle; and oh the sweet tranquillity that filled my mind! I thought it a foretaste of that glorious *rest* prepared for the children of God in His eternal kingdom.

At Durham, a clergyman came in a rage while I was preaching in a market place, wanting some of the people to hale me away; but they took little or no notice of him, and he passed on. Next day we appointed a meeting for First-day morning, in a hired room in this dark town; and, as was usual, posted up notices. These were torn down, and we were informed, that if we held the meeting, we should be heavily fined. The meeting was nevertheless held, and owned by the great Head of His own Church. At the close another was appointed for the evening of the same day, and a large heavenly meeting it was. We tarried there all that night, but heard no more of the threatened fine. This was but one of divers visits to Durham.

7. Anna Laetitia Barbauld, "The Rights of Woman," in *The Works of Anna Laetitia Barbauld*, 2 vols. (London, 1825), I:185-87.

With the events of the French Revolution the issue of "the rights of man" was in the air. But it was clear to Mary Wollstonecraft that very few understood these rights to apply to women; thus she entered this specific debate with *A Vindication of the Rights of Woman* in 1792. Anna Laetitia Barbauld (1743-1825), daughter and wife of liberal Dissenting ministers and a member of a group of learned ladies in London at the end of the century, picked up this theme in one of her poems.[31] Although occupied in literary activities and in private tutoring, Barbauld was also involved in other liberal causes as anti-slavery and the efforts to remove the civil disabilities suffered by Dissenters. As the poem indicates, Barbauld was concerned to defend women from attacks made against them. Much earlier, in a letter of 1771 to a friend, she had criticised Fordyce's suggestion that women's friendships were not sincere and declared that she wanted to burn his book because of that passage.[32]

But Wollstonecraft had herself criticised a poem of Barbauld's for contributing to the male tendency to restrict women to a particular sexual character which denied them the capacity of understanding and allowed them only instinct, "sublimated into wit and cunning, for the purposes of life." Barbauld's offending lines were, "nor blush, my fair to own you copy these; your best, your sweetest empire is—to please."[33] Barbauld was of a mixed mind, attracted to the talk of "rights," yet fearful of what they would do. Her vision of a society where men no longer rule women is one in which women rule men, and that disturbed her. "Equality" is curiously absent from her vision; the only mutuality is that of love, and in this relationship the need for separate rights disappears.

Yes, injured Woman! rise, assert thy right!
Woman! too long degraded, scorned, opprest;
O born to rule in partial Law's despite,
Resume thy native empire o'er the breast!

Go forth arrayed in panoply divine;
That angel pureness which admits no stain;
Go, bid proud Man his boasted rule resign,
And kiss the golden sceptre of thy reign.

Go, gird thyself with grace; collect thy store

Of bright artillery glancing from afar;
Soft melting tones thy thundering cannon's roar,
Blushes and fears thy magazine of war.

Thy rights are empire: urge no meaner claim, —
Felt, not defined, and if debated, lost;
Like sacred mysteries, which withheld from fame,
Shunning discussion, are revered the most.

Try all that wit and art suggest to bend
Of thy imperial foe the stubborn knee;
Make treacherous Man thy subject, not thy friend;
Thou mayst command, but never canst be free.

Awe the licentious, and restrain the rude;
Soften the sullen, clear the cloudy brow:
Be, more than princes' gifts, thy favours sued;—
She hazards all, who will the least allow.

But hope not, courted idol of mankind,
On this proud eminence secure to stay;
Subduing and subdued, thou soon shalt find
Thy coldness soften, and thy pride give way.

Then, then, abandon each ambitious thought,
Conquest or rule thy heart shall feebly move,
In Nature's school, by her soft maxims taught,
That separate rights are lost in mutual love.

8. Joanna Southcott: (A) *The Strange Effects of Faith* (Exeter, 1801), pp. 36-37, 104-106; (B) *The Trial of Joanna Southcott* (London, 1804), pp. 131-33.

"Is it a new thing for a Woman to deliver her people? Did not Esther do it? Did not Judith do it?"[34] So asked Joanna Southcott (1750-1814), who came from humble Devonshire beginnings to lead the most popular millenarian movement of the early nineteenth century. In her career and writings (sixty-five works published between 1801 and 1814) can be found glimpses of the world of the prophetess, wise woman, and witch—a world of dreams and visions, populated by spirits and demons, where divine processes are exhibited by signs and wonders and people are protected from evil and promised salvation through "seals." In this world, which was outside or on the fringes of respectability, since it veered too close to the dangers of "enthusiasm," women often played an important role. The French Prophets, who settled in England early in the century and included a number of women, and Ann Lee, who emerged from a sect of Quakers in the 1760s and later founded the Shaker movement in America, are some of Southcott's predecessors.[35] Other women, working only locally, including in their religion elements of magic, prophecy, and cures in an effort to make the world more controllable, are less visible to later view. Southcott was one of the few who wrote, and she attracted a national following.

In 1792, after working in domestic service and learning the upholstery trade, Southcott began to experience religious visions, together with an order from the Spirit to put these in writing. For a decade she was a prophetess in Exeter, predicting such events as bad harvests and wars and announcing the imminent second coming of Christ. She was rejected by the Methodists with whom she had been associated and received encouragement from only a few Anglican clergy. Another vision in 1800 charged her to publish her writings. The first, entitled *The Strange Effects of Faith*, appeared in 1801; a year later she moved to London, where her very modest following began to grow. In this and later works she assumed the mantle of "the woman clothed with the sun" (Rev. 12) to become the final instrument in the divine plan, the seventh mystery of God whose secrets would be fully revealed to the world. As sin came into the world through woman (Gen. 3), so redemption would be heralded by woman: "But now the woman's conq'ring seed shall break the serpent's head."[36]

The meaning of the "conquering seed" was unclear until Southcott announced another vision in 1814: she would give birth to a son, the Shiloh promised in Gen. 49. For months there was great interest among her followers and in the press; several doctors confirmed that she was pregnant. By late autumn, however, there had been no birth. She died in late December, and an autopsy showed no evidence of pregnancy. Initially stunned, many of her followers claimed that it had been a spiritual birth and continued on without her.

For many years Southcott proclaimed her religious orthodoxy and invited a jury of clergymen to test her writings. Although three such "trials" were held, the last in 1804, the jury of impartial clergy had never been assembled, and Southcottian worship drifted into independent sectarian status, complete with a liturgy drawn from the Anglican church, a form of communion, and hymnody based on her poetry. Her followers were drawn largely from the working classes, and almost two-thirds were women. In the two decades of her activity, amid threats of war, economic decline, frequent crop failures, and the turmoil of urbanization, certainly some were attracted by the promise of a glorious future and the certainty of salvation. Others responded to the new place given to women in the divine plan or to the compatibility of Southcott's visions with their understanding of the world. But from the established churches, where admonitions were frequently to be heard concerning feminine tendencies to delusive religious zeal, perhaps the memory of Joanna Southcott and her influence made them more reluctant to contemplate female leadership than they otherwise might have been.

(A)

These extraordinary things have been now explained to me.
"As she so boldly for her Master stand,
Then now in thunder I will answer men:
And first let thy original be trac'd,
And tell me now, what mighty thing thou wast,
When first I took thee from thy native dust,
And in the garden thou alone was plac'd,
Couldst thou brought forth the word as she hath done?
Or, like the woman, bear'd my only Son,
Without her aid, as she did without thine?
I tell you, men, the myst'ries are behind.
As from the woman you did all proceed,
Took from your side, man is pronounc'd the head,
But you must know, you are not the perfect man,
Until your bone is join'd to you again.
So both together must in judgment sit:
And tell me, men, if her disputes were right,
To say my honour I had still maintain'd,
And plead with Satan, as she hath began:
Then both together you shall surely know,
I have gain'd my honour by his overthrow,
For if the woman stands so much my friend,
You all shall find, I'll stand her's in the end.
If from herself this love and courage came,
I tell you plain, she is the head of man.
But if from me the spirit first did fall,
I tell you plain, I am the head of all:

And when her writings you have all went through:
Much greater mysteries must come to your view.
So by the woman now I will surely stand,
As for my honour she so long contend.
Ten days he held her with his blasphemy,
Ten days a hero she held out for me.
Then of these days I turn them now to years:
I'll prove her words, and man shall see it clear,
That every word was true what she had spoke:
I'll gain my honour, her words I'll never mock,
So if men mock them now, I'll tell them plain,
I'll gain my honour, to destroy such men."

. . . And now I am come to try the knowledge of the Gentiles, and find them as far from knowledge as the Jews, or they would have discerned from whence the Spirit came: but here is man lost in wisdom and understanding, and dead as to the knowledge of God. Now I will throw open the Bible unto all men. The woman, through her strange effects of faith, was betrayed by the serpent, and gave it to the man; the man betrayed his Lord; then followed the wondrous prophecies, that no man never understood, that as the serpent bruised my heel, so shall I bruise his head, by the same weak instrument he first betrayed to bring it on me, should in the end bring it back again; so I suffered what man cast on me, and satan shall suffer the blame the woman cast on him; and that man that will not own it just, shall go with his master the most praise, for now I will cut short my work in righteousness. Do these things appear too marvellous in the eyes of the readers to believe them? I answer, they appear to me so just, that the God of this world must so blind their eyes, that in seeing they cannot see, nor in hearing they cannot understand, if they do not see it clear: and every one must own the sentence just; for I may say with the thief upon the cross, satan received the just sentence passed upon him from the woman, but the Lord suffered an unjust sentence from the man, at first and at last; for if they thought it right to hearken to the woman at first, why not Pilate at last? So I cannot see but man is blameable, as well as the woman; but the author of the whole was the devil; he first rebelled in heaven, and as soon as man and woman were created, he studied arts and lies to betray them, and made them break the commands of God; and the best of men cannot shun all his arts, therefore it is impossible for the will of God to be done upon earth, as long as satan's power reigneth, for his arts are as many as his power is great. Now is it unlikely the Lord should pass so just a sentence on him, to turn back on his head the destruction he had brought on us all? He did not spare his Son, neither hath he spared man, and why should he spare the devil, who was the author of every evil? For we learn from Judas, that the devil entered into his heart before he betrayed his Lord, and it is plainly proved from his hanging himself afterwards; and I believe he entered into every heart, or they would never have betrayed the Lord Jesus Christ. Then why should it be marvellous in any one's eyes to say, the day of vengeance the Lord had in his heart turned on satan the spear, that he should receive his sentence from the woman, as Christ did from the man? This appeareth to me consistent with the mercy, wisdom, and the goodness of the Lord, who is wise in all his ways, and just and right in all his works, and when I disbelieve the one, I shall the other, for the prophecies are as clear of the one as the other. So here is my firm belief gone out into the world, and I believe this spirit as much came from the Lord, as I believe Christ died on the cross. Now let men of learning bring forth their arguments, and shew their strong reasons, why they believe the one and not the other; and I will bring forth mine, and shew my strong reasons, why I cannot believe the one without the other.

(B) . . .   About seven o'clock, wine and cakes were brought in, to be administered to the company, in the manner that Joanna had practised among her friends, and agreeably to the following communication:

"Now, Joanna, I shall give thee directions, as I am come to the fulfilment of the

Scriptures; and they shall be fulfilled in thee, and by thee. These that have not the Law, and do by nature the things contained in the Law, are a Law unto themselves: now, by the conduct of the ministers; and my Spirit being a ministring Spirit to thee, thou hast forsaken the Law of the Gospel of late, to meet in the churches and receive the Sacrament from the hands of men; yet thou hast been a Law unto thyself, in drinking the wine in remembrance of ME, with these words in thy heart, and on thy tongue:

> May I drink deep into the Spirit of Christ;
> And may his Blood cleanse me from all sin!

Now let all the believers join with thee in heart and tongue: let the wine be poured into one cup, and let it be handed round by the ministers; but let the words be repeated by every one that drinketh. First begin with thee; then follow with all the women, as I am come to redeem the Fall of women; then every man in his order, the ministers first, then go on to the twelve that were chosen with them; then to the Jury; then to the twenty-four Elders; then to the witnesses, every man in his order, one after the other, as the calling hath been. For though this is not a sacrament, yet let this be the desire of their hearts, if they wish for a double portion of my Spirit to be poured out upon them hereafter; for all that they have seen and heard, and any joy that they have felt, is but a shadow of what is to come; and let them know, from my disciples, whatever power of my Spirit they felt in my Life, they felt it much stronger by the power of the Holy Ghost, after my Death; for then came the days of Pentecost. And after thy death, I shall strengthen my disciples much stronger, when thou art gone; but while thou art living, all must come to thee; all must come through thee; and thou standest the Trial for the whole."

After every one had drank, and returned the cup, Joanna pronounced these words:—"As we all have drank in one cup, may we drink into one faith, and may that faith be in Christ!" This solemn and affecting ceremony being concluded, Joanna delivered a most impressive discourse upon the general tenor of her mission,

which brought her to this Trial. . . .   And as to her being called the Bride—
"This is but the shadow in ONE of what the substance will be to ALL, when the
BRIDEGROOM cometh." She dwelt with peculiar energy on this point; and which,
it is hoped, made a due impression upon the mind of every one present.

At nine o'clock Joanna sealed up the writings, which are to be kept till after
her death, and the signatures and seals of several present were also added; and the
packet was then delivered into the possession of one of the judges.

After this, as a part of the ceremony before described, Joanna handed cakes
to her female friends, which they broke among one another in token of love and
friendship; and the men helped themselves for the same purpose, and then all was
a scene of joy and mirth, in the midst of which Joanna took a final leave of her
friends and retired.

9. John Bowdler, "Thoughts on the Proposed Improvement of Female Education"
(1808), in *Select Pieces in Verse and Prose*, 2 vols., 4th ed. (London, 1820), I:244-46,
251-52, 256-57, 260-61, 269-71.

John Bowdler (1783-1815) was a London barrister whose ill health shortened
a promising career and led him into literary pursuits as well as the exploration of
contemporary philosophical, theological, and social questions. After his death his father
published a collection of his writings. Bowdler had no special expertise in these areas,
but does reflect the view of a literate, concerned Christian gentleman of his day. He
was open to new possibilities, although he wondered whether changes would produce
more harm than good. This ambivalence is particularly evident on the question of
improvements in female education, and his conclusion is at best patronizing to those
who sought further opportunities for women.

Three themes were central to later considerations of the issue. First, he feared that
greater attention to female intellectual development would undermine their capacity
to understand human nature through the affections. Secondly, he argued that since
the level of education reflects and parallels cultural opportunities, to provide the first
without more of the second would increase rather than reduce unhappiness. Thirdly, he

wondered if attention to the needs of women without corresponding interest in those of men would not adversely affect relations between the sexes. Such anxieties about what might happen did not mean that improvements could not be contemplated, but they did suggest that any changes would be received in the larger society only slowly and, even, grudgingly.

Among the persons who have engaged in discussions respecting female improvement, there subsists a great difference of sentiments; but both sides have, as by consent, proceeded on the assumption of the point which I wish to see more fully considered. They have each taken for granted, that the existing state of female attainments is very low. Proceeding on this hypothesis, one class of writers maintain, that thus it ought to continue. The other, with much more liberality, but perhaps with less of sound judgment than of good intention, contend that improvements are very desirable. I venture to doubt whether both bodies of disputants are not in error. The first indeed are so wrong, that they have no chance of ever getting right. Yet the mistake of the latter class may be the most serious, because it is a practical one. If the cultivation of female talents is at present, on the whole, about such as it ought to be, no interference is necessary, and tampering will probably do harm. At the least, this is a question which must be examined before we can advance a step securely; and this is just the question which, with their pardon be it said, all our worthy reformers have hitherto slipped by.

It may be as well here to dismiss at once those writers and talkers (thinkers they are not) who are pleased to insist, not only that women actually are ignorant and foolish, but that they ought always to be so. Nothing truly can be more impertinent than the liberties which such gentlemen take in this matter. They profess a jealousy of female improvement. It is natural, that, being stationary themselves, they should feel no pleasure in the advances of others: but what right have they to be thus jealous? Is the sex subject to their control? Are women bound to make choice of occupations according to their fancy? What concern have they with those whose discretion they think themselves authorized to question? This only—that they may some day wish to marry, and have therefore a slight interest in the character of the body from which they must then select. They need not, however, to feel any alarm. Were women much more highly educated than they generally are, there must still be very many of slender wit, and still more slender attainments, who will make them suitable companions. . . .

But the other body of writers on this subject are, in every view, well entitled to a grave reply; for professing, as I do, to agree with them, in respect to the general benefits of intellectual cultivation; and holding it clear that we have not the slightest right to debar women of those benefits if they wish to possess them; it is plain that my doubts, as to the soundness and safety of their conclusions, must arise from an original difference in our facts. If, however, they are mistaken in these, the inferences, of which they feel so secure, may not only be false, but dangerous; and the amendment they propose, nothing better than mischievous meddling.

In considering whether the present state of female knowledge is below its just level, we must bear in mind the infirmities and imperfections necessarily incident to the mechanism of society, and to man himself, the mechanist. Doubtless it would be very desirable to increase, in a ten-fold ratio, the wisdom and virtue now subsisting in the world; to make men, as well as women, much more knowing than they are. But this we are sure is impracticable by any sudden efforts. The whole of the social system must move on together; and though one part may accidentally, and for a short time, get the start of the rest, such an advantage is seldom great or lasting: chances come to all, and the race, in a long run, is pretty even. . . .

Upon general views then, without looking about for instances, there seems little reason to apprehend that women are at present less intellectual than they ought to be. If we turn to life, I cannot think we shall see reason to alter our judgment.

Women are not profound scholars and philosophers: it is admitted. They know but little of the Greek accents, of the doctrines of curves, of exchanges, and of paper credit; those learned ladies excepted, who are at home in every thing. But there is one sort of philosophy which they understand more practically and more deeply too, than any of us. I mean the philosophy of the human heart. This is their great field of inquiry; and the knowledge they here acquire is not gained by reading or thinking, but by observation on common life. . . .   Condemned as they are, partly by the ordinance of Providence, and partly by the ungenerous tyranny of men, to a state of dependence, their condition would be wretched indeed, if they possessed no resources by which to qualify or elude the domination of strength. But what they cannot attempt openly, they can, and frequently do, indirectly effect. As daughters, sisters, wives, and mothers, they have continual occasion to improve and exercise their knowledge of the heart, in foiling the passions and violence of men, in fixing or recovering their affections, in preserving the peace and animating the dulness of domestic life, and in training the infant mind to whatever is fair and amiable. Their attainments in *humanity* are their best arms, which serve for defence, and use, and ornament. Let us not insiduously or cruelly attempt to tear these from their hands, under the pretence of recommending a more regular system of mental discipline. They are necessary for the happiness of both sexes. Nor let us deceive ourselves and them, by the silly pedantry of fancying that human nature can only be studied to advantage in Hartley or Hutcheson. . . .

"I call that," says Milton, "a complete and generous education, which fits a person to perform justly, skilfully, and magnanimously, all the offices both of public and private life." In public life, women cannot be tried; but let the sufficiency of their education be judged by the general propriety of their behaviour, their constancy in distress, their moderation in prosperity, their fulfilment of every active and every passive duty. We talk freely of their love of follies, and delight to dwell on the foibles visible in the sex—foibles sometimes growing out of their very excellencies; but if the merits of education may be judged by the character and conduct of the students, Cambridge, and Oxford, and Edinburgh, must yield the palm to that course of female institution which has not hitherto been thought worthy even of being formed into a system. There are great mistakes about these matters. We deceive ourselves with the word education. Formerly this meant learning Latin and Greek at school, and going through the old courses of philosophy at college. It is still confined, with men, principally to intellectual discipline. But the present modes of instruction among women have this advantage, that the head and heart are trained together. Their dispositions are regulated; their manners are formed. Girls might be made excellent scholars as well as men; but then, other things must be neglected. . . . Let women be compared with men, in taste, curiosity, thirst of knowledge, and a quick relish of whatever is brilliant, lofty, or affecting; in propriety of manners, in their dispositions and affections, in prudential and moral conduct; and it may boldly be affirmed, that men would be "honoured by the rivalry." If such be the effects of their present system of education, I repeat with Milton, that "I call that a complete and generous education." . . .

Is it, then, desirable that women should sacrifice their present grace of mind and richness of imagination, in order to become forcible and accurate reasoners? If reason were a rare commodity, it would be necessary to procure it at any price; but, in the occupations of our busy world, there is such a constant demand for this great article of necessity, that we need not trouble ourselves to make laws and give bounties for providing a supply. On the contrary, it should seem prudent to secure, if possible, a fund of the more delicate faculties, which are not absolutely requisite for our existence, though they administer very largely to our happiness. Such are those which still flourish in the female world. Is there not also a natural affinity between that character of the understanding now peculiar to women, and the qualities we love to contemplate in the sex? Can we, without a sort of revulsion in our feelings, consider a timid, gentle, affectionate creature, disentangling all the mazes of metaphysics, floundering in the Serbonian bog of politics, lost in infinitesimals, or deep in dust and lore amidst the antiquities of history and languages? In a social view the matter is of great importance. "Manners make the man;" and women make the manners. Surely these are of some moment. A true delicacy in all the offices of social and domestic life is one of the best criteria, as it is one of the fairest fruits, of civilization. Woe to the nation that shall renounce it. They will descend fast into barbarism and brutality; for the gates of that dark passage stand open day and night—it is only the ascent which is difficult. Let us not rashly put in hazard that elegant refinement which is at once our honour and happiness. . . .

A few words only on religion, and these remarks shall be concluded. This indeed should be first, and last, and midst. Yet this too, I fear, is not likely to be benefited by the proposed alterations. We have been told, that "though Christianity does not require that every one should defend its authority, it seems to require that every one should understand its principles." It is granted. And who better understand those principles than pious females? I have heard of a zealous minister who said, that he had found a deeper acquaintance with Christianity in some old women of the lowest rank, than in any other persons of either sex. We are told, too, that "not one in a large proportion of pious women could advance any satisfactory reason for her belief." In one sense this is equally true of a great number of pious men; in another, it is true of neither. A satisfactory reason they have for themselves, in the peace and consolation they experience; but they have it not for others, because these are personal feelings. But it may even be doubted, whether "a systematic view of Christianity, with its various kinds of evidence," is needful; whether, in short, the religion of men and women ought to be exactly similar. In men, perhaps reason should preside; in women, affection. Thus each may improve the other. But if, by a novel system of discipline, the female character should be altered, and their feelings become cold, religion must lose its fervour, and with that, I fear, its life and energy. For though reason is the regulator, affection is the mainspring; and that devotion which resides only in the understanding, resembles rather the homage which a contemplative philosopher pays to his Creator, than the humble and grateful adoration which the repentant prodigal should render to his parent, the redeemed sinner to his God. In truth, a religion of mere reason is very suspicious. I once asked a French gentleman what were his guides in these matters. He replied, "Ma Bible, mes prêtres, et ma logique; et ma logique me serve plus que tout le reste." My readers will not be surprised to hear, that I found it impossible to convince my catholic that it was his duty to forgive some persons by whom he thought himself deeply injuried.

Reforms, however, in religion, can never be needless, whether for men or women. Let the latter then, since their improvement is in question, more seriously consider its inexpressible importance, and live more entirely under the influence of its precepts. Let them deeply and practically be persuaded, that the favour of God is far above every earthly blessing; that one act of charity or self-denial, one real exercise of humility or devotion, is better worth than the most flattering display of wit and accomplishments, with all the brilliancy of beauty to lend them lustre. So shall the loveliness of women be twice lovely; so shall the evening as well as the morn of life shine with unclouded brightness; and He, "before whose face the heavens and earth shall flee away," smile on them in that awful hour, when the charms of the fair and the wisdom of the wise shall alike be vain, and holiness alone retain its value.

CHAPTER 2

WOMEN AND THE EVANGELICAL REVIVAL

When one nineteenth-century Primitive Methodist preacher compared herself with John Wesley (1703-91), she felt the gap between them. He commanded respect and attention and could provide lodgings for himself. "But what am I? " she asked. "A poor 'Ranter' preacher, so termed, and a woman too."[1] Despite the tentativeness of the comparison, the opportunities for women in religious work fostered by the Evangelical Revival had been notable, though clearly not without external conflict and internal debate. The Revival in England was similar to the movements that had preceded it in Germany (Pietism) and America (the Great Awakening) in its emphasis on personal piety and holiness. The English version arose to fill a void created by the Anglican Church's prevailing posture of moderation and reasonableness in the faith, together with its difficulties in responding to the needs of the poor or ministering to the people of the growing industrial towns. Among its antecedents were the activities of the Oxford "Holy Club" of the late 1720s, which included as members John and Charles Wesley and George Whitefield. John Wesley's experience of religious re-direction in May, 1738 provide a beginning date for the Revival, which received its primary focus in his organizing genius.

Wesley's father, rector of Epworth in Lincolnshire, was a high church Tory. His mother had received an excellent education, especially in theology and the classics, and became a convinced Anglican in her teens as a result of her study. Both had been children of Dissenting ministers. A typically strict disciplinarian for her time,

Susanna Wesley also instilled in her children an interest in "serious Christianity." She even led religious services for a time. The occasion was her husband's absence in 1710 to attend Convocation. When the substitute minister proved to be unsatisfactory, she opened her family's Sunday evening worship to others in the parish and soon had a kitchen overflowing with people. In addition to leading in singing psalms and offering prayers, she read sermons from her husband's library. Upon receiving objections against such extraordinary activity, Samuel Wesley wrote to inquire if she were conducting something like a Dissenting conventicle. She denied all the accusations of impropriety, declared that she had done it only because of the people's entreaties, and defended herself on the basis of "the honour of Almighty God, the doing much good to many souls, and the friendship of the best among whom we live." In the end he did not forbid her to continue, and she stopped upon his return.[2] A young child at the time, John Wesley certainly participated in these services; but how much influence they had on his later views concerning the involvement of women in the Methodist movement is not known.

Wesley's work after his experience in 1738 was fully to recover "true Christianity" for England. Its several components, as he defined them, were that religion consists not so much in right opinions or in externals, but in possessing inward righteousness, "the image of God stamped upon the heart;" that the only way to this religion was to "repent and believe the gospel;" that this faith is justified freely by God's grace; and that the results of faith are to be "holy and happy."[3] In the organization of his work Wesley adopted some practices of the Moravian pietists, with whom he had first been associated on his voyage to Georgia in 1735, chiefly the divisions of the religious community into small bands for the sake of study, introspection, and prayer.[4] The pattern of composing bands by sex and marital status was also soon adopted; it seemed natural in terms of mutual interests as well as the distractions caused, as one man wrote, "by the too familiar intercourse at Societies with young women."[5] Wesley reported the creation of such bands in correspondence of 1738 after returning from a visit to the Herrnhut community: eight bands of men and two of women in mid-October (fifty-six and eight persons, respectively); six female bands by late November. He rejected a proposal to have monitors in each group, arguing that each person should be monitor to every other.[6] He also referred frequently to assistance provided in the movement by members of both sexes.[7]

By 1742 the organization was made more explicit with the formation of "classes" of twelve persons within a larger Methodist Society. Each had a leader, appointed rather than elected. Initially the leaders were to visit class members weekly in their homes. When that proved inexpedient the tasks of inquiring, comforting, reproving, and exhorting were accomplished in class meetings. Leaders also met regularly with the minister and the stewards of the Society, bringing in financial contributions, noting special needs of individuals, and reporting on the spiritual state of the members.[8]

Several aspects of this organization were particularly significant for women, the most basic being their religious equality with men. Further, the classes were divided for reasons of expediency, not to establish a hierarchy. Classes had no business to transact beyond the continuing interest in the spiritual welfare of the members, so there was no division of labor among them that could be differentiated according to sex. In addition, the class provided opportunity for the exercise of female religious leadership that had not been available in the Church of England in an official way. There was no formal preaching nor any occasions for the sacraments, since the meetings supplemented the regular parish services; thus there could be no constitutional objections to female leadership in these contexts, beyond those offered against the organization into classes itself. Finally, when "preachers" were added to the structure for pastoral oversight and itinerancy work, Wesley's authority at all levels of the movement did not change. He continued to meet with class leaders and stewards, as well as with all the men and all the women once each quarter.[9] Susanna

Wesley's leadership had been irregular; in Methodism the women's leadership was not.

From these relationships Wesley developed an extensive correspondence with women, who confided in him on spiritual as well as other matters. He encouraged and advised them generously. At the same time he cautioned his preachers against developing familiarity with women, partly from fear of scandal but partly also out of his own unfortunate experiences in close relationships with women.[10] Of course, women did not become "preachers." As the opening letter in this chapter indicates, Wesley at first found the Pauline injunctions determinative. He was also aware of the adverse effects of being too closely identified with the Quakers. Further, the life of the itinerants was hard. They travelled extensively alone, staying in Methodist homes, receiving little financial support beyond maintenance. Marriage was a burden on them, their families, and the Conference; and they were subject to harassment from mobs. It was not a life for a single woman, much less a married one.

But the evangelical life emphasized doing rather than being. Equality of class meetings meant that no specific religious character was assigned to women, no "ideal" required protection. The class meetings enabled women to exercise a kind of pastoral activity; they led Bible study, offered prayer, and testified to the power of the Gospel in their lives. Additional opportunities for service appeared, such as visiting the sick, talking with seekers, and helping the poor. It is not surprising that some women discovered special talents for this work, began to feel called by the Holy Spirit to enlarge their service, and received invitations to bring their witness to other Methodist groups. Wesley's letters show both his hesitation and his encouragement; if the Holy Spirit had called them, who was he to say no? At least he could urge them to be discreet so as not to raise needless complaints, and he could offer advice and counsel by way of monitoring their work. At times he feared it would get out of hand,[11] but in letters to individual women he regularly offered support.

We do not know enough about the religious work of particular women, partly because of the continuing ambivalence within Methodism concerning it. Without Wesley's personal encouragement there would have been fewer opportunities for service. After his death, and with greater institutionalization of the movement, even greater controls were exerted. Several of the new Methodist groups, from the Independent or Quaker Methodists in 1796 on, maintained a certain popular support for the ministry of women.[12] But again consolidation, institutionalization, and an adequate supply of male preachers worked against a prominent place for women. They continued as local preachers, class leaders, and Sunday School teachers, though less visible to a wider audience. To many Anglicans in the period it was little more than a matter for jest.[13]

Among Anglican Evangelicals there are few examples of any discussion concerning women and religion. The Countess of Huntingdon and Hannah More, the two most prominent women of that movement, were both very careful not to assume roles reserved for men. At the same time they took initiatives to respond to religious needs and did not hesitate to set up programs in the face of criticism from men. By their acceptance of the view that religion was action they were not inhibited by a religious "ideal" that made women observers of life rather than participants in it. However, neither of them provided avenues for the greater involvement of other women in the religious and social issues of the day. That was left for later generations to address.

1. *The Letters of the Rev. John Wesley*, edited by John Telford, 8 vols. (London: The Epworth Press, 1931).

One of John Wesley's most significant attributes was his ability to respond to the widely varied religious interests of those whom he came to lead. His approach to the participation of women in the Evangelical Revival is a prominent illustration of this.

From the early days of the movement women were used as class leaders. Although this created a new opportunity for developing religious leadership among women, Wesley had little intention of expanding it. On related matters he was similarly interested in maintaining the traditional views. For instruction on marriage he resorted to a treatise by the Puritan William Whately, *A Direction for Married Persons* (1619), which contained chapters on the husband's authority and the wife's inferiority.[14] And the Conference Minutes for 1765 record the following question and answer: "Q. Should the men and women sit apart every where? A. By all means. Every Preacher should look to this."[15]

But at this same Conference another question reflected concern over the place of women in the societies, and the answer indicated some shift in Wesley's position. The question was, "How can we encourage the women in the Bands to speak, since 'it is a shame for women to speak in the Church?' I Cor. xiv.35." Wesley's reply made two distinctions: first, he declared that "speaking" in the text referred only to *public teaching*, where authority over men is assumed; and secondly, he argued that the word "church" here meant the entire congregation. Thus, the practice of having women speak was allowable when it did not meet these two qualifications.

While Wesley could claim consistency with his earlier opposition to the Quaker employment of women, what is clear is that his context had been altered—from defense against external criticism to defense in relation to internal developments. By this time some women had not only enlarged on their earlier responsibilities and had been encouraged to do so; but Wesley had met women like Mary Bosanquet, Sarah Crosby, and Grace Walton, who were pressed by the extent of popular response to do more than lead class meetings and felt called by the Holy Spirit to continue this work. In most cases they took up the call reluctantly, and they anxiously inquired of Wesley for his judgment. He was impressed by their claim to the work of the Holy Spirit and decided that their experience fit the understanding of the "extraordinary call," which he asserted was applicable to all his preachers; but of course it was especially applicable to the women. Thus he encouraged, advised, and assisted them; and he suggested ways in which they could stave off criticism—do not call it preaching, do not identify a text, do not speak too long without a break. All this he managed without altering the visible structure of the Conference. It was a small step, then, but also a dramatic one, considering the context and the possibilities for expansion.

a) To Thomas Whitehead (?), February 10, 1748 (on the differences between Quakerism and Christianity):

. . .   'We judge it no ways unlawful for a woman to preach in the assemblies of God's people.'

In this there is a manifest difference: for the Apostle Paul saith expressly, 'Let your women keep silence in the churches; for it is not permitted unto them to speak. . . .   And if they will learn anything, let them ask their husbands at home; for it is a shame for women to speak in the church.' (I Cor. xiv. 34-5.)

Robert Barclay, indeed, says, 'Paul here only reproves the inconsiderate and talkative women.'

But the text says no such thing. It evidently speaks of women in general.

Again: the Apostle Paul saith to Timothy, 'Let the woman learn in silence with all subjection. For I suffer not a woman to teach, nor to usurp authority over the man' (which public teaching necessarily implies), 'but to be in silence.' (I Tim. ii. 11-12.)

To this Robert Barclay makes only that harmless reply: 'We think this is not anyways repugnant to this doctrine.' Not repugnant to this, 'I do not suffer a woman to teach'! Then I know not what is.

'But a woman "laboured with Paul in the work of the gospel."' Yea, but not in the way he had himself expressly forbidden.

'But Joel foretold, "Your sons and your daughters shall prophesy." And "Philip had four daughters which prophesied." And the Apostle himself directs women to prophesy; only with their heads covered.'

Very good. But how do you prove that prophesying in any of these places means preaching? (II:119-20)

b) To Sarah Crosby, February 14, 1761:

My Dear Sister,—Miss Bosanquet gave me yours on Wednesday night. Hitherto, I think you have not gone too far. You could not well do less. I apprehend all you can do more is, when you meet again, to tell them simply, 'You lay me under a great difficulty. The Methodists do not allow of women preachers; neither do I take upon me any such character. But I will just nakedly tell you what is in my heart.' This will in a great measure obviate the grand objection and prepare for J. Hampson's coming. I do not see that you have broken any law. Go on calmly and steadily. If you have time, you may read to them the *Notes* on any chapter before you speak a few words, or one of the most awakening sermons, as other women have done long ago. (IV:133)

c) To Grace Walton, September 8, 1761:

Sister,—If a few more persons come in when you are meeting, either enlarge four or five minutes on the question you had, with a short exhortation (perhaps for five or six minutes, sing and pray). I think, and always, its meaning is this: 'I suffer not a woman to teach in a congregation, nor thereby to assert authority over the man .   .   . , God has invested with this prerogative; whereas teaching. .   .   . (IV:164)

d) To Sarah Crosby, March 18, 1769:

I advise you, as I did Grace Walton formerly, 1) pray in private or public as much as you can. 2) Even in public you may properly enough intermix *short exhortations* with prayer: but keep as far from what is called preaching as you can: therefore never take a text; never speak in a continued discourse without some break, about four or five minutes. Tell the people, 'We shall have another *prayer-meeting* at such a time or place.' If Hannah Harrison had followed these few directions, she might have been as useful now as ever. (V:130)

e) To Mary Bosanquet, June 13, 1771:

My Dear Sister,—I think the strength of the cause rests there—on your having an *extraordinary* call. So I am persuaded has every one of our lay preachers; otherwise I could not countenance his preaching at all. It is plain to me that the whole work of God termed Methodism is an extraordinary dispensation of His providence. Therefore I do not wonder if several things occur therein which do not fall under the ordinary rules of discipline. St. Paul's ordinary rule was, 'I permit not a woman to speak in the congregation.' Yet in extraordinary cases he made a few exceptions; at Corinth in particular. (V:257)

f) To Sarah Crosby, December 2, 1777:

My Dear Sister,—I hope you will always have your time much filled up. You will, unless you grow weary of well doing. For is not the harvest plenteous still? Had we ever a larger field of action? And shall we stand all or any part of the day idle? Then we should wrong both our neighbour and our own souls.

For the sake of retrenching her expenses, I thought it quite needful for Miss Bosanquet to go from home. And I was likewise persuaded (as she was herself) that God had something for her to do in Bath and Kingswood; perhaps in Bristol too, although I do not think she will be called to speak *there* in public.

The difference between us and the Quakers in this respect is manifest. They flatly deny the rule itself, although it stands clear in the Bible. We allow the rule; only we believe it admits of some exceptions. At present I know of those, and no more, in the whole Methodist Connexion. You should send word of what our Lord is doing where you go to, dear Sally. (VI:290-91)

g) To Sarah Mallet, August 2, 1788:

. . . I do not doubt but you have given God your heart, and do in all things wish to do His holy and acceptable will. But if so, it is no wonder that you should meet with crosses, both from the devil and his children, especially as you believe you are called of God to bear a public testimony against him. But you are in far greater danger from applause than from censure; and it is well for you that one balances the other. But I trust you will never be weary of well doing. In due time you shall reap if you faint not. Whoever praises or dispraises, it is your part to go steadily on, speaking the truth in love. I do not require any of our preachers to license either themselves or the places where they preach. Indeed, a forward young man in Northamptonshire brought some trouble on himself by preaching in church time, and so near the church as to disturb both the minister and the congregation. But that need not fright any other of our preachers. They are just as safe as they were before. Go on, therefore, and fear nothing but sin. . . .   (VIII:78)

2. John Wesley, "On Visiting the Sick," *The Works of John Wesley*, 14 vols. (1872; Grand Rapids: Zondervan, n.d.), VII:125-27.

> With the involvement of women in Wesley's organization of classes and bands within the larger societies, one might expect to find frequent reference to a greater place for them in the life and work of the Christian community. Yet there are few such references. However, at the end of one rather ordinary sermon on the obligation of visiting the sick, Wesley made some bold assertions about the Christian responsibilities of women. It is not that equality in Christ is a social fiction, but that such equality must challenge society's view and expectations of women. It is not that equality as "image of God" can co-exist with intellectual inferiority, but that being "image of God" affirms women, as well as men, to be rational creatures. In view of some eighteenth-century claims made about women, that was more unusual than it may at first seem. Wesley encouraged women to a life of service, on the model of the early church's deaconesses and William Law's Miranda (see chapter 1), carefully limited to work with their own sex but not limited to a life within the home. That life could itself participate in the modification of the larger society's expectations of women, even though the primary concern was that of one's relationship to God.

. . .   "But may not *women*, as well as men, bear a part in this honourable service?" Undoubtedly they may; nay, they ought; it is meet, right, and their bounden duty. Herein there is no difference; "there is neither male nor female in Christ Jesus." Indeed it has long passed for a maxim with many, that "women are only to be seen, not heard." And accordingly many of them are brought up in such a manner as if they were only designed for agreeable playthings! But is this doing honour to the sex? or is it a real kindness to them? No; it is the deepest unkindness; it is horrid cruelty; it is mere Turkish barbarity. And I know not how any woman of sense and spirit can submit to it. Let all you that have it in your power assert the right which the God of nature has given you. Yield not to that vile bondage any longer! You, as well as men, are rational creatures. You, like them, were made in the image of God; you are equally candidates for immortality; you too are called of God, as you have time, to "do good unto all men." Be "not disobedient to the heavenly calling." Whenever you have opportunity, do all the good you can, particularly to your poor, sick neighbour. And every one of *you* likewise "shall receive *your* own reward, according to *your* own labour."

It is well known, that, in the primitive Church, there were women particularly appointed for this work. Indeed there was one or more such in every Christian congregation under heaven. They were then termed Deaconesses, that is, servants; servants of the Church, and of its great Master. Such was Phebe, (mentioned by St. Paul, Rom. xvi. 1,) "a Deaconess of the Church of Cenchrea." It is true, most of these were women in years, and well experienced in the work of God. But were the young wholly excluded from that service? No: Neither need they be, provided they know in whom they have believed; and show that they are holy of heart, by being holy in all manner of conversation. Such a Deaconess, if she answered her picture, was Mr. Law's Miranda. Would any one object to her visiting and relieving the sick and poor, because she was a woman; nay, and a young one too? Do any of you that are young desire to tread in her steps? Have you a pleasing form, an agreeable address? So much the better, if you are wholly devoted to God. He will use these, if your eye be single, to make your words strike the deeper. And while you minister to others, how many blessings may redound into your own bosom! Hereby your natural levity may be destroyed; your fondness for trifles cured; your wrong tempers corrected; your evil habits weakened, until they are rooted out; and you will be prepared to adorn the doctrine of God our Saviour in every future scene of life. Only be very wary, if you visit or converse with those of the other sex, lest your affections be entangled, on one side or the other, and so you find a curse instead of a blessing.

3. The Journal of Mary Bosanquet Fletcher, in Henry Moore, *The Life of Mrs. Mary Fletcher*, 3rd ed. (London: Methodist Conference Office, 1818), pp. 38-39, 96-97, 119-20.

Mary Bosanquet Fletcher (1739-1815) made many contributions to the Methodist movement, not the least of which was that she was one of the women who by dint of their sense of urgency in the Christian life compelled Wesley to reassess his position on female preachers. Born to a wealthy and lukewarm Anglican family, she encountered serious religion as a youth through a maid and a family friend who were Methodists. Eventually, tensions within the family over her religious convictions forced her out of her home at the age of twenty-one and into her own residence. Freer now to practice her religion she entered actively into Methodist circles. In 1763 she moved to her home village, Leytonstone in Essex, and soon had a thriving Methodist society, a school for orphans, and a small community of women who shared in the work, wore a common uniform, and practiced a daily office. Support came primarily from her personal income. The work was based on the model of the German Pietist A. H. Francke's work with orphans at Halle earlier in the century. Wesley visited frequently, noting the parallels with Halle and recording in his journal that he "found one truly Christian family; that is, what that at Kingswood should be, and would, if it had such governors."[16]

Both of Bosanquet's parents died in 1766. Two years later she moved her "family" to Cross Hall, a farm near Leeds in Yorkshire. Because of her responsibilities with the school, community, and farm, she did not travel as some other Methodist women did. But she continued to work with Methodist societies and spoke in public on many occasions, stopping short of calling herself a "preacher." Financial difficulties in the late 1770s forced her to contemplate selling the farm and dispersing the community, which she did after receiving a proposal of marriage from John Fletcher, vicar of Madeley and Wesley's most prominent associate. They were married in 1781; she continued to live at Madeley after her husband's death in 1785, travelling some to such places as Bristol and Bath for religious work but mainly working with her own classes at home, which numbered from sixty to a hundred persons. After her death her journal, edited by Henry Moore, provided a model of the saintly life for those who followed after her.

On March the 24th, the same year [1763], we removed to Layton-stone. From the first hour we found much of the presence of God; and stood still to see his salvation. In order to supply the want of public means, (which we could not have but when we went to London,) we agreed to spend an hour every night together in spiritual reading and prayer. A poor woman, with whom I had formerly talked, came to ask if she might come in, when we made prayer? We told her, at seven every Thursday night she should be welcome. She soon brought two or three more, and they others, till in a short time our little company increased to twenty-five. One night, just before the time of meeting, a poor woman called with a basket of cakes to sell. On our refusing to buy any, she stood still a long time at the gate. We began to converse with her about her soul, when she expressed a great desire to stay the meeting, and in so doing was so greatly blessed, that she would fain have left us part of her goods in return. We now thought it would be well to converse with each in particular, and that the time was come for it. Some few were offended, and came no more; but most appeared under conviction, and those we appointed to meet on Tuesday night, reserving the Thursday for the public meeting, which still kept increasing, and in which we read a chapter, and sometimes spoke from it.

The first time we met on the Tuesday night, two were set at liberty. We now thought it expedient to apply to Mr. Wesley for a preacher. He approved our plan, and sent Mr. Murlin the next Sunday; and within a fortnight, we had twenty-five joined in society. Much opposition now arose from all sides, (though more from the rich than the poor,) and one Thursday night, as I was speaking to a pretty large company in my own kitchen, the bell at the fore-gate was rung very hard. Our servant, who was a pious woman, went to see who was there. In the mean time, four shabby-looking men, with great sticks in their hands, came in at the back door, and so into the kitchen. The servant soon returned with some emotion, and whispered me, "It is Mr. W. who is come to inform you, you must, if you please, break off, for here is a great mob coming; and the ring leaders are four men with clubs." Turning to the people, I answered her aloud, "O, we do not mind mobs when we are about our Master's business." *Greater is he that is for us, than all that can be against us.* I then went on till I had concluded my subject. Having a few of the rules of the society, which I intended to disperse that night, I addressed myself first to the four men, who stood before me, explaining what they were, and asked if they would choose to accept one? They received them with a respectful bow, and went out. Who they were, and what was their purpose, I do not know to this day. We heard no more of the mob. At this time the hand of the Lord was much with us, supporting and comforting us under every trial. . . .

After a few days [1773], I was asked to go to Pannel, (about a mile from Harrowgate,) in order to hold a meeting at the house of a poor woman, who had taken the preachers in once or twice; at which I found many had been offended, and threatened much, so that I did not know what sort of treatment I was likely to meet with. Nevertheless I did not dare to refuse. We had a profitable time, and all was quiet. Two days after, I heard that some of the chief opposers were much affected; Glory be to God!—While we were holding the meeting a drunken man came by, and stopped a little while, then went on to the inn where I lodged, and told some of the gentlemen, that the lady who lived upstairs was preaching at Pannel. He repeated also some of the words he had heard me speak. When we came home they watched us in, and my maid, (who was a pious young woman,) going into the kitchen, they flocked about her, asking, in many questions, what her mistress had been doing at Pannel?

The following Sunday the company sent me a message upstairs; "That they unanimously requested I would have a meeting with *them* in the great ball-room." This was a trial indeed! It appeared to me, I should seem in their eyes as a bad woman, or a stage-player;—and I feared they only sought an opportunity to behave rudely. Yet, I considered,—I shall see these people no more till I see them at the judgment-seat of Christ, and shall it then be said to me,—"You might that day have warned us, but you would not!"—I answered them immediately, That I would wait on them at the time appointed. They behaved very well, and the presence of the Lord was with us. The following Sunday they made the same request. Much more company came in, even from High-Harrowgate:—but the Lord bore me through, and, glory be to him, we had some fruit. The next day I returned home, better in health, and comfortable in mind. All praise be to the Lord! . . .

October 1 [1776]. I was to-day at Clackhigh-town, and saw the hand of the Lord in many things. I have been more abundantly led to reflect on the difficulties of the path I am called in. I know the power of God which I felt when standing on the horse-block in the street at Huddersfield; but, at the same time, I am conscious how ridiculous I must appear in the eyes of many for so doing. Therefore, if some persons consider me as an impudent woman, and represent me as such, I cannot blame them. Again, many say, if you are called to preach, why do you not do it constantly, and take a round as a preacher? I answer, Because that is not my call. I have many duties to attend to, and many cares which they know nothing about. I must therefore leave myself to His guidance who hath the sole right of disposing of me. Again, they say, "Why do you not give out, I am to preach? Why call it a meeting?" I answer, Because that suits my design best. First, It is less ostentatious. Secondly, It leaves me at liberty to speak more or less as I feel myself led. Thirdly,

It gives less offence to those who watch for it. Others object, "Why, yours is a Quaker call; why then do you not join them at once? You are an offence to *us*. Go to the people whose call is the same as your own; here nobody can bear with you." I answer, Though I believe the Quakers have still a good deal of God among them, yet, I think the Spirit of the Lord is more at work among the Methodists; and while I see this, though they were to toss me about as a foot-ball, I would stick to them like a leech. Besides, I do nothing but what Mr. Wesley approves; and as to reproach thrown by some on me, what have I to do with it, but quietly go forward, saying, *I will be still more vile*, if my Lord requires it? Indeed, for none but thee, my Lord, would I take up this sore cross. But thou hast done more for me. O do thy own will upon me in all things! Only make me what thou wouldst have me to be. Only make me holy, and then lead me as thou wilt.

4. "An Account of S. Mallitt," *The Arminian Magazine*, 11 (1788), pp. 186-88, 238-41.

One of Wesley's most prominent women preachers at the end of his life was the young Sarah (or Sally) Mallet (b. 1768?). After a period of religious struggle, which included extended physical illness (described as "fits"), she felt called to preach in 1785-86. At first she preached locally, encouraged by her uncle, and soon received the Wesley's support. Joseph Harper, superintendent of the Norfolk circuit, gave her permission to preach in 1787 "by order of Mr. Wesley and the Conference," in the following notice: "We give the right hand of fellowship to Sally Mallet, and shall have no objection to her being a preacher in our connexion so long as she continues to preach the Methodist Doctrine and attends to our Discipline."[17] She traveled primarily in Norfolk and Suffolk, preaching wherever invited—in chapels, barns, and the open air. Later she married a Methodist local preacher and continued for a time to preach with him. Wesley was extremely solicitous in letters to her, encouraging her work, asking if she needed money, and giving advice. In 1789 he wrote, "Never continue the service above an hour at once, singing, *preaching*, prayer, and all. You are not to judge by your own *feelings*, but by the word of God. Never scream. Never speak above the natural pitch of your voice; it is disgustful to the hearers. It gives them pain, not pleasure. And it is destroying yourself. It is offering God murder for sacrifices."[18] And in response to some of the trials she had encountered in her work, he declared, "God is on your side."[19]

In the beginning of March [1785], the Lord set my soul at full liberty, by applying those words, *I will, be thou clean!* Now all darkness was dispersed, every doubt fled away, and I was filled with joy unspeakable. At this time I began to see more clearly, the work I came back to do. It was impressed on my mind, to speak in public for God; and those words were continually before me, *Reprove, rebuke, exhort!* Nor could I by any means drive them out of my thoughts. But I could not bear the thought, having been in time past no friend to women's preaching. I therefore resolved never to do any such thing, be the consequence what it would. From that moment it seemed as if the powers of darkness overwhelmed my soul: and I was forced to withdraw from the family, and pour out my soul before God. I entreated a portion of his word, that I might know what to do! And opened the book on these words, *No man lighteth a candle to put it under a bushel.* Yet I struggled with the devil six hours before he fled from me; and I gave myself up into the hands of God, to do with me what he pleased. He then broke in upon my soul. And as the room seemed a little before to be filled with the powers of darkness, it seemed now filled with the glory of God. I spent that night in prayer and praise. One of my sisters, being in the room with me, bid me hold my peace. But I told her, if I held my peace, the stones would cry out. I then showed her the need she had of a farther work in her own soul. And she cried unto the Lord for a clean heart, and received the petition which she asked of him.

But my conflict with Satan, and the abundant pouring out of the Spirit of God upon me, were more than my body could bear; I was tortured with inexpressible pain for some hours: my mother asked, What she should do for me? I answered, "Nothing. The Lord himself will remove it when it pleases him." While I was speaking, the pain was taken away, and I rose from bed immediately. I now returned to Long-Stratton, where in the beginning of April, my leg was restored as the other, without any outward help. I was grieved to leave two young women with whom I had met in band. But I believed God called me, and so on the tenth of May, I returned to my uncle's. But I had still a burden upon my mind, not seeing what I came thither for: for I still reasoned against the conviction which followed me, That I must speak in public. Meantime my soul was filled with darkness and distress: while I was more and more convinced, that I ought to speak for God. I had none to reveal my mind to, and I knew not how to begin, being kept back by fear and shame. Many times *my eyes gushed out with tears, because men kept not God's law,* many times I said, *O that my head was water, and mine eyes a fountain of tears, that I might weep day and night for the sins of my people.* . . .

In September the Lord visited me again with affliction. . . . For during my fits I was utterly senseless; but when I came to myself I could well remember, the place where I had been preaching, and the words I had been speaking from. I grew weaker and weaker, and expected to die soon; but death was a welcome messenger: and the foretaste of those joys to which I thought I was just going, took off the edge of my pains. In my sharpest pains I thought, what is all this to what I should have suffered, had not the Son of God suffered for me? And I continually said, "Lord, give me thyself, and then deal with me as thou pleasest!" In this affliction he weaned me from the creature, from all created good: so that the world was utterly dead to me, and I unto the world.

And in this affliction God made known, notwithstanding all my resistance, the work he had called me to do; and not to me only, but to all that were round about me, by opening my mouth, whether I would or no. While every sense was locked up, the Lord prepared me for the work which he had prepared for me. And I thought, if he should restore me, I would spend my latest breath in declaring his dying love to sinners. From this time my strength continually increasing, my uncle asked, "Have you any objection to speaking in public?" I answered, "Whatever is in your mind concerning me, I consider as appointed of God." So in the beginning of February 1786, he desired me to speak in his Preaching-House. Fear and shame caused me to tremble at first. But the Lord gave me strength and loosed my tongue. At this Satan was much displeased. I had fighting without and within. Professors and profane seemed engaged against me. And I had no earthly friend to give me any encouragement, but those with whom I lived. These words had followed me for near a year, "Ye shall be hated of all men for my name's sake:" and so did those, "Fear not; for I am with thee: be not afraid: for I am thy God. I will strengthen thee, yea, I will help thee: I will uphold thee with the right hand of my righteousness."

I now gave myself up to prayer and much watchfulness. I saw a greater need of close walking with God than ever, having the eyes of all upon me; and above all, the eyes of God. He showed me daily more of my own weakness, and of his willingness to strengthen me. Yet I often broke out, *O Lord God, behold I am a child!* And often, sensible of the importance of the work, I said, "Why me, Lord? What am I, or my father's house?"

I was now appointed to speak in my uncle's house, every other Sunday evening. The Lord gave me light and liberty, and I had great peace in my soul, and more nearness to God than ever. I walked continually in the light of his countenance: and sometimes meditating on the dying love of Jesus to a guilty world, I have had such manifestations of his love to my soul, as were more than my body could bear. In this state I continued for some time. But then Satan came in like a flood, endeavouring to persuade me, that I was not called of God to this work. Not prevailing this way, he tempted me to spiritual pride: and when he was not able to lift me up, he strove to cast me down, telling me, I had neither learning nor sense for such a work, and that all I said was mere foolishness. I entreated the Lord, to stand by me in the trying hour: and those words were powerfully applied to my soul, *If any man lack wisdom, let him ask of God—and it shall be given him.* During these temptations I scarce knew what it was to have one whole night's sleep in a week. Sometimes also my soul was so engaged with God, that my sleep departed from me. And sometimes I spent whole nights in reading, chiefly the Holy Scriptures. . . .

Being to preach on the 22d of October, and having a violent headache, I was almost persuaded to give it up; especially as I could find but one text to speak from, and had but little light on that. One of my friends coming in, I told him my distress, and said, "I fear you will have no Preacher tonight." He said, "Will you be on the devil's side? Be on God's side." I thought, So I will. I laid my cause before the Lord, and looked to him for strength. As soon as I begun speaking, the darkness fled away, and the Lord removed my pain, and gave me light and liberty with a particular blessing to the people.

5. George Eliot, *Adam Bede* (New York: Harper & Bros., 1859), Chapter II, pp. 18-23, 26-27.

In 1859 the publication of *Adam Bede* revived the image of the Methodist female preacher, by this time only a memory among the Wesleyans. George Eliot (1819-80) set her novel in the year 1799. The picture of Dinah Morris reflected the experience of her aunt, Mrs. Elizabeth Evans, who had been a Methodist preacher, as well as Eliot's study of such works as Southey's biography of Wesley and the life of Mrs. Fletcher. The character was so authentic that many contemporaries and later commentators thought the correspondence to Eliot's aunt was exact in the substantive details.[20] Eliot's own religious skepticism intruded at the novel's end; Dinah has given up preaching to conform to the Wesleyan restriction of 1803 (see selection 6) and married the only modestly religious Adam Bede. But the narrative of Dinah's preaching from a cart on the village green of Hayslope, complete with its declaration of God's love to sinners and its invoking of the law followed by the gospel, provides a vivid glimpse of the religious zeal of female preachers and the popular response to it that is almost impossible to duplicate from other sources.

"Dear friends," she said, in a clear but not loud voice, "Let us pray for a blessing."

She closed her eyes, and hanging her head down a little, continued in the same moderate tone, as if speaking to some one quite near her:—

"Saviour of sinners! when a poor woman, laden with sins, went out to the well to draw water, she found Thee sitting at the well. She knew Thee not; she had not sought Thee; her mind was dark; her life was unholy. But Thou didst speak to her, Thou didst teach her, Thou didst show her that her life lay open before Thee, and yet Thou wast ready to give her that blessing which she had never sought. Jesus! Thou art in the midst of us, and Thou know'st all men: if there is any here like that poor woman—if their minds are dark, their lives unholy—if they have come out not seeking Thee, not desiring to be taught; deal with them according to the free mercy which Thou didst show to her. Speak to them, Lord; open their ears to my message; bring their sins to their minds, and make them thirst for that salvation which Thou art ready to give.

"Lord! Thou art with Thy people still: they see Thee in the night-watches, and their hearts burn within them as Thou talkest with them by the way. And Thou art near to those who have not known Thee: open their eyes that they may see Thee—see Thee weeping over them, and saying, 'Ye will not come unto me that ye might have life'—see Thee hanging on the cross and saying, 'Father, forgive them, for they know not what they do'—see Thee as Thou wilt come again in Thy glory to judge them at the last. Amen."

Dinah opened her eyes again and paused, looking at the group of villagers, who were now gathered rather more closely on her right hand.

"Dear friends," she began, raising her voice a little, "you have all of you been to church, and I think you must have heard the clergyman read these words: 'The spirit of the Lord is upon me, because he hath anointed me to preach the gospel to the poor.' Jesus Christ spoke those words—he said he came *to preach the Gospel to the poor.* I don't know whether you ever thought about those words much; but I will tell you when I remember first hearing them. It was on just such a sort of evening as this, when I was a little girl, and my aunt, as brought me up, took me to hear a good man preach out of doors, just as we are here. I remember his face well: he was a very old man, and had very long white hair; his voice was very soft and beautiful, not like any voice I had ever heard before. I was a little girl, and scarcely knew anything, and this old man seemed to me such a different sort of a man from anybody I had ever seen before, that I thought he had perhaps come down from the sky to preach to us, and I said, 'Aunt, will he go back to the sky to-night, like the picture in the Bible?'

"That man of God was Mr. Wesley, who spent his life in doing what our blessed Lord did—preaching the Gospel to the poor—and he entered into his rest eight years ago. I came to know more about him years after, but I was a foolish thoughtless child then, and I remembered only one thing he told us in his sermon. He told us as 'Gospel' meant 'good news.' The Gospel, you know, is what the Bible tells us about God.

"Think of that now! Jesus Christ did really come down from heaven, as I, like a silly child, thought Mr. Wesley did; and what he came down for, was to tell good news about God to the poor. Why, you and me, dear friends, are poor. We have been brought up in poor cottages, and have been reared on oat-cake, and lived coarse; and we haven't been to school much, nor read books, and we don't know much about anything but what happens just round us. We are just the sort of people that want to hear good news. For when anybody's well off, they don't much mind about hearing news from distant parts; but if a poor man or woman's in trouble and has hard work to make out a living he likes to have a letter to tell him he's got a friend as will help him. To be sure we can't help knowing something about God, even if we've never heard the Gospel, the good news that our Saviour brought us. For we know everything comes from God: don't you say almost every day, 'This and that will happen, please God?' and 'We shall begin to cut the grass soon, please God to send us a little more sunshine?' . . .

"But perhaps doubts come into your mind like this: Can God take much notice of us poor people? Perhaps he only made the world for the great, and the wise, and the rich. It doesn't cost him much to give us our little handful of victual and bit of clothing; but how do we know he cares for us any more than we care for the worms and things in the garden, so as we rear our carrots and onions? Will God take care of us when we die? and has he any comfort for us when we are lame and sick and helpless? Perhaps, too, he is angry with us; else why does the blight come, and the bad harvests, and the fever, and all sorts of pain and trouble? For our life is full of trouble, and if God sends us good, he seems to send bad too. How is it? how is it?

"Ah! dear friends, we are in sad want of good news about God; and what does other good news signify if we haven't that? For everything else comes to an end, and when we die we leave it all. But God lasts when everything else is gone. What shall we do if he is not our friend?"

Then Dinah told how the good news had been brought, and how the mind of God towards the poor had been made manifest in the life of Jesus, dwelling on its lowliness and acts of mercy. . . .

"Well, dear friends, who *was* this man? Was he only a good man—a very good man, and no more—like our dear Mr. Wesley, who has been taken from us? . . . He was the Son of God—'in the image of the Father,' the Bible says; that means, just like God, who is the beginning and end of all things—the God we want to know about. So then, all the love that Jesus showed to the poor is the same love that God has for us. We can understand what Jesus felt, because he came in a body like ours, and spoke words such as we speak to each other. We were afraid to think what God was before—the God who made the world and the sky and the thunder and the lightning. We could never see him; we could only see the things he had made; and some of these things was very terrible, so as we might well tremble when we thought of him. But our blessed Saviour has showed us what God is in a way us poor ignorant people can understand; he has showed us what God's heart is, what are his feelings towards us.

"But let us see a little more about what Jesus came on earth for. Another time he said, 'I came to seek and to save that which was lost;' and another time, 'I came not to call the righteous, but sinners to repentance.'

"The *lost*! . . .   *Sinners*! . . .   Ah, dear friends, does that mean you and me?"

Hitherto the traveller had been chained to the spot against his will by the charm of Dinah's mellow treble tones, which had a variety of modulation like that of a fine instrument touched with the unconscious skill of musical instinct. The simple things she said seemed like novelties, as a melody strikes us with a new feeling when we hear it sung by the pure voice of a boyish chorister; the quiet depth of conviction with which she spoke seemed in itself an evidence for the truth of her message. He saw that she had thoroughly arrested her hearers. The villagers had pressed nearer to her, and there was no longer anything but grave attention on all faces. She spoke slowly, though quite fluently, often pausing after a question, or before any transition of ideas. There was no change of attitude, no gesture; the effect of her speech was produced entirely by the inflections of her voice; and when she came to the question, "Will God take care of us when we die?" she uttered it in such a tone of plaintive appeal that the tears came into some of the hardest eyes. The stranger had ceased to doubt, as he had done at the first glance, that she could fix the attention of her rougher hearers, but still he wondered whether she could have that power of rousing their more violent emotions, which must surely be a necessary seal of her vocation as a Methodist preacher, until she came to the words, "Lost!—Sinners!" when there was a great change in her voice and manner. She had made a long pause before the exclamation, and the pause seemed to be filled by agitating thoughts that showed themselves in her features. Her pale face became paler; the circles under her eyes deepened, as they do when tears half gather without falling; and the mild loving eyes took an expression of appalled pity, as if she had suddenly discerned a destroying angel hovering over the heads of the people. Her voice became deep and muffled, but there was still no gesture. Nothing could be less like the ordinary type of the Ranter than Dinah. She was not preaching as she heard others preach, but speaking directly from her own emotions, and under the inspiration of her own simple faith.

But now she had entered into a new current of feeling. Her manner became less calm, her utterance more rapid and agitated, as she tried to bring home to the people their guilt, their wilful darkness, their state of disobedience to God—as she dwelt on the hatefulness of sin, the Divine holiness, and the sufferings of the Saviour, by which a way had been opened for their salvation. At last it seemed as if, in her yearning desire to reclaim the lost sheep, she could not be satisfied by addressing her hearers as a body. She appealed first to one and then to another, beseeching them with tears to turn to God while there was yet time; painting to them the desolation of their souls, lost in sin, feeding on the husks of this miserable world, far away from God their Father; and then the love of the Saviour, who was waiting and watching for their return. . . .

But now Dinah began to tell of the joys that were in store for the penitent, and to describe in her simple way the divine peace and love with which the soul of the believer is filled—how the sense of God's love turns poverty into riches, and satisfies the soul, so that no uneasy desire vexes it, no fear alarms it: how, at last, the very temptation to sin is extinguished, and heaven is begun upon earth, because no cloud passes between the soul and God, who is its eternal sun.

"Dear friends," she said at last, "brothers and sisters, whom I love as those for whom my Lord has died, believe me I know what this great blessedness is; and because I know it, I want you to have it too. I am poor, like you: I have to get my living with my hands; but no lord nor lady can be so happy as me, if they haven't got the love of God in their souls. Think what it is—not to hate anything but sin; to be full of love to every creature; to be frightened at nothing; to be sure that all things will turn to good; not to mind pain, because it is our Father's will; to know that nothing—no, not if the earth was to be burnt up, or the waters come and drown us—nothing could part us from God who loves us, and who fills our souls with peace and joy, because we are sure that whatever he wills is holy, just, and good.

"Dear friends, come and take this blessedness; it is offered to you; it is the good news that Jesus came to preach to the poor. It is not like the riches of this world, so that the more one gets the less the rest can have. God is without end; his love is without end—

'Its streams the whole creation reach,
So plenteous is the store;
Enough for all, enough for each,
Enough for evermore.'"

Dinah had been speaking at least an hour, and the reddening light of the parting day seemed to give a solemn emphasis to her closing words. The stranger, who had been interested in the course of her sermon, as if it had been the development of a drama—for there is this sort of fascination in all sincere unpremeditated eloquence, which opens to one the inward drama of the speaker's emotions—now turned his horse aside, and pursued his way, while Dinah said, "Let us sing a little, dear friends;" and as he was still winding down the slope, the voices of the Methodists reached him, rising and falling in that strange blending of exultation and sadness which belongs to the cadence of a hymn.

6. The Methodist Conference of 1803, from *Minutes of the Methodist Conferences,* 16 vols. (London: Wesleyan Conference Office, 1812-68), II:188-89.

Despite Wesley's gradual change of mind and the success of a number of women preachers among the Methodists, women were never accepted into the regular itinerancy. They were thus both supplementary and extraordinary to the institutional structure of ministry, conditions which made them less visible but which also gave those who sought to preach a certain amount of freedom as well. After Wesley's death support and encouragement from the leadership declined, and pressure to regularize the place of women preachers grew. Reflecting the increase of opposition to women preaching, a debate took place on the issue at the Irish Conference of 1802, concluding with a resolution which declared "that it is contrary both to Scripture and prudence that *women* should preach or should exhort in public; and we direct the Superintendents to refuse a Society Ticket to any woman in the Methodist Connexion who preaches, or who exhorts in any public congregation, unless she entirely cease from so doing."[21] At least one of the Irish women preachers, Alice Cambridge, refused to give up her work and continued to preach before large congregations; she was readmitted by Conference resolution in 1811.[22]

The Conference of 1803 did not forbid the preaching of women, but it made two claims which Wesley in his later years would have repudiated, namely, that its status depended largely on whether there was an adequate supply of male preachers, and that it normally should address an audience of women only. The further regulations regarding permission to preach brought their previous freedom under the control of the local authorities. Although some women continued to minister under these regulations, the Conference direction was clearly against them.

Question. Should women be permitted to preach among us?

Answer. We are of opinion that in general they ought not. 1. Because a vast majority of our people are opposed to it. 2. Because their preaching does not at all seem necessary, there being a sufficiency of preachers whom God has accredited, to supply all the places in our connexion with regular preaching. But if any woman thinks she has an extraordinary call from God to speak in public, (and we are sure it must be an *extraordinary* call that can authorize it,) we are of opinion she should, in general, address her *own sex*, and *those only*. And, upon this condition alone, should any woman be permitted to preach in any part of our connexion; and when so permitted, it should be under the following regulations: 1. They shall not preach in the circuit where they reside, until they have obtained the approbation of the Superintendent and a Quarterly meeting. 2. Before they go into any other circuit to preach, they shall have a *written* invitation from the Superintendent of such circuit, and a recommendatory note from the Superintendent of their own circuit.

7. A Letter of Jabez Bunting, 1836, in T. P. Bunting, *The Life of Jabez Bunting*, 2 vols. (London: T. Woolmer, 1859, 1887), II:307.

Some women preachers were able to accommodate themselves to the 1803 resolution, but others simply defied it. Best known among the early nineteenth-century Wesleyan women preachers was Mary Barritt Taft, who travelled widely in the north of England. She married Zechariah Taft, a Methodist itinerant, who encouraged his wife in this work and wrote several tracts defending women's preaching. But the towering leadership of Jabez Bunting (1779-1858) over the Conference from 1814 until his death prevented this question from becoming anything more than a matter of local concern. Bunting's letter in 1836 was a response to a Superintendent who wrote for advice on how to interpret the 1803 regulation in relation to the wife of a ministerial colleague. Not only did he oppose any public (that is, advertised or officially sanctioned) ministry for women, but he denied the legitimacy of an appeal to the work of the Spirit, which was the theological claim that had moved Wesley to support it. Bunting's commitments to the authority of the Pastoral Office and to the discipline necessary to sustain the Conference had by this date also been challenged by some men. Rejecting the extraordinary appeal of the Spirit, however, did not disrupt the foundation of their ministry the way it did that of women.

Mrs. _____ I fully believe to be a talented and excellent woman; but I agree with you that St. Paul has expressly prohibited the *public* teaching of women; and therefore I could never conscientiously sanction it, or, where I had official responsibility, allow it in any case. Prayer and private teaching of those of their own sex are different questions. . . . Even our standing Rules (see Minutes of 1803), though more lax in their principle than, I think, is scrupulously correct, are opposed to your compliance with the request to which you refer. They limit a woman's preaching, even under that vague and perilous condition of an 'extraordinary call' (which is every fanatic's plea) to her own sex.

8. Hugh Bourne, "Remarks on the Ministry of Women" (1808), from *Memoirs of the Life and Labours of the Late Venerable Hugh Bourne,* by John Walford; ed. by the Rev. W. Antliff; 2 vols. (London: T. King, 1855), I:172-77.

The two decades following Wesley's death was a period of considerable ferment in the Methodist movement, producing denominational independence from the Church of England as well as several schisms and offshoots from the movement itself. Among the latter groups the Primitive Methodists, led by Hugh Bourne (1772-1852) and William Clowes, and the Bible Christians, founded by William O'Bryan, gave a prominent place for the ministry of women. Bourne was the son of a Staffordshire farmer and first worked as a carpenter and timber-cutter. He experienced religious conversion after many years of searching and soon became a local Wesleyan preacher. After several years in this work he helped to lead a series of open-air meetings in the summer of 1807 on the model of the American camp meeting. This activity was not well received by the Wesleyan leaders, and a year later he was expelled by his circuit's quarterly meeting.

Between those events two incidents helped to make the issue of women in ministry an important dimension of his differences with the Wesleyans. First, in the course of his ministry he talked with two men who were disturbed by the exclusion of a female preacher named Mary Dunnell from the pulpit of the local chapel in Tunstall. They pressed for secession, but Bourne persuaded them not to take such extreme action. Secondly, he attended the Conference of Independent Methodists at Macclesfield in 1808, where he heard a discussion on the ministry of women in the societies. These people were also called Quaker Methodists; they permitted no distinction between ministers and laity and freely admitted women to the ministry, following the Quaker pattern. Each incident compelled Bourne to wrestle with the topic, to consider the biblical evidence, and to assess the work of women he knew who engaged in preaching and teaching. Shortly after the Macclesfield Conference he produced his tract on the ministry of women.[23] In 1812 the name "Primitive Methodists" was chosen for the emerging society composed of followers of Bourne and those of Clowes.

In the early years of these groups a number of women were employed as itinerants. Thirteen were listed in the Primitive Methodist Conference Minutes of 1832, and fourteen (out of thirty) at the first Bible Christian Conference in 1819. Many more were local preachers and class leaders. Among the more notable were Sarah Kirkland (1794-1880), the first woman itinerant in the Primitive Methodists; Elizabeth Bultitude, a minister for thirty years from 1832 who served a total of seventeen stations; Mary Porteous, who wrote a narrative of her ministry; and O'Bryan's wife Catherine and daughter Mary. Yet despite initial affirmation and the enthusiasm of a later generation of denominational historians,[24] the number of travelling women preachers declined steadily. Elizabeth Bultitude was the last within the Primitive Methodists, and among the Bible Christians there was only one listed in 1872, compared with 127 men. The shift reflected the evolution from a revival society to a more institutionalized denomination, as well as the fact that a sufficient number of men were available. Further, the various levels of resistance to female participation had not easily gone away; women itinerants of the Bible Christians, for example, had never had votes in its business meetings.[25] Some later leaders would conclude that the ministry of their women was only an exception to the general scriptural rule against female preaching.[26] Some participants were also reluctant. It was reported of Ann Shaw (1792-1857) that despite the urgings of others, "she would only pray and exhort sinners to flee from the wrath to come, and believers to claim their emancipation from sin. No argument could induce her to ascend the pulpit or give out a hymn."[27] That was quite a contrast to the claims made earlier by Bourne.

. . . We find in Joel ii.28: "And your sons and your daughters shall prophesy." In order to enter more easily into the subject, we must first find out the precise meaning of the word prophesy: and on this head you will find full satisfaction in a sermon on the Christian Prophet and his work, by Adam Clarke, which may be had of the methodist preachers, price six-pence. It was first published in the magazine, for 1800. To this I will add the explanation given by Parkhurst, whose authority ranks very high. . . .

We see here that a prophet was simply one who was employed in the service of God, and that whether as one that sung the praises of God, or one that preached, exhorted, or instructed the people; and these last were said to preach the gospel. . . .

I shall now endeavour to follow your friend's propositions. The first of which may be comprised in the following words:—"Is the preaching of women authorized by Jesus Christ?"

Answer. I think it is. I think he authorized Miriam, (Micah vi. 4,) Deborah, Huldah, and perhaps many others not recorded; and the gospel was preached in those days, (Heb. iv. 2,) and he is the same God now, and acts in the same way.

But, perhaps, you wish for an example when our Lord was upon earth. Well, besides the Virgin Mary and Elizabeth, you have Anna, the prophetess, who testified of Jesus in the Temple; and this I take to be strong preaching. Well, but you say, whom did he authorize personally? Ans. The Woman of Samaria. I believe she was commissioned by the Holy Ghost to preach Jesus, and she did preach him with extraordinary success; and he authorized her ministry, for he joined in with it, and acted accordingly.

But, perhaps, you want a personal commission,—very well, then you have Mary Magdalene. She was commissioned by an angel to preach, and then by Jesus Christ himself. It is said of Paul, in one place, that he preached Jesus and the resurrection,—so did Mary to the apostles themselves. Thus our Lord ordained her an apostle to the apostles, a preacher to the preachers, and an evangelist to the evangelists.

The second proposition may be stated thus:—"Was women's ministry countenanced by any of the apostles?"

Answer. Philip, the evangelist, had four daughters, virgins, that prophesied—preached. Acts xxi. 9. Secondly, Aquila and Priscilla took Apollos, and expounded to him the way of God. Acts xviii. 26. St. Paul says, "Help those women which laboured with me in the gospel." Phil. iv. 3. He there joins them with Clement and his other fellow-labourers. He also says, I Cor. xi. 5, "Every woman that prayeth or prophesieth with her head uncovered," &c. This is rather decisive. He here lays down rules and regulations for this very thing; and even if any woman who prayed or prophesied would not submit to rule, he did not say let her be stopped, but let her be shorn.

The third proposition is about historical documents, which I think is pretty well answered above. And in Acts, Phoebe is called a deaconess. Now a part of the office of deacons was preaching, as appears by the customs of the churches, and by the example of St. Stephen. . . .

The fifth proposition may be stated thus:—"Is not women's preaching interdicted by apostolic authority?" I Cor. xiv. 34. I Tim. ii. 11. Answer. It is rather harsh to suppose that an apostle interdicted what had been the practice of the church of God in all ages, what had been personally sanctioned by our Lord himself, and what even the same apostle had just been establishing, by giving rules for it. I Cor. xi. 5, 6, 7. The question, then, is, "What are we to understand by these scriptures?" I shall not endeavour to give you on this any opinion as my own; for having never studied them very closely, I could not in conscience do it.

But I am told that these speak of church discipline, and of establishing church authority; and truly, if women must ordain or set apart the men for the ministry, it would be usurping authority, for the greater would be blessed of the less.

I have heard it stated further, that he there says, "If they will learn any thing, let them ask their husbands at home." This they say settles the meaning, for he must be speaking of something that the husbands can inform them of. This well applies to discipline, but if it extends to preaching also, then all who have ungodly husbands are inevitably bound over to eternal damnation, because they are restricted from learning any thing from any but their husbands.

If also this must be stretched out so as to exclude women from teaching men religion, it would reach too far,—it would break the order of God,—it would interdict mothers from teaching their sons; and I believe that I owe my salvation, under God, in a great degree, to a pious mother. . . .

I have been many years in the methodist society, during which I frequently heard of Mrs. Fletcher's exercising the ministry, before I was favoured with an opportunity of sitting under it, and she had Mr. Wesley's approbation, as appears by his letters to her, and I never heard any person express his disapprobation of it. Now supposing her ministry had been stopped by arbitrary measures, what a loss that part of the country would have sustained.

I think all the objections that can be brought may be confined to this, that the woman is the weaker vessel. But this is so far from making against, that it is strongly in favour of it. See I Cor. i. 27. And as God chose the ministry of women under darker dispensation, it would be strange if they are incapable of ministering, on account of being weaker vessels, now the gospel shines with a brighter light.

9. Letters of Selina Hastings, Countess of Huntingdon, in [A. C. H. Seymour], *The Life and Times of Selina, Countess of Huntingdon*, 2 vols. (London: William Edward Painter, 1844), II:399-401, 432, 324-25.

Selina Hastings, Countess of Huntingdon (1707-91), took advantage of an opportunity available to peers of the realm and used her wealth and managerial skills to promote the Evangelical Revival. She was not the only person to do this,[28] but she is the best known, as the association of congregations which she organized and supported became known as The Countess of Huntingdon's Connexion. In 1728 she married

Theophilus, the ninth Earl of Huntingdon, and entered a life of raising a family, managing estates, and mixing in fashionable society. During an illness in 1739 she experienced an evangelical awakening which changed her life. Attracted to the preaching of George Whitefield, she invited him, the Wesleys, and other preachers to her estate to preach the gospel to family, workers, and friends. In 1748, two years after her husband's death, she appointed Whitefield as her chaplain. It was this rather common practice among titled families which she gradually expanded after 1760 into a network of chaplains and other clergy who took assignments from her, a group of private chapels in several towns, and an extensive correspondence with people who sought her aid or advice on matters relating to the Revival. All this was done within the framework of the established Church. In 1768 she opened a college for the training of ministers at Trevecca in south Wales and appointed Wesley's associate, John Fletcher, as its first president. But as her theological sympathies were with Whitefield, the Methodist critique of predestination irritated her. After Whitefield's death in 1770 the debate between the parties became more heated; she dismissed Fletcher, and the relations between her associates and the followers of Wesley deteriorated badly.[29]

The pattern of adding to the number of her private chapels, sending ministers to groups of Evangelicals who requested them and planning lengthy preaching tours for others, eventually ran afoul of the Church of England's parochial structure. Disgruntled clergy brought suit in ecclesiastical court against the use of unconsecrated buildings for worship and of ministers preaching without regular call from a particular parish or the approval of either bishop or local vicar. Although the Countess protested, ecclesiastical law went against her, and she and a group of supporters felt their only alternative was to secede from the Church of England and take refuge in the protection provided by the Toleration Act. They would try to remain neutral between the Church and Dissent, as they accepted the doctrine and ceremonies of the Church but not its discipline. This took place in 1781, and it was followed in 1783 with an ordination service for six men from the college (there being less possibility of using Anglican clergy in the seceded structure) and the acceptance of a confession of faith.

In this work the Countess was administrator, governor, financial supporter and manager, but neither minister nor theologian. She remained firmly in control of the operation of the Connexion until her death, when the rights of property she possessed were transferred to four trustees (chiefly Lady Anne Erskine, her closest associate), who continued to appoint ministers and chapel managers. In 1791, there were seven chapels in trust and approximately a hundred more in some degree of association with the Countess; a century later the number stood at thirty-three. After her death, with the lease expiring, the college was moved to an estate near London and opened as Cheshunt College in 1792, where it continued the ecumenical tone begun by the Countess at Trevecca.

a) To Mr. Hallward, April 27, 1775:

. . . I am persuaded that the wisdom from above is as free from partiality as it is from hypocrisy; and for this reason, our fears relative to either ought to be as much indulged as in any other apparent contradiction to the word of God, in the most solid experiences of an humble mind. The present Reformation has been owned by the Lord under the general idea of *irregularity*; but I humbly think his orders are more regularly observed by this conduct than by any other means. You must allow me, dear Sir, the freedom this great subject obliges me to. The express word of God orders and directs his servants, as messengers of peace to the whole world; and they are either under the necessity of obeying, or they are not. If he has not the authority of even an earthly master to engage the obedience, place, and time of his servants, his precepts must be vain, and, of course, every degree of their obedience vain also; but we, as wretched bond-slaves, redeemed, by a love stronger than death, to liberty and life, seem to have no conditions to make in the service of such a friend; and any composition for body, soul, or spirit, must imply an insensibility of the purchased blessing, or the debt from us for ever due to such a heavenly purchaser. This, to each individual, seems the state of our case. What shall we say, then, when still further favoured, as ministers, not only to *know this* for their own everlasting comfort, but are also honoured by a commission to declare such glad tidings of rich, free, covenanted mercy to every creature? Should thousands attempt to restrain such by any supposed power, found inferior to that which they have received, in order to make them hold their peace, we venture to circumscribe their commission. Alas! where is their appeal to be made? Never, but with perpetual shame to Him who gave the authority. . . .   You must allow me every sincerity for the contempt I feel for any or every reserve in my own wretched heart, and which begets the just impatience I own against myself, as well as the littleness and meanness of all that can be done by me for such a faithful, suffering, and eternal friend. It is from so believing I thus speak. He claims me to the ends of the earth, and every breath to suffer for him; and there is, I do know (from experience), more cowardice than humble fear or real conscience in every retreat we make. Simple, child-like obedience, while the heart is led by the Spirit of God, and consistently disposed and united with the precepts, never can, or ever did, essentially err, as the tenderest protection is ever in the Lord's hands for such, while cold and lukewarm spirits, and the enthusiasm of false fire kindled by nature's pride, have alike been the reproach of Christ's Church in the world. My point is, I fairly own, for myself a universal devotedness through all, and such as would make me, by disposition, and not by plausible appearances, the honest and simple disciple of Jesus Christ; neither formality nor legal bondages having any part of my care, but the pure truth, according to the Bible, verified and understood, by being actually possessed and experienced, and as by this only God is most glorified. When this becomes the real state of the heart, whether in the Church or out of it, is no material matter; and may your heart and mind, my dear Sir, be ever thus the ready servant of Jesus Christ, and then all men's sentiments (as such) will be as the tow that held Sampson. The superior strength will soon burst such cords asunder.

. . . A true conversion of the soul to God, by the power of the Holy Ghost, is in no want how to pay the tithe of mint, annise, and cummin, when the weightier matters are the point for all their views. Without this, I would for ever be silent on religion; in my esteem, it brings all things to a sensible moral mind, or worse than nothing in any other. In this light you must but judge the importance I see for every possible sacrifice being joyfully made by Christians once fully convinced of what they are about. Rational influence or divine we must be under; the former makes but a Pagan, the latter only a Christian.

b) Circular Letter to the Societies, July 17, 1781:

My worthy Friends,—From the various calls of many of the counties in England, it appears an important consideration to us, and alike to all, that every means in our power should be engaged for those many thousands lying in darkness, and in the shadow of death, that the voice of the gospel by our faithful ministers should, by every means in our power, reach them also. For this best end it was concluded, at a late meeting, that the only means effectually, to reach the multitudes, was, that the four principal ministers, Mr. Glascott, Mr. Wills, Mr. Taylor, and Mr. Piercy, should for three months visit universally, in four different departments, and thus severally taken, preach through the towns, counties, and villages of the kingdom, by a general voice or proclamation of the glorious gospel of peace to lost sinners. My dear Friends, you and I have tasted the blessedness that is to be found in such a Saviour for our lost and perishing souls, and how know you but you may have many scattered friends and relations in various parts of the land, where these faithful servants of God are proclaiming the glad tidings of salvation, and that this glorious sound of heavenly and everlasting peace may reach their precious, though perhaps, yet guilty souls, and who, in the great day of the Lord, shall eternally rejoice with you? It therefore calls upon us loudly to use all diligence for the thousands that know not our God. The trifling contributions of many, may render this a universal blessing to all, and, by a free and liberal engagement in this matter, thousands may be made to rise up to praise the Lord, through your means, at the great day. The expense of the ministers as given in, will be before you, for any that may choose to examine them. The contributions of the various congregations will be transmitted to our worthy Committee at Spafields; and wishing to share in the blessings attending the glorious and universal intention of serving many, many thousands, allow me to cast in my poor mite of fifty pounds, with your much more, begging our gracious Lord to accept it from you and from me, for his glorious Name's sake. Let us ever remember that it is not constraint, but the willingness of a cheerful giver he only delights in. May you share many consolations in your own souls, by many being called by this means out of darkness into his marvellous light! I make this request in my own name to you all: as it is the first request, so my few remaining days may make it the last from me, for my dear Master's sake, but in which we shall have jointly and alike cause to rejoice over sinners converted, with the angels in heaven.

c) To the Committee of Spafields Chapel (undated):

My worthy Friends,—You must allow me to assure you that the pleasure I had in reading the conclusion of your letter did abundantly outweigh those many complaints, and, I hope, needless fears, which our gracious Lord is forced to try us by, and *that* in order that we may see the only hand worthy to expect our blessing from, and yield him all the praise. More I want not than to find our Lord own our assemblies as *his*. No good thing shall be withheld while the Lord of Hosts remains the tender father of us his Israel, and will afford us our meal in due season. I thought the shortest way to explain my thoughts was sending them as communicated to the Norwich committee, and fully agreed to those of Bath and Bristol. I lament a complaint should come on Mr. Taylor's account, and have sent a direction to provide for him from my own property, as no collection can be had at Tunbridge Wells, owing to the great poverty of the people. The income of an estate of mine has been ever freely given to support the gospel in that part of Kent, with an allowance for the winter food of a student, as no minister can pay this out of what is received. Mr. Taylor cannot have more for his support for four months there than is allowed through all the churches; and in case of his absence, a minister is to be boarded by him, as is the student supported in part by the people all the winter. The purpose that is intended (and kindly so to me by you all) bears no proportion of difficulty to me, who only am the responsible person for the debt or deficiencies that may arise upon the chapel. I am still willing to trust my dear and faithful Master—he has dealt ever kindly by his poor old worthless servant, and I don't find I want a better bank to maintain food and raiment for me, or those proper and just supplies he shall afford for his various little household, which he orders or may order for my ignorant care of them. As to the minister's board, your allowance of two guineas a week just comes to what you have stated. As to a reader, we have no such example among us. The Gardens have one for the sake of the prayers when a student preaches, but no one minister has ever had a single difficulty; and, it appears to me, allowing the minister *ten guineas* who stays a quarter with you, to find a reader if he likes, will be less expense than the burden of regularly maintaining one. Many choose to read the prayers; and I must say that the air of superiority and importance thus manifested has not that simplicity, that means neither show nor parade. The more apostolic we are, the better; and I must say, as a most remarkable blessing, I know of none anxious or discontented among us, even when it might justly have been excused, seeing myself unable to do what my heart so much desired. My best advice to you, is to be wisely cautious upon this point, and either collections or private subscriptions from honest and devoted hearts, privately applied to for this purpose (and this latter above all others to be preferred) as a little loan to the Lord, and not necessity, will go further to bless such means than the many affected shows supposed liberality wears. I am sure you expect a faithful answer from me, and 'such as I have give I unto you all.' . . .

10. Hannah More: (A) *Strictures on the Modern System of Female Education*; (B) "On the Importance of Religion to the Female Character;" in *The Works of Hannah More*, 11 vols. (London: Henry G. Bohn, 1853), III:46-54; VI:335-39.

Moderate Evangelicals within the Church of England who set themselves against the worldliness and lax religion of the eighteenth century found a significant ally in Hannah More (1745-1833). By the time of her introduction to "serious religion" in the 1780s through the influence of John Newton of Olney and William Wilberforce, she was a well-known playwright and literary figure in London society. Through her many writings and her activities on behalf of educational reform she became a spokesperson of Evangelicalism to the poor as well as to the great. She combined a strong social critique with a great fear of revolution and unbelief, a perspective which both in her day and after brought criticism from those who thought she had gone too far and others who complained she had not gone far enough. In religion More sought to avoid controversy by eschewing doctrinal labels and concentrating on essentials. Against the theological orthodoxy and general decency of behavior in the majority of Anglicans, the tendency of high Calvinists to dismiss the importance of good works for one's religious life, and the deist limitation of religion to morality, she countered with a religion rooted in the affections: "It is not casting a set of opinions into a mould, and a set of duties into a system, which constitutes the Christian religion. The circumference must have a centre, the body must have a soul, the performances must have a principle." That principle was an inward devotedness of ourselves to God's service; "it is being transformed into the image of God."[30] For this she was criticised as well, especially for her lack of attention to the sacraments and the episcopacy. But she was firmly committed to the established Church; and during the controversy over what was being taught in the schools she and her sisters had set up in the Mendips, she vigorously disclaimed any interest in either Methodism or Dissent.

Much of More's writing addressed the condition of women. Here again she found herself between extreme positions. She deplored the education of women in the upper classes, for it promoted attention to "accomplishments" and vanity rather than substantial knowledge or usefulness. But she also had no use for talk of "the rights of women," either; she was interested in equipping women for their duties, for the life of a devoted believer in the sight of God. A special link was forged between women and religion which continued the perspectives developed earlier by Law and Fordyce, but which also extended the opportunities seen by them. Christianity is a practical religion, women are inherently religious, and the education of women should be practical; these theses, together with the conviction that religion is the foundation of society led her to claim an important place for women in a truly reformed society. In her only novel More provided a model of the ideal woman in the character of Lucilla Stanley and a charge to those who would take it up:

> Charity is the calling of a lady; the care of the poor is her profession. Men have little time or taste for details. Women of fortune have abundant leisure, which can in no way be so properly or so pleasantly filled up, as in making themselves intimately acquainted with the worth and the wants of all within their reach.[31]

Widely embraced in the nineteenth century, it was double-edged advice: it was stylized, restricted to a small segment of women, and dependent upon capacity to influence rather than access to power; yet it urged women to be more than ornamental, opened to them the field of benevolence (and its attendant pastoral dimensions), and provided opportunities for activity and organization that would lead to changed lives as well as to a changed society.

(A)   It is far from being the object of this slight work to offer a regular plan of female education, a task which has been often more properly assumed by far abler writers; but it is intended rather to suggest a few remarks on the reigning mode, which, though it has had many panegyrists, appears to be defective, not only in certain particulars, but as a general system. There are indeed numberless honourable exceptions to an observation which will be thought severe; yet the author would ask, whether it be not the natural tendency of the prevailing and popular mode to excite and promote those very evils which it ought to be the main end and object of Christian instruction to remove? Whether the reigning system does not tend to weaken the principles it ought to strengthen, and to dissolve the heart it should fortify? Whether, instead of directing the grand and important engine of education to attack and destroy *vanity, selfishness,* and *inconsideration,* that triple alliance, in strict and constant league against female virtue; the combined powers of instruction are not sedulously confederated in confirming their strength and establishing their empire? . . .

Since then there is a season when the youthful must cease to be young, and the beautiful to excite admiration; to learn how to grow old gracefully is perhaps one of the rarest and most valuable arts which can be taught to woman. And it must be confessed it is a most severe trial for those women to be called to lay down beauty, who have nothing else to take up. It is for this sober season of life that education should lay up its rich resources. However disregarded they may hitherto have been, they will be wanted now. When admirers fall away, and flatterers become mute, the mind will be driven to retire into itself; and if it find no entertainment at home, it will be driven back again upon the world with increased force. Yet, forgetting this, do we not seem to educate our daughters, exclusively, for the transient period of youth, when it is to maturer life we ought to advert? Do we not educate them for a crowd, forgetting that they are to live at home? for the world, and not for themselves? for show, and not for use? for time, and not for eternity? . . .

Not a few of the evils of the present day arise from a new and perverted application of terms: among these, perhaps, there is not one more abused misunderstood, or misapplied, than the term "accomplishments." This word, in its original meaning, signifies *completeness, perfection.* But I may safely appeal to the observation of mankind, whether they do not meet with swarms of youthful females, issuing from our boarding schools, as well as emerging from the more private scenes of domestic education, who are introduced into the world, under the broad and universal title of "accomplished young ladies," of *all* of whom it cannot very truly and correctly be pronounced, that they illustrate the definition, by a completeness which leaves nothing to be added, and a perfection which leaves nothing to be desired.

This frenzy of accomplishments, unhappily, is no longer restricted within the usual limits of rank and fortune; the middle orders have caught the contagion, and it rages downward with increasing and destructive violence, from the elegantly dressed but slenderly portioned curate's daughter, to the equally fashionable daughter of the little tradesman, and of the more opulent but not more judicious farmer. . . . [T]his class of females, in what relates both to religious knowledge and to practical industry, falls short both of the very high and the very low. Their new course of education, and the indolent habits of life, and elegance of dress, connected with it, peculiarly unfits them for the active duties of their own very important condition; while, with frivolous eagerness, and second-hand opportunities, they run to snatch a few of those showy acquirements which decorate the great. This is done apparently with one or other of these views; either to make their fortune by marriage, or, if that fail, to qualify them to become teachers of others: hence the abundant multiplication of superficial wives, and of incompetent and illiterate governesses. . . .

But, to return to that more elevated, and, on account of their more extended influence only, that more important class of females, to whose use this little work is more immediately dedicated. Some popular authors on the subject of female instruction, had for a time established a fantastic code of artificial manners. . . . Another class of contemporary authors turned all the force of their talents to excite *emotions*, to inspire *sentiment*, and to reduce all mental and moral excellence into *sympathy* and *feeling*. These softer qualities were elevated at the expense of principle; and young women were incessantly hearing unqualified sensibility extolled as the perfection of their nature; till those who really possessed this amiable quality, instead of directing, and chastising, and restraining it, were in danger of fostering it to their hurt, and began to consider themselves as deriving their excellence from its excess. . . .

Fashion then, by one of her sudden and rapid turns, instantaneously struck out both real sensibility, and the affectation of it, from the standing list of female perfections; and, by a quick touch of her magic wand, shifted the scene, and at once produced the bold and independent beauty, the intrepid female, the hoyden, the huntress, and the archer; the swinging arms, the confident address, the regimental, and the four-in-hand. Such self-complacent heroines made us ready to regret their softer predecessors, who had aimed only at pleasing the other sex, while these aspiring fair ones struggled for the bolder renown of rivaling them: the project failed; for, whereas the former had sued for admiration, the latter challenged, seized, compelled it; but the men, as was natural, continued to prefer the more modest claimant to the sturdy competitor.

It would be well if we, who have the advantage of contemplating the errors of the two extremes, were to look for truth where she is commonly to be found, in the plain and obvious middle path, equally remote from each excess; and, while we bear in mind that helplessness is not delicacy, let us also remember that masculine manners do not necessarily include strength of character nor vigour of intellect. Should we not reflect also, that we are neither to train up Amazons nor Circassians, but that it is our business to form Christians? that we have to educate not only rational, but accountable beings? and, remembering this, should we not be solicitous to let our daughters learn of the well-taught, and associate with the well-bred? In training them, should we not carefully cultivate intellect, implant religion, and cherish modesty? Then, whatever is engaging in manners would be the natural result of whatever is just in sentiment, and correct in principle; softness would grow out of humility, and external delicacy would spring from purity of heart. Then the decorums, the proprieties, the elegancies, and even the graces, as far as they are simple, pure, and honest, would follow as an almost inevitable consequence; for to follow in the train of the Christian virtues, and not to take the lead of them, is the proper place which religion assigns to the graces.

(B)   A man must be an infidel either from pride, prejudice, or bad education: he cannot be one unawares, or by surprise; for infidelity is not occasioned by sudden impulse or violent temptation. . . .   But though the minds of men are sometimes fatally infected with this disease, either through unhappy prepossession, or some of the other causes above mentioned, yet I am unwilling to believe that there is in nature so monstrously incongruous a being as a *female* infidel. The least reflection on the temper, the character, and the education of women, makes the mind revolt with horror from an idea so improbable, and so unnatural.

May I be allowed to observe that, in general, the minds of girls seem more aptly prepared in their early youth for the reception of serious impressions than those of the other sex, and that their less exposed situations in more advanced life qualify them better for the preservation of them? The daughters (of good parents I mean) are often more carefully instructed in their religious duties than the sons, and this from a variety of causes. They are not so soon sent from under the paternal eye into the bustle of the world, and so early exposed to the contagion of bad example: their hearts are naturally more flexible, soft, and liable to any kind of impression the forming hand may stamp on them; and, lastly, as they do not receive the same classical education with boys, their feeble minds are not obliged at once to receive and separate the precepts of Christianity, and the documents of pagan philosophy. . . .

It is presumed that these remarks cannot possibly be so misunderstood, as to be construed into the least disrespect to literature, or a want of the highest reverence for a learned education, the basis of all elegant knowledge: they are only intended, with all proper deference, to point out to young women that, however inferior their advantages of acquiring a knowledge of the belles-lettres are to those of the other sex, yet it depends on themselves not to be surpassed in this most important of all studies, for which their abilities are equal, and their opportunities perhaps greater.

But the mere exemption from infidelity is so small a part of the religious character, that I hope no one will attempt to claim any merit from this negative sort of goodness, or value herself merely for not being the very worst thing she possibly can be. Let no mistaken girl fancy she gives a proof of her wit by her want of piety, or that a contempt of things serious and sacred will exalt her understanding, or raise her character even in the opinion of the most avowed male infidels. . . .

With whatever ridicule a polite freethinker may affect to treat religion himself, he will think it necessary his wife should entertain different notions of it. He may pretend to despise it as a matter of opinion, depending on creeds and systems; but, if he is a man of sense, he will know the value of it as a governing principle, which is to influence her conduct and direct her actions. If he sees her unaffectedly sincere in the practice of her religious duties, it will be a secret pledge to him that she will be equally exact in fulfilling the conjugal; for he can have no reasonable dependence on her attachment to *him*, if he has no opinion of her fidelity to God; for she who neglects first duties, gives but an indifferent proof of her disposition to fill up inferior ones; and how can a man of any understanding (whatever his own religious professions may be) trust that woman with the care of his family, and the education of his children, who wants herself the best incentive to a virtuous life, the belief that she is an accountable creature, and the reflection that she has an immortal soul.

Cicero spoke it as the highest commendation of Cato's character, that he embraced philosophy, not for the sake of *disputing* like a philosopher, but of *living* like one. The chief purpose of Christian knowledge is to promote the great end of a Christian life. Every rational woman should, no doubt, be able to give a reason of the hope that is in her; but this knowledge is best acquired, and the duties consequent on it best performed, by reading books of plain piety and practical devotion, and not by entering into the endless feuds, and engaging in the unprofitable contentions of partial controversialists. Nothing is more unamiable than the narrow spirit of party zeal, nor more disgusting than to hear a woman deal out judgments, and denounce vengeance, against any one who happens to differ from her in some opinion, perhaps of no real importance, and which, it is probable, she may be just as wrong in rejecting, as the object of her censure is in embracing. A furious and unmerciful female bigot wanders as far beyond the limits prescribed to her sex, as a Thalestris or a Joan d'Arc. Violent debate has made as few converts as the sword, and both these instruments are particularly unbecoming when wielded by a female hand.

But, though no one will be frightened out of their opinions, yet they may be persuaded out of them: they may be touched by the affecting earnestness of serious conversation, and allured by the attractive beauty of a consistently serious life. And while a young woman ought to dread the name of a wrangling polemic, it is her duty to aspire after the honourable character of a sincere Christian. But this dignified character she can by no means deserve, if she is ever afraid to avow her principles, or ashamed to defend them.

CHAPTER 3

NINETEENTH-CENTURY VIEWS OF WOMEN

The nineteenth century did not immediately bring changes in the status of women or in the place of women in the religious consciousness. Mary Wollstonecraft's protests made little public impact, and John Bowdler's anxieties continued to prevail. But over the century some old questions were more directly debated, new opportunities created, adjustments made in the law (chiefly concerning divorce and property rights), and additional issues raised. The next four chapters will consider several aspects of these developments.

Along with the specific issues, from education to philanthropy and from employment questions to suffrage, came the consolidation of an "ideal of womanhood" as well as defenses and modifications of it. The ideal had its roots in the previous century, of course; but there its supporters often set the argument in relation to what they perceived as widespread frivolity among women. It therefore had the force of a critique. In the nineteenth century the dimension of criticism was less evident. Its shaping depended to a great extent on the transformations effected by the Industrial Revolution (see chapter 4). The ideal contained a model of education, a goal of marriage and motherhood, a set of appropriate activities for life within the home, as well as proscriptions concerning what must not be attempted, much less contemplated.

When the realities of life did not correspond to the ideal, or when complaints were offered from several quarters, many defenders simply refused to take them seriously. Margaret Oliphant, the novelist, thought the claim to equality was "the mightiest of humbugs" and added, "God has ordained visibly, by all the arrangements of nature and of providence, one sphere and kind of work for a man and another for a woman. He has given them different constitutions, different organizations, a perfectly distinct and unmistakable identity."[1] Not much could be done, she thought, to enlarge employment opportunities for women beyond those of teaching, needlework, domestic service, and novel writing; perhaps the best solution was emigration. And Cardinal Manning, for all of his involvement in social issues, refused even to meet with women who wanted to discuss the question of the place of women in society because he believed that their proper sphere was the home.[2]

The ideal was important for religion for at least two reasons: it was based on divine sanctions and it helped to preserve religion in an increasingly secular world. Robert Southey accepted as a maxim "that if religion were every where else exploded, it would retain its place in the heart of woman."[3] The relation was reciprocal, many argued; for just as true religion depended on women for its propagation within home and family, so women owed their moral, intellectual, and social position in Western culture to the fact that Christianity had elevated them from their position in the pagan world. If the negative religious associations of an earlier era were not entirely discarded, the positive ones now clearly surpassed them. The two aspects of this relationship are indicated in the titles of two popular works published before mid-century. Mrs. John Sandford's *Female Improvement* gave a prominent place to religion in educating women and preparing them for their duties, while Anne R. Dryden boldly asked, *Can Woman Regenerate Society?*[4]

Such interests fed naturally into a growing attention to the "mission" or "ministry" of women in the 1830s and 1840s. It had to be discussed carefully, so as not to confuse or project false expectations. The Quakers provided the model to be opposed; the Bible made that clear! As one writer put it, "Nature is forced, when the woman usurps the authority over the man. We may resist, and strive against this, but it is part of the scheme of creation."[5] But, again, subordination did not necessarily imply inferiority. Properly understood, then, the ideal made woman more than merely decorative; it gave her meaning and purpose. The emergence of maternal associations and "mothers' magazines" in this period underscored the new interest, with several variations on the charge, "Some of you may be ready to say, '*My* influence will neither do much good nor evil; I am of no importance in the world.' No importance! *All mothers* are of great importance."[6] But not only in the home; there was a larger world as well. Mrs. Boyd Carpenter wrote later in the century, "The Church sends her servant, but what can he do among so many over so wide an area? He must neglect the work, or he must seek help; and it is amongst the women of his flock that he will chiefly find it. Except in the actual ministry of the sanctuary there is hardly a department in which women cannot take their part."[7] Some might well wonder if this transformation of consciousness was too much of a good thing, for piety now had to be defended as an appropriate manly virtue, not as something simply for women and beneath the notice of men.[8]

Throughout the century two broad and interrelated issues lay beneath the general religious discussion of the ideal of womanhood. One was how to understand the biblical passages relating to women; the other, whether finality or change was a more appropriate image for understanding "woman's place." On the first, the dominant point of view saw absolutes which expressed the divine will in creation and were confirmed by reason and experience, together with prohibitions against public speaking and assuming authority over men. But some evangelicals had modified this view in subtle but significant ways, and the gradual emergence of an historical sense in reading the Bible brought out possibilities of cultural conditioning as well as that Jesus could be used against Paul. The old answers did not suffice for everyone, and the questions had to be asked once more. In part, attention focused again on the several creation motifs discussed in chapter 1 and their implications for the current situation (see selections by James, Fletcher, and Cobbe). The second issue also contained theological dimensions, but was more responsive to the realities of social and economic change. Do altered conditions require new solutions? Must the ideal be maintained at all costs, or can it be modified? The following selections indicate that the questions were seriously debated in at least some religious circles, and that was itself a major change from the previous century.

Almost all who sought new foundations for the place of women in society saw religion as a dubious ally. Small wonder, if one looks at sermons and lectures by the clergy. Few there were like the Rev. Benjamin Parsons (1797-1855), a Congregational minister in Ebley (Gloucestershire), who supported several social causes, including anti-slavery, Chartism, suffrage, and temperance. He wrote *The Mental and Moral Dignity of Woman* to counter the widespread belief that their intellectual powers were greatly inferior to those of men. Citing evidence from Scripture, reason, and experience to oppose this, he declared, "Neither sex nor gender belong to intellect. Here, as in the gospel of Christ, there is 'neither male nor female.'"[9] He concluded that women must be educated as broadly and deeply as possible, for through education they will be more able to influence the nation for good.

More typical were the views expressed by the Rev. H. P. Liddon, canon of St. Paul's, and Bishop Wordsworth of Lincoln. To the Association for Parochial Mission Women in 1877 Liddon affirmed, "The social position of women is fixed by the natural laws of God, and not by any human and arbitrary conventionalisms of later date. It is not of man's appointment that differences, mental as well as physical, divide the sexes. These differences are rooted in the original constitution of our race."[10] While Liddon considered the question of appropriate work for women, Wordsworth took up the issues of authority and education in a sermon dedicated to his daughter, principal of the newly-founded women's college, Lady Margaret

Hall, in Oxford. Woman's true strength, he contended, "is in loyal submission; her true power is in tender love and dutiful obedience." Therefore, the kind of education provided them should be carefully related to fundamentals. Without any apparent awareness of many women's need for employment, but with considerable anxiety over the growing split between Christian and secular education, Wordsworth concluded that the church must declare "that to stimulate women to exercise their intellects, and to strive by eager ambition and emulation to acquire knowledge merely for the sake of knowledge, or for the sake of glory, or of gain and a means of livelihood, would be a betrayal of her trust, and of the honour and dignity of woman."[11]

There were, of course, many opponents to any new possibilities for women. But these church leaders just cited, and others like them, thought of themselves as "friends," since they supported various dimensions of the "ministry of women" in the context of "ideal womanhood" and its religious foundation. Yet a number of them showed a petulant side when observing those who pressed for more than was thought proper. They encouraged women by defending the ideal, and they used the ideal to engage what they saw as the secular spirit of the age. In this they were the more serious opponents, for their negative spirit was usually hidden. The problem for them was the ideal itself, grounded as it was in a sense of divine purpose and not challenged by the pressures that events in society, demands for greater participation, or organized protests were bringing to bear upon it.

With the publication of John Stuart Mill's *The Subjection of Women* (1869), another theme received a philosophical and programmatic foundation. Its thesis, while not a new claim, was simple and direct: "That the principle which regulates the existing social relations between the two sexes—the legal subordination of one sex to the other—is wrong in itself, and now one of the chief hindrances to human improvement; and that it ought to be replaced by a principle of perfect equality, admitting no power or privilege on the one side, nor disability on the other."[12] As society had progressed, Mill argued, this was the one significant area resistant to change. Physical force as an operative social principle had been discredited, except in relation to women; instinct rather than reason continued to dominate the patterns of relationship; and the modern conviction of individual choice had not yet been applied to women. But now it was possible to understand that women suffer disabilities "from the mere fact of their birth" and to reconstruct male-female relationships on the moral foundations of justice and social good. For Mill the benefits would be more social than individual, for the simple reason that the number of those available for service to society would be doubled: "In all things of any difficulty and importance, those who can do them well are fewer than the need, even with the most unrestricted latitude of choice; and any limitation of the field of selection deprives society of some chances of being served by the competent, without ever saving it from the incompetent."[13]

Besides the moral claims, argued without reference to religion, Mill challenged traditional arguments concerning the inequality of women. Discussion of "the nature of women" was both artificial and based on conjecture, he contended, depending less on views of women than of men! We need, rather, to learn from the experiences of women: "What women by nature cannot do, it is quite superfluous to forbid them from doing."[14] We know something about women's capacities for work, and we are more aware of cultural variations in perceptions of women. Thus, absolutes are not helpful; preparation, opportunity, and experience are the factors that will allow women to exhibit their individual talents.

To speak of justice and of "women's rights" was still rather strange. Everyone had *duties*, but who had *rights*? With voting based on property qualification, participation in the political process was a privilege and a responsibility, but not a right. With one's career largely determined by one's station in life—education, access to a profession, etc.—it made little sense to most people to complain that one had no freedom of choice. While recognizing the question of rights to be an issue worth discussing, one woman wrote, "If anything urged in behalf of women tends to taking them out of their true sphere, I wish that it may be promptly and completely refuted."[15] To another commentator the "rights of woman" was "the vexed question;" but they would be better obtained through increased work for social improvement than through demands, for men would be "more ready to yield the Rights which they will then feel to be her due."[16] Acknowledging the deeply rooted prejudices against the social advance of women, he did not state how women should participate in efforts at social improvement, or if they did, whether what they earned from men could be called rights.

But some, at least, within the churches were impressed with Mill's argument. Charles Kingsley contrasted John Knox' sixteenth-century blast against women with Mill's critique of their subjection as a way of noting society's progress. On the status of independent single women, he declared, "They are in fact in exactly the same relation to the State as men. Why are similar relations, similar powers, and similar duties not to carry with them similar rights?"[17]

Reflecting on a century of development as well as frustration, Helena Swanwick spoke for many women who were burdened by what she called "the tyranny of the ideal." It had submerged individuality into a whole and "unsexed" those who would not or could not conform. What was often held to represent the glory of womanhood actually prevented women from wider opportunities and created a world where "the mass of women have been degraded by the narrowness and irresponsibility of their lives." A new ideal and a new foundation must replace the image of separate spheres, she contended. "The analogy of division of labour won't work when it is human beings that are being made. 'Male and female created He them,' and both are indispensable. Therefore both must be equipped with knowledge and given liberty."[18]

1. The Journal of Elizabeth Fry, in Susanna Corder, *Life of Elizabeth Fry* (Philadelphia: Henry Longstreth, 1855), pp. 134-35, 178, 244, 285-86, 375-76, 449-50, 547.

Elizabeth Gurney Fry (1780-1845) was perhaps England's first non-royal national female hero. In her early years that prospect would have been regarded as most unlikely. Born to a prominent Quaker family in Norwich, her father a merchant and banker, she agonized about religious faith as a youth, married in 1800, gave birth to six children in nine years (she had eleven in all), and experienced a renewed sense of religious vocation at the time of her father's death in 1809. She was accepted as a minister at her Monthly Meeting in 1811 and travelled extensively to Meetings around London and East Anglia, where she became known for her preaching ability. A visiting Friend, Stephen Grellet, introduced her to the horrors of prison conditions and persuaded her to visit women inmates at Newgate prison in 1813.

Although family responsibilities prevented her from taking up the cause of prison reform for three more years, Fry found her life's work here. In 1817 she persuaded prison officials and inmates to let her begin a program of education for children and employment and instruction for the women; and she established a committee of twelve with the title, The Association for the Improvement of the Female Prisoners in Newgate. Initially she was very successful, completely re-organizing prison life with a set of inmate-approved rules for conduct, including the appointment of a matron and monitors from the inmates who would superintend the work and exercise discipline. Within two years she had given testimony before a parliamentary committee and her fame had spread abroad. In 1821 The Ladies' British Society for Promoting the Reformation of Female Prisoners was founded, with the Duchess of Gloucester as president, to encourage the local and foreign associations that were being established and to promote more humane conditions on the female convict ships bound for Australia.

The strain of her public ministry (for it was always that to her) was very hard on Fry, and she confided in her diary about the conflicts that occurred between her ministry and her family responsibilities, the criticism she received from family and the Society of Friends, the ambivalence felt as a woman at being a public figure, and the continuing anxiety experienced in attempting to discern her religious vocation. After the initial burst of public enthusiasm her prison reform work was a persistent struggle against magistrates who resisted the idea of female visitors, against legislators who objected to her attacks on capital punishment, and against prison officials who came to prefer greater punishment to rehabilitation as a deterrent to crime. Additional personal trials were suffered in the financial collapse of 1828 and in the alienation of some of her children from the Society of Friends. Although her views on prison reform were not accepted by the authorities, she continued to advocate her cause at home and, in her later years, on several tours to the continent.

I have been married eight years yesterday. Various trials of faith and patience have been permitted me; my course has been very different to what I had expected, and instead of being, as I had hoped, a useful instrument in the Church Militant, here I am a careworn wife and mother, outwardly, nearly devoted to the things of this life. Though, at times, this difference in my destination has been trying to me, yet, I believe those trials (which have certainly been very pinching) that I have had to go through, have been very useful, and brought me to a feeling sense of what I am; and at the same time have taught me where power is, and in what we are to glory; not in ourselves, nor in anything we can be, or do, but we are alone to desire that He may be glorified, either through us, or others, in our being something, or nothing, as He may see best for us. I have seen, particularly in our spiritual allotments, that it is not in man that walketh to direct his steps; it is our place, only to be as passive clay in His holy hands; simply and singly desiring, that He would make us what He would have us to be. But the way in which this great work is to be effected, we must leave to Him, who has been the Author, and we may trust will be the Finisher of the work: and we must not be surprised to find it going on differently, to what our frail hearts would desire.

I may also acknowledge that, through all my trials, there does appear to have been a particular blessing attending me, both as to the fatness of the land and the dew of heaven; for though I have been at times deeply tried, inwardly and outwardly, yet I have always found the delivering Arm has been near at hand, and the trials have appeared blessed to me. The little efforts, or small acts of duty, I have ever performed, have often seemed remarkably blessed to me; and where others have been concerned, it has also, I think, been apparent in them, that the effort on my part, has been blessed to both parties. Also, what shall I say when I look at my husband and my five lovely babes? How I have been favoured to recover from illnesses, and to get through them without material injury in any way. I also observe, how any little care towards my servants appears to have been blessed, and what faithful and kind friends to me, I have found them. Indeed, I cannot enumerate my blessings; but I may truly say, that of all the blessings I have received, and still receive, there is none to compare to believing that I am not yet forsaken, but notwithstanding all my deviations, in mercy cared for. And (if all the rest be taken from me) far above all, I desire, that if I should be led through paths I know not of, which may try my weak faith and nature, I may not lose my faith in Thee; but may increasingly love Thee; delight to follow after Thee, and be singly Thine; giving all things up to thee, who hast hitherto been my only merciful Protector and Preserver. . . . (August 20, 1808)

The prospect I have had for some months, of going into Norfolk, to attend the Monthly and Quarterly Meetings, is now brought home to me, as I must apply to my next Monthly Meeting for permission. It is no doubt a sacrifice of natural feeling, to leave the comforts of home, and my beloved husband and children; and to my weak, nervous habits, the going about, and alone (for so I feel it in one sense without my husband) is, I have found from experience, a trial greater than I imagined; and my health suffers much I think, from my habits being necessarily so different. This consideration, of its being a cross to my nature, I desire not to weigh in the scale; though, no doubt, for the sake of others, as well as myself, my health being so shaken is a serious thing. What I desire to consider most deeply is this:—Have I authority for leaving my home and evident duties? What leads me to believe I have? for I need not doubt that when away, and at times greatly tried, this query is likely to arise. The prospect has come in that quiet, yet, I think, powerful way, that I have never been able to believe I should get rid of it; indeed hitherto I have hardly felt anything but a calm cheerfulness about it, and very little anxiety. It seems to me as if, in this journey, I must be stripped of outward dependences, and my watchword appears to be,—"My soul, wait thou ONLY upon God; for my expectation is from Him." (February 3, 1812)

My mind too much tossed by a variety of interests and duties—husband, children, household, accounts, Meetings, the Church, near relations, friends, and Newgate—most of these things press a good deal upon me. I hope I am not undertaking too much, but it is a little like being in the whirlwind, and in the storm; may I not be hurt in it, but enabled quietly to perform that which ought to be done; and may it all be done so heartily unto the Lord, and through the assistance of His grace, that if consistent with His Holy will, His blessing may attend it, and if ever any good be done, that the glory of the whole work may be given where it is alone due. (March 11, 1817)

Since I last wrote, much has happened to me; some things have occurred of an important nature. My prison engagements have gone on well, and many have flocked after me, may I not say of almost all descriptions, from the greatest to the least; and we have had some remarkably favoured times together in the prison. The Yearly Meeting was a very interesting one to me, and also encouraging. I felt the unity of Friends a comfort and support. I had to go into the Men's Meeting, which was a deep trial of faith, but it appeared called for at my hand, and peace attended giving up to it. The unity which the women expressed at my going, and the good reception I found amongst the men, were comforting to me; but it was a close, very close, exercise. Although I have had much support from many of my fellow-mortals, and so much unity expressed with me, both in and out of our Society—yet I believe many Friends have great fears for me and mine; and some, not Friends, do not scruple to spread evil reports, as if vanity or political motives led me to neglect a large family. I desire patiently to bear it all, but the very critical view that is taken of my beloved children, grieves me much. . . .   (July 1, 1818)

I think that I am under the deepest exercise of mind that I ever experienced, in the prospect of a Meeting to be held this evening, for all the young people assembled at the Yearly Meeting. It is held at my request, my brother Joseph uniting in it. In a remarkable degree it has plunged me into the depths, into real distress; I feel so unfit, so unworthy, so perplexed, so fearful, even so sorrowful, so tempted to mistrustful thoughts, ready to say, "Can such an one be called to such a service?" I do believe that "this is my infirmity;" and I have a humble hope and confidence, that out of this great weakness I shall be made strong. As far as I know it has been in simple obedience to manifested duty, that I gave up to this service, and went through the ordeal of the Yearly Meeting. If I know my own deceitful heart, it has been done in love to my Lord and to His cause. Lord, preserve me through this depth; through this stripping season! If it should please Thee to grant me the garments of Thy salvation, and the help of Thy Spirit, further enable me wholly to give unto Thee the glory, which is due unto Thy name. If thou makest use of Thy handmaid to speak in Thy name, be Thou Thyself her help and her strength, her glory, and the lifter up of her head. Enable her to rely on Thee, on Thy might, and on Thy mercy; to commit her whole cause unto Thee, and keep in the remembrance of Thy handmaid, that the blessed cause of truth and righteousness is not *her's*, but *Thine*. (May 23, 1825)

We returned home from our journey last Sixth-day evening, having been absent just five weeks. We visited several places in the south of Ireland, a good many in Wales, and some in England. I think I never remember taking a journey, in which it was more frequently sealed to my own mind, that we were in our right places; through much difficulty, our way was opened to go, and to continue out. Though I believe we have scripture authority for it—still further confirmed by the internal evidence of the power of the Spirit, and its external results,—yet, I am obliged to walk by faith, rather than sight, in going about as a woman in the work of the ministry; it is, to my nature, a great humiliation, and I often feel it to be "foolishness," particularly in large Public Meetings, before entering upon the service; but generally, when engaged in the ministry, I find such an unction, and so much opening upon Christian doctrine and practice, that after a Meeting, I mostly say in my heart, "It is the Lord's doing, and marvellous in our eyes." (September 18, 1832)

. . . I have for some time believed that duty would call me to have a meeting in London or the neighbourhood, previous to leaving home. I see many difficulties attached to it, and perhaps none so much, as my great fear of women coming too forward in these things, beyond what the Scripture dictates; but I am sure the Scripture most clearly and forcibly lays down the principle that the Spirit is not to be grieved, or quenched, or vexed, or resisted; and on this principle I act; under the earnest desire that whatever the Lord leads me into by his Spirit may be done faithfully to Him, and in His name; and I am of opinion, that nothing Paul said, to discourage women's speaking in the Churches, alluded to their speaking through the help of the Spirit, as he clearly gave directions how they should conduct themselves under such circumstances, when they prayed or prophesied. (February 1, 1840)

2. Alfred, Lord Tennyson, *The Princess* (1847), 15th ed. (London: Edward Moxon & Co., 1866), Part VII.

In the 1830s and 1840s "the woman question" received considerable attention from a number of perspectives. One of its primary foci was a renewed interest in the education of women, and it led eventually to the establishment of colleges for women in 1848 and 1849 (see chapter 5). But behind the wider support for education was a troubling concern that had continued from the eighteenth century: what would education do to women and to the existing relationship between women and men? There was a widespread fear that education, especially if it were no different for women than for men, would encourage rivalry between the sexes, make women dissatisfied with their divinely-appointed roles in society, and disrupt the complementarity that is at the heart of the marriage relationship. Tennyson (1809-92), poet laureate of England from 1850 until his death, took this issue as the central theme for his poem, *The Princess*. The notion of separate spheres is expressed by Gama in Part V:

Man for the field and woman for the hearth:
Man for the sword and for the needle she:
Man with the head and woman with the heart:
Man to command and woman to obey;
All else confusion.

Ida attempts to challenge this view by the creation of a university for women, independent of male involvement. The attempt fails, and the Prince responds to her disappointment with what is Tennyson's summary judgment on the issue, that there are innate differences which make women gentler and more moral than men and that society is strengthened when these are present in complementarity rather than in rivalry.

The force of this claim is seen when one compares the challenge to religious orthodoxy found in Tennyson's *In Memoriam* (1850) to the acceptance of the social orthodoxy concerning women in *The Princess*. The influence of Tennyson's view later led Thomas Holloway, a wealthy seller of patent medicines, to establish Holloway College as a separate residential women's university. It opened in 1886, but soon had to affiliate with London University for examination purposes.[19] The idea of creating a distinctively feminine curriculum for higher education continued to be discussed as a way of advocating a particular view of womanhood, but with an increasing focus on

credentials achieved through examinations and degrees it became less and less possible
to implement.

> "Blame not thyself too much," I said, "nor blame
> Too much the sons of men and barbarous laws;
> These were the rough ways of the world till now.
> Henceforth thou hast a helper, me, that know
> The woman's cause is man's: they rise or sink
> Together, dwarf'd or godlike, bond or free:
> For she that out of Lethe scales with man
> The shining steps of nature, shares with man
> His nights, his days, moves with him to one goal,
> Stays all the fair young planet in her hands—
> If she be small, slight-natured, miserable,
> How shall men grow? but work no more alone!
> Our place is much: as far as in us lies
> We two will serve them both in aiding her—
> Will clear away the parasitic forms
> That seem to keep her up but drag her down—
> Will leave her space to burgeon out of all
> Within her—let her make herself her own
> To give or keep, to live and learn and be
> All that not harms distinctive womanhood.
> For woman is not undevelopt man,
> But diverse: could we make her as the man,
> Sweet love were slain: his dearest bond is this,
> Not like to like, but like in difference.
> Yet in the long years liker must they grow;
> The man be more of woman, she of man;
> He gain in sweetness and in moral height,
> Nor lose the wrestling thews that throw the world;
> She mental breadth, nor fail in childward care,
> Nor lose the childlike in the larger mind;
> Till at the last she set herself to man,
> Like perfect music unto noble words;
> And so these twain, upon the skirts of Time,
> Sit side by side, full-summed in all their powers,
> Dispensing harvest, sowing the To-be,
> Self-reverent each and reverencing each,
> Distinct in individualities,
> But like each other ev'n as those who love,

Then comes the statelier Eden back to men:
Then reign the world's great bridals, chaste and calm:
Then springs the crowning race of humankind.
May these things be!"
                     Sighing she spoke "I fear
They will not."

3. S. A. J., "In What Way Can Wives and Mothers Best Promote the Revival of Piety in the Church?," *The British Mothers' Magazine*, IV (December, 1848):265-68.

The London Central Maternal Association began publishing *The British Mothers' Magazine* in 1845, aiming to be "purely evangelical in sentiment and entirely free from any sectarian bias." Its two primary objects were "to direct attention to the high and important position the mothers in our country hold and to promote, in some degree, their education and fitness for that post." As such it was a forerunner of organizations like the Mothers' Union (see chapter 4) and one of the first agencies to argue aggressively for the religious responsibilities of mothers. An early article, entitled "The Power of Christian Mothers," bluntly noted, "Fathers have power, ministers have power, Sabbath-school teachers have power; but in the earliest stage of human existence, a mother's power exceeds them all."[20] Apart from a variety of practical advice there was considerable interest in female education and concern about restrictions that had been placed on opportunities for women. Contrary to much earlier discussion of domestic responsibility, the journal included articles which argued that the greater education available to women, the greater the possibilities for good. "Never will it be known what woman's *sphere* is," declared W. B. Hodgson,

till the powers with which she has been gifted by our common Creator shall have been unfolded to the utmost, and till she shall have been qualified too for the situation which she may be destined to fill. It may be that in every succeeding phase of our social condition, woman's sphere is proportioned to woman's merit. Let us increase the merit of the woman then, and trouble not ourselves about her sphere; it may be safely left to provide for itself.[21]

Although women now had responsibility for meeting the awesome challenges of "open infidelity and lukewarm profession," the occasion for this was to come largely through their indirect influence—keeping the faith within the home for their husbands, children, and servants. Woman's work would be seen through her effect on others.

No one who has reflected on the subject, will deny that the times in which we live are solemnly momentous. They are, indeed, to use the Apostle's expression, "perilous times." The age of persecution for righteousness' sake has passed away; but the danger was then of a very different character to that which threatens the Church now. The professors of Christianity were few and scattered; no honourable idea was connected with the belief of its glorious truths—its followers were even wondered at, despised, persecuted unto death. It offered no allurement to the worldly or the selfish to profess its holy doctrines. Yet even then there was a noble army of martyrs, who counted not their lives dear unto them, so that they might know *Him* and the power of *His* resurrection who had loved them and given Himself for them. Their witness is in heaven, and their record is on high. Far different is the aspect which the Church presents in these days. Religion (in the general acceptation of the term) is no longer a thing despised; its possession is accounted creditable; its professors have multiplied, but, alas! for the character of many.

The word of God is no longer esteemed as the sole standard of judgment; a temporizing expediency has usurped the place of single-hearted Christianity, and the high and holy principles of the Gospel, are made subservient to the trifling conventionalities of society. The noble declaration of the apostle Paul, "I am crucified unto the world," would not bear application to all the *professed* adherents of the Redeemer; of some it might with greater propriety be said, that having a form of godliness, they are denying the power thereof. It is this spirit of ungodly compromise—this attempt to amalgamate religion and the world—to serve God and Mammon, this continual struggle to unite what God has *eternally separated*, which has struck at the root of vital godliness; the word of truth cannot be gainsayed, "Whosoever will be the friend of the world, is the enemy of God."

The religion of Jesus demands the *entire* relinquishment of earthly preference, and the *undivided* consecration of every talent. Were we to examine closely, we might find the habit of self-gratification to be the foundation of much that is cold and lukewarm in our own profession; and if we follow its influence still further, becoming from unrestrained indulgence an impulsive principle, it would not be difficult to trace much of the infidelity and licentiousness which surrounds us, to its unhallowed source. It is not that men *cannot*, but that they are not *willing* to believe a revelation which requires of them that they should mortify the flesh with its affections and its lusts; that they should deny themselves, take up their cross and follow Him, who "pleased not Himself." Granting, then, that open infidelity and lukewarm profession are the unequivocal characteristics of our times, does it not become those who occupy the responsible position of wives and mothers, seriously to inquire how they may best aid in stemming the torrent of evil, and reviving the languishing spirit of that which is essentially good? In order to this we may do well to consider the causes of this declension, and its manifestations. An age of luxury has ever been detrimental to the interests, not only of true piety, but also of pure morality. Rome is an illustration of this; in proportion as she grew luxurious, she became effeminate and corrupt—her real greatness was impaired, for her moral energies were paralyzed. The all-absorbing character of business, and the nature of its transactions, is a great barrier to spirituality. Occupying as it almost necessarily does so much of time and thought, the mind becomes secularized, and a callousness of feeling and conscience is too often the result. What can a wife and mother do to modify its ungenial influence? Whilst she sympathizes in cares and anxieties which it is her duty to share, it should be hers to seek to raise the minds of those in whom she is so tenderly interested, to objects of higher and purer contemplation. . . .

There is much danger arising from the manner in which social parties are frequently conducted; friends seem to meet together more for the purposes of show and display, and the gratification of vanity, than for the pleasures of rational intercourse, or the refreshment and invigoration of mental and spiritual energy.

Scenes of amusement are frequented, and frivolous pursuits sanctioned, by which wrong passions are excited, and hallowed emotions deadened, and *this* amongst those who *profess* to have chosen Christ in preference to the world. Is this the non-conformity which He requires of His people? Is it not rather a melancholy proof that men are lovers of their own selves—lovers of pleasure more than of God? The piety that would be vigorous and healthy, must be independent of worldly aid or extraneous excitement; its source must be love to God; its aim must be God's glory; its anticipated reward must be God's approval. But the conduct of many would induce us to think, that they have scarcely yet made up their minds which world they shall choose as their portion; whether God or Mammon shall claim their affection. . . .

There are objects of active and public interest, closely connected with the revival of piety in the Church, which demand our sympathy and support; true religion is an expansive principle—its sphere of vision comprehends the world. But the secret influence of a wife and mother, that influence which will tell most powerfully on the Church and the world, must have its spring in the sanctified associations of the domestic circle. Let our light so shine before our household. Let the atmosphere of single-hearted piety be breathed in our homes. Let our children detect no inconsistency between our profession and our practice, (they soon will perceive it.) Let them from early childhood be taught to rely on established principles in religion, and to weigh their conduct by the unerring standard of the word of truth—not by the changing policy of the world's maxims. God's requirements, and man's obligations, are the same yesterday, to-day, and for ever. They shift not as the panoramic scenes of earth. A religion of expediency will never stand the test of an omniscient gaze.

It might not be out of place to advert to the moral and religious influence which a right appropriation of the day of rest exerts in a well-ordered family.

How much confusion and irregularity might be spared by a judicious adjustment of household matters on the evening preceding the Sabbath. With what strictness was the "preparation day" observed amongst the Jews; surely in the midst of a purer light, and with more animating motives, its observance should not be less sacred. A husband will generally rejoice in reaping the fruits of such arrangements; if not from higher motives, it is at least a grateful repose, after six days' buffeting with the cares and anxieties of time. Children will learn to estimate more highly the privilege of one day in seven, set apart for more exclusive consecration to God and preparation for eternity. Servants will become more impressed with the value of that religion, which thus as it were breaks in upon the engrossing concerns of earth, and gives space for the toil-worn spirit to recruit its wearied energies, and to seek its surest refuge. It is no easy matter to be a Christian indeed; to maintain a high-toned consistency of principle and action amidst the active, bustling scenes of everyday excitement; to keep up uninterrupted intercourse with heaven, whilst struggling with an evil heart of unbelief. "I am the Lord that helpeth thee:" "My grace is sufficient for thee," can alone insure the victory. "Be not weary in well-doing, for in due season ye shall reap if ye faint not," is an encouragement peculiarly needful to a Christian wife and mother, amidst discouragements of mind, and weakness of body, which none but herself can enter into. But her reward is sure, not only in the favour of Him who regardeth with complacency the humblest efforts to promote His glory, but "her children arise up and call her blessed, her husband also, and he praiseth her."

4. John Angell James, *Female Piety; or, The Young Woman's Friend and Guide Through Life to Immortality*; in *The Works of John Angell James*, edited by his Son, 17 vols. (London: Hamilton Adams and Co., 1860-64), IV:78-80, 83-85.

> John Angell James (1785-1859), one of the outstanding Independent (Congregation-
> al) ministers of his day, spent his entire ministry of fifty-four years at Carr's Lane
> Chapel, Birmingham, and was active in the public arena as well. He became a leading

advocate of the Evangelical Alliance, founded in 1846. Among his many published writings, chiefly works of pastoral guidance to a lay audience, was *The Anxious Inquirer After Salvation* (1834), widely distributed by the Religious Tract Society. *Female Piety* was first published in 1853. There he took up the popular theme of "Woman's Mission" to claim authority from Christianity and reason to exclude women from all public offices and from suffrage and to proclaim female supremacy within the home. The woman is there because she wants to be and because she is particularly suited to those responsibilities. She is superior to man in many areas, but her power is "passive"—that is, it is shown indirectly in its effect on others rather than for what she can do herself. Such a view was to be significantly challenged in the following two decades (see chapter 4), but it continued to be influential within evangelical circles until well into the twentieth century.

. . . . What shall I say of those women who claim on their own behalf, or of their advocates who claim for them, a participation in the labours, occupations, rights, and duties, which have usually been considered as exclusively appertaining to men? There are those who would expunge the line of demarcation, which nearly all nations have drawn, between the duties and the occupations of men and women. Christianity has provided a place for woman for which she is fitted, and in which she shines; but take her out of that place, and her lustre pales and sheds a feeble and sickly ray. Or to change the metaphor, woman is a plant, which in its own greenhouse seclusion will put forth all its brilliant colours and all its sweet perfume; but remove it from the protection of its own floral home into the common garden and open field, where hardier flowers will grow and thrive, its beauty fades and its odour is diminished. Neither reason nor Christianity invites woman to the professor's chair, or conducts her to the bar, or makes her welcome to the pulpit, or admits her to the place of ordinary magistracy. Both exclude her, not indeed by positive and specific commands, but by general principles and spirit, alike from the violence and license of the camp, the debates of the senate, and the pleadings of the forum.

And they bid her beware how she lays aside the delicacy of her sex, and listens to any doctrines which claim new rights for her, and becomes the dupe of those who have put themselves forward as her advocates only to gain notoriety, or perhaps bread. They forbid us to hear her gentle voice in the popular assembly; and do not even suffer her to speak in the Church of God. They claim not for her the right of suffrage, nor any immunity by which she may "usurp authority over the man." The Bible gives her her place of majesty and dignity in the domestic circle: that is the heart of her husband and the heart of her family. It is the female supremacy of that domain, where love, tenderness, refinement, thought and feeling preside. . . . A woman who fills well the sphere assigned to her, as a wife, a mother, and a mistress; who trains up good citizens for the state, and good fathers and mothers of other families which are to spring from her own; and so from generation to generation in all but endless succession, need not complain that her sphere of action and her power of influence are too limited for female ambition to aspire to. The mothers of the wise and the good are the benefactresses of their species. What would be gained to woman's comfort, respectability, or usefulness, or to the welfare of society, and how much would be lost to each, by withdrawing her from her own appropriate sphere, and introducing her to that for which she has no adaptation? Who, but a few wild visionaries, and rash speculatists, and mistaken advocates of woman's rights would take her from the home of her husband, of her children, and of her own heart, to wear out her strength, consume her time, and destroy her feminine excellence in committee-rooms, on platforms, and in mechanics' or philosophical institutions? But may not woman, in every way in her power, benefit society by her talents and her influence? Certainly, in every legitimate way. Her sphere is clearly assigned to her by Providence; and only by very special and obvious calls should she be induced to leave it. Whatever breaks down the modest reserve, the domestic virtues, the persuasive gentleness, of woman, is an injury done to the community. Woman can be spared from the lecturer's chair, the platform of general convocation, and the scene of public business; but she cannot be spared from the hearth of her husband and the circle of her children. Substitutes can be found for her in the one, but not in the other. In the bosom of domestic privacy she fulfils with truest dignity and faithfulness the first and highest obligations of her sex. . . . .

Now look at woman's natural adaptation for her sphere. If the view here given of woman's mission be correct, we can in a moment perceive what is required to enable her to fulfil it. There must be, what indeed there generally is pervading the sex, a consciousness of subordination, without any sense of degradation, or any wish that it was otherwise. Woman scarcely needs to be taught, that in the domestic economy, she is second, and not first, that "the man is the head of the woman." This is a law of nature written on the heart, and coincides exactly with the law of God written on the page of revelation. It is, first of all, an instinct, and then confirmed by reason. Without this law deeply engraven and constantly felt, as well as known, her situation would be endured as a slavery, and she would be constantly endeavouring to throw off the yoke. Her condition would be wretched, and she would make all wretched around her. With such a sense of oppression, or even of hardship, pressing upon the mind, no duty could be well performed, and the family would be a scene of domestic warfare. But she generally knows her place, and feels it her happiness as well as her duty to keep it. It is not necessity, but even choice, that produces a willing subjection. She is contented it should be so, for God has implanted the disposition in her nature.

Then her gentleness is another part of her qualification for her duty. She should have, must have, really has, influence, power of impulsion, if not compulsion. Were she utterly powerless, she could do nothing. Her influence, however, is a kind of passive power; it is the power that draws, rather than drives, and commands by obeying. Her gentleness makes her strong. How winning are her smiles, how melting her tears, how insinuating her words! Woman loses her power when she parts from her gentleness. . . .   She vanquishes by submission. . . .

Tenderness is another of her characteristics. The former relates more to manner, this more to disposition; that to habitual conduct, towards all persons and all cases, this to the occasional exercise of sympathy with distress. Tenderness is so characteristic of the female heart, than an unfeeling woman is considered a libel upon her sex. If compassion were driven out from every other habitation, it would find there its last retreat. Her heart is so made of tenderness, that she is ever in danger of being imposed upon by craft and falsehood. How suitable such a disposition for one who is to be the chief comforter of the domestic commonwealth. . . .

Self-denial is no less necessary for this domestic mission than anything I have yet mentioned. How much of ease, comfort, enjoyment, must she surrender, who has to consult her husband's comfort and will, before her own: whose happiness is to consist, in a great measure, in making others happy: who has first to endure all that is connected with giving birth to her children, and then all that is involved in nursing, watching, comforting, and training them! One of the most striking instances in our world of endurance and self-denial both as to the extent and the cheerfulness with which it is born, is the busy, tender, and contented mother of a rising family. God has given the power, yet I sometimes wonder how she can exercise it.

And then see her fortitude in this situation. In that courage which leads man to the cannon's mouth, to mount the breach, or to encounter some terrific danger of any other kind, she is inferior to man; but in the fortitude manifested by enduring bodily suffering, the ills of poverty, the wasting influence of long-continued privations, the gloom of solitude, the bitterness of injustice, the cruelty of neglect, the misery of oppression, is she not in all these as superior to man, as man is to her in all that appertains to brute force?

5. "The Social Position of Women," *The Churchman's Magazine*, October, 1857, pp. 201-207.

In contrast to the views of James, others in the 1850s were calling attention to problems regarding the social position of women and urging clergy to speak out for reform. Education and employment were central issues in this discussion, and they were beginning to receive some broader national interest (see chapters 4 and 5). The anonymous author of the following article could not, as James had, revel in the elevation accomplished by Christianity. Quite the contrary, the patterns which prevented the full development of women, inhibited their contributions to society, and created faulty images for men to hold commanded the view. The passive condition of woman and her limited power in the public sphere were conditions to be corrected, not ideals to be defended.

Besides stressing the triviality and limited character of female education, which had been criticised in the eighteenth century by Law, Fordyce, and More, the author also contended that the rigidly separate education of boys and girls prevented mutual understanding as adults. All of these factors encouraged the judgment that woman is inferior and limited the resources available for social, moral, and intellectual progress. The argument against James' position was enhanced by allusion to the contributions of Elizabeth Fry, Florence Nightingale, and their associates in prison and hospital reform, two areas where men had previously failed to improve conditions. A clear implication of the article is that other possibilities certainly await us if there is appropriate imagination and preparation. Although considered within the framework of what was "the especial appropriation of the sex," it was a clarion call for involvement by church people in the reconsideration of dominant perspectives of womanhood and their effects on women and the larger society.

It is a generally true observation that the degree of national civilization may be calculated by the condition of the women. As we approach the savage state we find the feminine portion of the community reduced to slavery and moral degradation, converted into vassals to domineering sensuality, or into mere serfs to supply the drudgery of physical existence. As we soar higher, however, the elevation of the female sex after a certain point does not bear adequate proportion to the other characteristics of moral advancement, and thus some countries are certainly not to be compared with our own in the progress of intellect and science, yet evince more respect for women, and beyond all question recognize her rights and privileges more. It is remarkable that in America, not excepting even those states which are still disgraced by slavery, the deference paid to free women by all classes far exceeds what they receive here; whilst as to admission into what we may denominate the privilege of their heritage, namely, to become helpmates to men in ways of usefulness, spheres of occupation are opened to them from which in England they are selfishly debarred.

Whether, therefore, it be from fear that our ladies should far exceed ourselves in intelligence, were we to educate them thoroughly,—a fear not without foundation when we consider what self-educated women have accomplished in the ranks of science and literature, the great social improvements they have effected, and the daily augmenting influence they are bringing to bear upon the amelioration of our criminal, or sick, or pauper population; or whether we allow the national plague-spot of English selfishness to cause us to absorb every source of influence we are not shamed out of engrossing, certain it is that our neglect of female education generally is neither more nor less than a flagrant public error. A woman's education at the present day, we speak of the upper and middle classes as well as of the lowest, is stamped with perversion or inutility. In the lowest classes our endeavours are chiefly to make house-maids comprehend the relative bearings of the sun to the equator, or to render clod-poles and hinds first-rate mathematicians. . . .   In our middle ranks from the well-to-do farmer, through the professional orders up to the verge of aristocracy, woman is treated as though her whole end were a successful, that is to say, a lucrative marriage, without any reference to intellectual or social advancement or aptitude whatever. . . .   Our female aristocracy, having at fashionable schools been taught to regard a husband as a mere necessary step to position, when primed to the very brim with boarding school French, foreign airs, and very questionable continental literature, are "brought out" as it is termed, with the thoroughly well understood notion that not the most moral man, not the most intellectual, is to be chosen for a partner through life, but a ducal heir, however profligate, or a rich manufacturing parvenu, though reeking of the ill-bred atmosphere where the letter "H" comes not. After this daily, hourly exhibition, shall we wonder that we have no servants on the one hand, or on the other that men should ignore the rightful position of women, seeing that they have so few specimens of real worthiness which can stand the brunt of such inimical education?

Now it is an unassailable axiom that no law of God's creation can be violated without certain detriment to the offender. It matters not whether the guilty party be an individual or a nation, the pernicious penalty is certain in either case. Woman has her duties, her privileges, her social powers. Whatever keeps her low in the scale of moral advancement impedes those duties by violating those privileges, and society loses the benefit of her powers. If she were only a doll, or a plaything to be dandled for an hour's amusement, the allowance of exertion apportioned to her might be as insignificant as man has made it, but the instant we recognize the great fact that she is not only a moral responsible agent herself, but that upon her watchfulness, capability, and example, the moral training as well as physical culture of our children depend, it is the height of selfish infatuation to either limit her mental development, to misappropriate our intellectual culture of the sex to the station it is called on to fill, or to deprive it of those means of labour and employment which may legitimately be suited to her constitution.

Before we pass on, however, to the injustice done to women upon the score of employment, we must remark that the gross anomalies at present constantly lamented in society cannot be removed until the education of the sexes be assimilated. At present men and women have no means of attaining real knowledge of each other, are neither occupied in the same pursuits nor live in a medium of common interest nor of combined activity. Hence a wide gulf opens between the two prime elements of society, depriving the latter of its finer vitality, and leaving the power of growth only to a money-getting spirit and other rude springs of character.

. . . True it is that women may be censured for encouraging the ill by almost invariably taking part against their own sex, but this is nothing more than the bias of our common human nature to side with the strong against the weak. In other words, they purchase a temporary and false security as individuals by leaguing with men against themselves collectively. And even were it a more glaring anomaly, this treatment by women of their own sex, man is still responsible for it, in the sense of impairing by the vitiated education and treatment of woman, her true appreciation of right and wrong. The late debate in the House of Commons upon divorce, proved the tyrannical injustice with which woman's most sacred rights are treated; it is not to be wondered at then, that she herself should in the hopelessness of remedy strengthen by her foolish connivance what under more favourable circumstances her perfect moral development would expunge.

But without entering more fully into the question of her education, public enquiry has, in spite of men's resistance, been wrenched down to the amelioration of her condition as a fellow-labourer for not this world only but the next. The Church has in all ages, whilst holding inviolate the Divine law that the man should be the head of the woman, ratified to her the fullest equality of justice in respect of treatment and admission to labour. Of late years, the acknowledged helplessness of man in several most important public works; his utter incompetency to deal with sickness without female aid; the scandalous extravagance, irreligion, and cruelty of our workhouses when removed from educated female influence, contrasted with the admirably humane, economical, and devotional treatment found in those asylums or reformatories where woman's surveillance is exhibited; the shameful neglect and mismanagement under official male commissioners in the Crimea, remedied by the quiet tact and self-devotion of heroic but most gentle spirits in the fairer sex; the long array of well-conducted prisons abroad and hospitals under womanly management, showing that other nations have not only long ago ascertained woman's mission but encouraged her in its discharge; these, and a thousand similar proofs have at last forced Englishmen to admit to woman a scope of good, which she never could have reached under any other pressure than heavy parochial taxation, incident to the obtuse intellect and feeling of gross and boorish poor-law guardians. Man starts upon the principle that violence and force must succeed; woman knows the oil penetrates much further than the vinegar. It is not in man's nature to sympathize with individual suffering, to pour anodyne into particular woe; he deals with ills by the gross, and files down by harsh discipline (at once costly and self-destructive,) want and guilt by the myriad. Hence, in prisons, workhouses, hospitals, he has signally and totally failed. Religion has been practically inefficient, though most officially applied, while the swearer has merely been converted into a hypocrite, because the soft place in his heart, which the greatest villain still possesses, has not been won.

So now in the year of grace 1857, we are beginning to mend our ways, and not only with respect to hospitals and prisons, but we have been absolutely wise enough to discover and admit that a restriction of feminine employment to merely sewing, washing, or cooking, to factory work or millinery, is to cast out thousands of unwilling votaries to vice upon the streets, to rob society of the best manual labour, and to give it prostitution in exchange. This is no overcharged statement. The merest tyro in political economy knows that our streets swarm with women who are driven there to eke out a pittance *for their families*, because they are debarred more general means of employment, whilst on the other hand the numbers driven into the only recognized channels hitherto of woman's employment, reduce the wages to a minimum price. Members of Parliament representing the manufacturing towns are often ashamed at the undeniable statistics given of the enormous fortunes, obtained from human blood, it may be said, out of those hives of vice and consumption, the factories, wherein the Lilliputian wages are in inverse proportion to the colossal debauchery, or the Titanic strain upon the labour. Ill indeed would the clergy of this country have done their duty if they had not aided the miseries of the overtaxed and ill-paid workwoman: but as to resisting the greed of her oppressor, the latter, alas! is represented with all honour to gold, in Parliament, to which the voice of God's heritage is inadmissible! Hence the evil went on, until profit and loss, the only considerations influencing the manufacturing mind, appeared to cast a balance in favour of woman being admitted into a better status of employment, since though her soul was of little consequence, her vices swelled the poor rates!

In an ecclesiastical view, the employment of women should of course be encouraged in regard to the education of the young, attendance on the sick, and the various other elements of usefulness which the church in all ages has recognized as the especial appropriation to the sex. But though women have a sad perversion of taste which leads our fashionable dames, with very spurious perception of propriety, to prefer the attendance of men in several offices far more fitting for the female sex, we doubt not but sarcasm, if no better weapon will serve, will convert (as it partly has already done,) the public mind to a better bias. To see man, the noblest work of creation, perverted into a measurer of tape, a counter-skipper after bobbins and laces, is a sadly hard hit at the portals of our self-love; as to witness a greasy, perfumed, and frizzled up coxcomb manipulating the tresses of our most fastidious dames or young women, is a spectacle so utterly indelicate that nothing but the authority of our impure custom can account for it. The fact that ladies prefer these hirsute effeminates to female attendants is itself one of the strongest proofs of the innate corruption of the system. Evidently, linen-drapery, and hairdressing for ladies, ought to be assigned to women. Again, the delicate machinery of watches, and the fine drawing required for architectural designs, or wood engraving, are eminently appropriate to feminine manipulation. We may add that invention is a strong feminine characteristic, and that had architecture been studied by female artists, we should not have had the grievous and grotesque exhibition of our national incapability to furnish a fitting memorial of our greatest warrior, simply from the designs being executed only by men. The subject of woman's employment has, however, taken such a hold upon every right-minded person, that each day will corroborate its adjustment; all we desire is that the clergy should give the impulse its right bias, by directing the national education of both sexes upon more common-sense principles, and assure to women that proper moral and intellectual culture, and those spheres of useful employment, which are her rightful inheritance from the Lord of the Vineyard, to whom both "woman and her master" are responsible.

6. John W. Burgon, "Woman's Place. A Sermon   . . .   , February 12, 1871" (Oxford: James Parker and Co., 1871), pp. 3, 6-10.

Frequently the most strident claims for a point of view are made when those very claims are most under attack. On the heels of women voting in borough elections in 1869 came the Education Act of 1870, giving women the rights to vote for and serve on municipal school boards. The election of Miss Eleanor Elizabeth Smith to the first Oxford school board brought out the ire of the Rev. John W. Burgon (1813-88), vicar of St. Mary's and fellow of Oriel College, Oxford, in a sermon which advanced assertions about "woman's place" that were beginning to be extreme even for that time. Burgon later became dean of Chichester, where he continued to oppose such developments as the abolition of religious tests in the universities, the revised translation of the Bible, and the admission of women to the universities to be educated with men and under the same course of study. While now more of a rear-guard sentiment, especially in the absoluteness of its claims, these views, together with the religious sanctions on which he based them, made it difficult for gains to be made for women in the universities or in the society very rapidly. The theological foundations for his position made it more likely that when gains were made, they would not come first in the churches.

When I desire to know the truth on any point of conduct or of morals, I turn instinctively to Holy Scripture as my one only infallible guide; and inquire,—What light does Scripture throw upon the subject under consideration? [Here follows a discussion of the injunctions of St. Paul.]

. . . It appears that in the very dawn of Christianity it was judged necessary to repress forwardness of self-assertion in the other sex: while at the same time Woman's actual duties; Woman's appointed sphere; Woman's legitimate channels of influence and methods of occupation,—these were carefully prescribed to her. I need hardly rehearse the familiar words,—or do more than remind you that Home is clearly and emphatically "Woman's *place*;" and the duties which belong to Home, Woman's special and peculiar duties. The primeval utterance will never lose its force while sun and moon endure,— to be "*an help.*" Next, as perforce when two wills clash there must needs follow either conflict or else submission, all doubt is removed as to the side on which the submission (S. Paul calls it *subjection*) must be found. The Christian training-up of Children is indicated, obviously enough, as the special care and privilege of as many as are Mothers. Shamefastness and modesty of apparel are again and again required of all. In lieu of costly array, good works are suggested as the more becoming apparel; and instead of broided hair, gold, and pearls, the ornament of a meek and quiet spirit, which in the sight of God is declared to be of great price.

But, as already hinted, it is generally in the sweet sanctities of domestic life,— in home duties,—in whatever belongs to and makes the happiness of *Home*, that woman is taught by the SPIRIT to find scope for her activity,—her sphere of most appropriate service. "*To guide the house*," and so to guide it as "to give none occasion to the adversary to speak reproachfully:" *this* is her province! "*To be a keeper at home*;" and so to keep *at* home as to be the keeper *of* home, the watcher *for* the home, as well: *this* is her duty! Home, in a word,—*Home* is "Woman's *place.*" . . .

I have considered this as a question of Authority and Right. Viewed on the side of Experience and Expediency, we shall be conducted to the same result, only in a more summary way. . . .

Woman's strength is her weakness. She rules,—at all events she reigns,—because it is perfectly well understood that she consents—*has vowed*, in fact—to obey. We show her such invariable deference, such chivalrous consideration, such punctilious homage, because we know very well that she has no power whatever to enforce it;—cannot produce a shadow of proof that she has any right to exact it;—is without remedy, (except of course the remedy of making herself disagreeable,) if we withhold it, even if we show her a slight. We follow her advice and are guided by her opinion,—at least we are influenced by both to an extent we should hardly care to confess,—because she neither dictates, nor argues, nor for a moment claims *the right* to guide. She makes one believe—(*that* is a part of her wisdom and her tact)—that she does not expect we shall care for what she says. And so she generally carries her point. And really no harm comes of it. She is generally right, after all, because she *feels* so justly; her *instincts* are so capital. But she is a bad reasoner. Logic,—I was going to say she has none: but that would not be true. Hers is the Logic of *conclusions*, irrespective of *premisses*. . . .

See you not plainly then, that if the mischievous fashion of which I complained at first is suffered to proceed unchecked at its present rapid rate of progress, it must in the end, (and the end will be before long,) prove fatal to the happiness of *both* parties? The rival Professor;—the competing Institution;—the conflicting interest;—the challenge which used to be addressed to our Christian chivalry, addressed to our mercy or to our pity;—the plea which used to be urged with undisguised weakness, now enforced with the feeble semblance of official prerogative:—See you not plainly that all this kind of thing can only serve to disgust and alienate as well as permanently to weaken the ties which at present are the strongest? In a word, when Woman, instead of being a gentle, modest, and *most* unselfish helper, makes herself a bustling, forward, and in fact inconvenient rival; she must not be astonished to find herself treated as such. When, instead of rejoicing in the sacred retirement of her home and the strict privacy of her domestic duties, she is found to be secretly longing for the publicity of print and the notoriety of the platform:—when this, or any approach to this, becomes a common thing,—Woman will too late discover that she has, as far as in her lay, unsexed herself; lost her present unique social position; come to be regarded only as an inferior kind of Man. Man, with all his hardness: Man, without his manliness. She will be no longer a help and a consolation. She will inevitably find that she has dethroned *herself*, and degraded *herself*,—to her own heavy harm and loss; to our abiding sorrow and unceasing discomfort.

7. C. J. H. Fletcher, "Woman's Equality with Man in Christ. A Sermon . . . , March 19, 1871" (London: Rivingtons, 1871), pp. 3-10.

One indication of the changes that had taken place by 1871 regarding views of women within the Church of England is that Burgon's sermon received a public rebuttal. The curate of St. Mary Magdalene, Oxford, the Rev. C. J. H. Fletcher, preached his sermon a month later as a direct rejoinder. His main theme was not new; in fact, it reproduced George Fox's understanding of the salvation process and its implications for the position of women. But this had seldom been presented from an Anglican pulpit. A further point took up a contemporary issue and argued that recent changes in society—e.g., many women working and many not married—required an enlarged sense of "woman's place" in God's plan for humankind. The recognition that contemporary conditions had to be addressed in the determination of a "proper" Christian perspective on the issue contributed greatly to a reconstruction of the position represented by Burgon. Fletcher continued to believe, as did the vast majority of people, that there were differences of temperament and ability between men and women which were best united in marriage. But he was also aware that the traditional view of womanhood was both restrictive and increasingly unrealistic for a growing number of

women in the society and that a reassessment of the biblical basis for it was essential
to the development of an alternative perspective.

It has been lately asserted from the pulpit that [the Woman's] movement is opposed to God's Word, that the Bible confines Women to duties to be done in their own homes or in the homes of others, and that Woman's relation to Man is declared by the same authority to be one of subjection. Now there is one thing, I venture to think, of which in these days it especially behoves Christ's ministers to beware: they must carefully avoid identifying His Gospel with anything that is not essentially part of it. Christianity has been retarded by being misrepresented to involve bad morality and false astronomy and geology; its interpreters should not further hamper it by making it the ground of opposition to what may be the cause of social justice and moral progress. It is not my purpose now to consider the expediency of the movement in question, whether or not it is likely to be beneficial to society—*that*, it seems to me, must be determined by experience rather than by discussion—I merely propose to show you that the Bible has not prejudged the matter, that it does not say that Home is Woman's *only* place or that her *true* relation to Man is one of subjection or submission.

The first point you should clearly understand is this, that, according to the Bible, Woman's original condition was one of equal co-operation with Man, and that it is sin that has degraded her from this position of equality into being the slave and instrument of his selfishness and pleasure. The proof of this is to be found in the first three chapters of Genesis. . . . [In the first chapter] the word "man" means humanity, or the human race, comprehending men and women. The passage teaches that Man and Woman are the two halves of one humanity, which is the likeness of God; that the sexes, possessing innate moral as well as physical differences, are complements of each other, and that their spiritual function is to perfect one another by the interchange of their respective characteristics. The relation of Man and Woman, therefore, as defined in this first chapter, is that of mutual educators, of equal co-operators in the education of humanity. There is not a word subordinating the one to the other or limiting the province of either. If we pass to the actual creation of the first Man and Woman described in the second chapter, we shall find a confirmation of what has just been said. Eve is there said to be Adam's helper, an office which neither in itself nor by scriptural use implies subjection to him; Adam is drawn by love to Eve as to her who could supply a want in him; the two together form a unity. The additional truth to be gathered from the second chapter is, that marriage is a necessary condition of Man and Woman's mutual education. If there were any doubt that the primeval relation of the sexes was one of equality, it would be removed by the third chapter, which declares that Woman's subjection to Man is a consequence of sin; "thy desire shall be subject to thy husband, and he shall rule over thee." The connection between sin and Woman's degradation is obvious. . . .

The second point you should understand is, that Woman's original equality with Man is recovered in Christ. The true ground of her restored dignity is often misrepresented. It does not rest on the fact that the Virgin Mary was the divinely selected instrument of the Incarnation. . . . Nor is Woman's elevation in Christ derived from her relation as Wife being (according to S. Paul) a sacramental sign of the Church's relation to Christ. Its true cause lies deeper. It is found, first, in this, that Christ's character manifested the womanly virtues—purity, sympathy, gentleness, obedience—which had died out of the world with Woman's degradation. You must never forget that Christ is neither Man nor Woman, He is the divine likeness, the whole humanity, Manhood and Womanhood in one. It is found, next, in Christ's reverence for Woman, in His tender care for the weak, the suffering, the oppressed. It is also found in the power there is in Christ's character, example, and spirit gradually to eradicate the selfishness that had degraded woman. "There is neither Jew nor Gentile, male or female; for ye are all one in Christ." Christ does not destroy characteristics of race or sex, but He will destroy the selfish exclusiveness of race and sex, the oppression of one race or sex by another. Woman's elevation in Christ is slow and gradual, part of the general progress of society. The method of Christianity is to remove abuses by removing their causes. It attacks them indirectly. It works a social revolution, but it takes ages to do it in. It took above 1800 years to abolish slavery in Christendom; it has not yet abolished cruelty to animals; it has done much for Women, but much remains for it to do.

If, however, Christ has regained for Woman her original equal dignity with Man, how are we to account for S. Paul and S. Peter so frequently and urgently exhorting Women to home privacy, avoidance of publicity, and submission to Men? This brings me to the third point, that in these passages the Apostles aimed at checking the disposition of the Christian Women of their time, prematurely to vindicate their rightful social rank; but that they had no intention of preventing Woman's gradual elevation to equality with Man, by the progress of Christian society. . . .

The duties of Wife and Mother are unquestionably the highest a Woman can discharge; they form the noblest field of her co-operation with Man, for by these she leavens with Womanly virtue two generations at once. If the state of society allowed of every Woman becoming a Wife on arriving at marriageable age, the question of Woman's place would perhaps never have arisen. Society, however, is not so happily constituted, nor is there any present prospect of its being so. When we glance at the Women of our lower classes, what do we see? Are they all Wives and Mothers, all keepers at home—doers of home duties? No; we see many earning their subsistence in the field, the factory, and the shop. Do we think their doing so contrary to God's Word? Do we blame their working out of the home-circle? Do we deem their lives unlovely by self-assertion and publicity? No; we honour them for thus using the talents God has given them. Why should Women of a higher grade be judged differently? Does God's Word vary with classes? Does it forbid in one class what it allows in another? Or is the condition of Women of the middle class such as to render needless other than home occupations? Let us glance at that condition. Are there not in our middle-class homes thousands of young Women doing nothing but waiting to be married, which a large proportion of them never can be? Are not some leading useless, frivolous, and dissipated lives? Are not some, painfully conscious of this, striving to make their weary lives worthier by work? Are these to be rebuked, and told to work at home? . . . Our Church, indeed, might make greater use of her Women than she does; she might organize societies in which they should be taught to educate, to nurse, and to visit, and might direct their skilled labour to these ends. But if this were done, it would not be enough. What right have men to say that women, if they leave home, shall do nothing but nurse, educate, and visit? Suppose God has fitted them for other things? Has He not endowed some with genius to adorn literature? What a loss, if these had shrunk from the publicity of print! Neither God's Word, nor reason, as it seems to me, justifies the imposition of limits to Woman's work. What God has fitted them for, they ought to be allowed to do, and what He has fitted them for can only be ascertained by giving them full liberty to follow their bent and choose their work. God has so made us that inclination and fitness for particular work usually go together. We may trust Him not to incline Women to any work of which they are incapable, or which would injure Womanhood. We trust Him so in Men—why should we not in Women? . . .

Some suggestions may be offered to young Women arising out of what has been said. Every Woman is endowed with the qualities that make womanhood—with purity, sympathy, gentleness, endurance—qualities in which Men are weak. Her Womanhood is a trust from God, and her first duty is to let it shine through her life, and to diffuse it in her intercourse with others, and especially with Men. But, as where she is strong Man is weak, so where Man is strong she is weak. Her next duty, therefore, is to know her defects, to learn of Man his virtues—justice, truth, courage, public spirit. Without some measure of these added to her Womanhood, she is but half the image of God. Let her, in looking forward and preparing for life, contemplate that she may become Wife and Mother, but let her also contemplate that she may not. . . . She must not . . . so plan her life, as that it will seem a failure unless she marry. She must endeavour to find or make some work for herself. If inclination points to some new line of activity, and parents sanction her pursuing it, let her not be discouraged by vulgar sneers or conventional intolerance; let her wed herself to her work, and beautify it by her Womanhood, and she may then rest assured that, so doing, she will not be out of Woman's place.

8. Charlotte Mary Yonge, *Womankind* (London: Mozley and Smith, 1877), pp. 1-8.

Charlotte Yonge's (1823-1901) views of womanhood reflected her life, which was focused on the institutions of family and church. She spent her entire life in a small Hampshire village, taught Sunday School for seventy years, edited a magazine for Anglican girls (*The Monthly Packet*) for some forty years, and did not marry. She was greatly influenced by John Keble, who became vicar of Hursley in 1836 and for thirty years was her tutor in the Christian faith, critic and supporter of her literary endeavors, and close friend and guide. In a long career she wrote some 250 works, including novels, stories for children, histories and biographies, and books of religious instruction. But before she was allowed to publish, a family council took up the question and agreed only when it was decided that the earnings would be devoted to charity. Her writings reflect the religious and moral perspectives of her high church convictions, and many of her novels were widely read in Victorian society.

Yonge had no sympathy for notions of women's emancipation or for efforts to enlarge the participation of women in society. She thought that possession of the vote would be a greater burden on women than the lack of it, and she objected to women trying to be doctors when they could be nurses or teachers. She feared what Liberals would do to church and state. Readily accepting the inferiority of women, she affirmed the qualities of humility, meekness, and submission as "the true strength and beauty of womanhood." Yet she disdained the notion that women are more moral or more religious than men as an offense to Christianity, which had restored woman to her original role as helpmeet to man and had provided a meaningful vocation for the single woman. Though acknowledging her secondary position, a woman should seek to be an active helpmeet and complement to her husband or to the church. The married woman needs to pursue a serious education, be alert to political and theological issues, and be willing to assume authority and responsibility as needed. A single woman will have a number of outlets for her talents, especially through the church. For both, as for Yonge personally, a woman's religion is her center and her consolation.

A woman can hardly arrive at middle age without having thought over some of the duties and opportunities placed in the hands of her sex. *To think* is in the present day almost equivalent with *to express*; and it is in the hope that the expression of some of my thoughts may be in some degree an assistance to a few readers, that I venture to throw a fresh contribution into the seething cauldron of sayings and opinions with which we are regaled in the present day.

Not that I have anything new to say—only that which is so old that it may seem new. I have no hesitation in declaring my full belief in the inferiority of woman, nor that she brought it upon herself.

I believe—as entirely as any other truth which has been from the beginning— that woman was created as a help-meet to man. How far she was then on an equality with him, no one can pretend to guess; but when the test came, whether the two human beings would pay allegiance to God or to the Tempter, it was the woman who was the first to fail, and to draw her husband into the same transgression. Thence her punishment of physical weakness and subordination, mitigated by the promise that she should be the means of bringing the Redeemer to renovate the world, and break the dominion of Satan.

That there is this inequality there is no reasonable doubt. A woman of the highest faculties is of course superior to a man of the lowest; but she never attains to anything like the powers of a man of the highest ability. There is a difficulty, however, in generalizing; because, owing to difference of climate, habit, and constitution, there is less inequality between the sexes in some races than there is in others. . . .

Savage life renders the woman the slave. . . . Perhaps the very first stage from savagery to civilization is marked by the preponderance of ornament on the female side. As soon as woman ceases to be the mere squaw, adornment is viewed as primarily her due. Her condition, where there is civilization without Christianity, is extremely variable, and chiefly dependent on the national character; and everywhere, in the very lowest classes, there is the tendency to bring her to the squaw level. In the upper ranks and among classes fairly at ease, the usual tendency has been to regard the splendour and indolence of the chief wife as testimonials to the wealth and grandeur of her lord and master. . . .

The position of woman was at once recognized in Gospel teaching. The Blessing conferred upon the holy Mother of our Lord became the antidote to the punishment of Eve's transgression; and in proportion to the full reception of the spirit of Christianity has woman thenceforth been elevated to her rightful position as the help-meet.

There, however, comes in the woman's question of the day—Is she meant to be nothing but the help-meet? If by this is meant the wife, or even the sister or daughter, attached to the aid of some particular man, I do not think she is. It is her most natural, most obvious, most easy destiny; but one of the greatest incidental benefits that Christianity brought the whole sex was that of rendering marriage no longer the only lot of all, and thus making both the wife and the maiden stand on higher ground.

"Thy desire shall be to thy husband, and he shall rule over thee," had been said to Eve. Without a husband the woman had hitherto been absolutely nothing. Wife, mother, or slave, were her sole vocations; and if her numbers became superfluous, polygamy and female infanticide were the alternatives.

But the Church did away with this state of things. Wifehood was dignified by becoming a faint type or shadow of the Union of the Church with her Lord. Motherhood was ennobled by the Birth that saves the world; and Maidenhood acquired a glory it had never had before, and which taught the unmarried to regard themselves, not as beings who had failed in the purpose of their existence, but as pure creatures, free to devote themselves to the service of their Lord; for if His Birth had consecrated maternity, it had also consecrated virginity. . . .

So began the vocation of the dedicated Virgin, the Deaconess, the Nun. The life in community became needful when no security could be had save in a fortress; and this, together with the absolute need of the feminine nature for discipline and obedience, led to the monastic life being, with rare exceptions, the only choice of the unwedded throughout the middle ages; but this safe and honourable refuge for the single daughters of families did, to take it on the very lowest grounds, much to enhance the estimation in which their secular sisters were held.

It is not, however, my purpose here to dwell on monasticism. All I want to do is to define what I believe to be the safe and true aspect in which woman ought to regard herself—namely, as the help-meet of man; not necessarily of any individual man, but of the whole Body whom Christ our Lord has left to be waited on as Himself. He is her Lord. He will find her work to do for Him. It may be that it will lie in the ordinary course of nature. It is almost certain that she will begin as help-meet to her father or brothers; and to many, there comes the Divinely-ordained estate of marriage, and the duties and blessings it entails, all sanctified through Him. It may be, again, that her lot is attendance on a parent—still a work of ministry especially blest by Him; and so with all those obvious family claims that Providence marks out by the mere fact of there being no one else to undertake them. And for those who are without such calls, or from whom their tasks have fallen away, what is there left? Nay, not left as a remnant, for He has been there through all. Their Lord is ready for their direct, complete, uneclipsed service in whatever branch seems their vocation. His Church is the visibly present Mother to guide them; and as daughters of the Church their place and occupation is found.

Previously they had no status, except as appendages to some individual man. Now, as members of one great Body, each has her place and office, whether domestic or in some special outer field. And in proportion as this is recognised, the single woman ceases to be *manqué*, and enjoys honour and happiness.

The change makes less visible difference to the married woman . . . But the woman destitute of such a direct object for her obedience, cares, interests and affections, is apt, when her first youth is over, to crave for something further, unless she have recognised her relation to the universal Body and to its Head. . . . [L]et her feel herself responsible to the one great Society of which she is a part, and let her look for the services that she can fulfil by head or by hands, by superintendence or by labour, by pen or pencil, by needle or by activity, by voice or by music, by teaching or by nursing—nay, by the gentle sympathy and earnest prayers of an invalid; and the vague discontent is appeased. She has found a vocation, or it has been found for her. It may be an outwardly secular life that she lives, and there is no visible difference between her pursuits and those of others; but they are dedicated, they have their object; and if her heart rests in Him, she is content. . . . It is only as a daughter of the Church that woman can have her place, or be satisfied as to her vocation.

9. Frances Power Cobbe, *The Duties of Women* (London: Williams and Norgate, 1881), pp. 21-27.

There could hardly be a greater contrast between two persons who had virtually identical life spans and a common vocation as writer than that seen in Charlotte Yonge and Frances Power Cobbe (1822-1904). Cobbe was born in Dublin to devout Evangelical parents and educated by governesses until sent to a school in Brighton in 1836, where, as she later recalled, "everything was taught us in the inverse ratio of its true importance. At the bottom of the scale were Morals and Religion, and at the top were Music and Dancing."[22] By the age of twenty she had rejected orthodox Christianity, but gradually through her interest in moral questions came back to religion, affirming a moral theism but not identifying herself directly with any religious group. Many of her later writings were concerned with theological issues, as she sought to resolve the contemporary problems of faith and doubt and yet avoid the extremes of traditionalism and rationalism. She was considerably influenced in her development by the thought of Immanuel Kant.

Cobbe lived at her family home, which she managed after her mother's death in 1847, until her father died ten years later. With the estate in the hands of her brother, she left with a modest inheritance and soon joined Mary Carpenter's "Ragged School" enterprise in Bristol, educating working-class children and visiting workhouse inmates. Poor health prevented her from staying longer than a year, and she eventually turned to writing. But that experience opened her for the first time to a wider world, which continued to be reflected over the rest of her life in essays and social reform activities. She became interested in issues of education and employment of women, in the rising suffrage movement, in the plight of battered women (see chapter 5), and in anti-vivisection activities. On this latter issue she devoted the last thirty years of her life.

Cobbe did not know about "women's rights" until she went to Bristol. Her own experience made her sensitive to the inadequate education, the limited opportunities, and the legal disabilities that prevented women from taking a full place in society and created in many men an underlying attitude of contempt. Her broadest contribution was to attack the theory of womanhood on which these limitations were built and to construct an alternate theory based on a religious conception of duty. This meant that women were first human beings and secondly women; justice could thus be appealed to against all laws or conventions which restricted women because of their being women. Next, it meant that women had to take care of themselves (personal duties came before social duties). Thirdly, it meant that social duties included attention not only to the home, but to the larger spheres of society, state, and world. Finally, it meant the eventual realization of a common humanity for men and women, which she once pictured in terms of a marital ideal of mutuality and the sharing of virtues.[23]

We learn to bear in mind that whatever be the aim and end of the creation of a Man—the end which he ought steadfastly to contemplate and towards which he should guide the whole voyage of his life,—that *same* aim and end is ours, and we too must keep it prominently before our eyes. I think we women have reason to thank Milton for having so distinctly and lucidly set forth the opposite and prevailing error—the great moral *heresy* (as I reckon it) on this point, so that we can recognize it in a moment and renounce it distinctly. Milton's doctrine, as you all know, is, that Man only is made directly for God's service;

"*He* for God only—*she* for God in him,"

or, as he elsewhere makes Eve say to Adam—

"God is thy law—thou mine!"

Now, if we women are to advance one step forward, our very first leap must be over this abominable and ridiculous doctrine! For once in my life I find myself able to avail myself of the words of the Westminster Catechism, and I say that we are made "to know God and enjoy Him for ever," to live for Him and make ourselves like Him, and advance His kingdom, which means the reign of justice, truth, and love—and all this directly and immediately, and not for God "*in*" any man alive.

Here is the root of the misplacement of women, that they have been deemed by men, and have contentedly deemed themselves, to have only a secondary purpose in the order of things. Brigham Young's doctrine that only a woman *sealed* to a man in marriage can possibly be saved, is little more than a carrying out of our British legislator's idea, that women who do not marry (and so do not immediately contribute to the comfort of some particular man) are *"Failures."* They have no *raison d'etre* in creation, any more I suppose, than the mistletoe without the apple-tree! The Hindoos formerly carried out this idea to its logical conclusion by suttee. When the man died, it was time to burn the widow. When we cut down the tree, the mistletoe dies. Of course there is a sense in which every created being is made for others. Creation is like one of those vast suspension bridges in which every bar and chain tends to support the whole structure. But in *this* sense man also is made for woman, the father for the son, the daughter for the mother, and so on *ad infinitum.* There is no degradation to any, but honour to all, in this view of the solidarity of the family, the State and Humanity. And why? Because every one recognizes that it is only the secondary purpose of each to help the other. The primary *raison d'etre* of every one is his own existence, and only in a secondary sense he exists for others. . . .

Let us take it once for all thoroughly to heart. We women have before us the noblest end to which a finite creature may attain; and our duty is nothing else than the fulfilment of the whole moral law, the attainment of every human virtue.

How shall we now, for our present purposes, map out this vast field of morality? Necessarily I must do it merely in outline. . . .

Practical Morality includes three branches of Duty: RELIGIOUS DUTY, PERSONAL DUTY, and SOCIAL DUTY. All Duties are, in one sense, Religious. We owe it to God to lift our souls up to the blessed end of union with Himself for which He has created us; and we owe it to Him to love and serve our fellow men who are His children, and to be kind to the brutes which are His creatures. But in speaking here of Religious Duty as a branch of ethics, I refer to the special Duties owed *directly* by man to God, whenever he recognizes that there is above him such a Being, his Creator and Benefactor, the Lord of Conscience, the absolutely Holy One, the Alpha and Omega of his existence: "Path, Motive, Guide, Original, and End."

These, strictly speaking, RELIGIOUS DUTIES may be classified under the heads of Thanksgiving, Repentance, Prayer, Faith, Adoration, and Self-Consecration, and may be summed up on the canon "Thou shalt love the Lord thy God."

The second branch of Morals is PERSONAL DUTY, the duty directly concerning ourselves, the pursuit of the proper End of our being; inward rather than outward virtue; *being* good as distinguished from *doing* good. These Personal Duties may be classified under the heads of Chastity, Temperance, Veracity, Courage, and the conservation of our Freedom (whereby alone any other duty can be performed). They may be summed up in the canon "Be Perfect."

The third branch of Morals is SOCIAL DUTY, the Duty which concerns all our fellow creatures. These duties may be classified in various ways; in these Lectures we shall treat them in order as regards the objects of each Duty, viz.—Duties of the Family; Duties of the Household; of Society; and of the State. All these Social Duties may be summed up by the canon "Thou shalt love thy Neighbour as Thyself."

Now of this great trinity of human duties, Religious, Personal, and Social, we need not concern ourselves in these lectures with the first, seeing that no one in Christian countries has been silly enough to suggest that there is any difference between the Religious Duties of a man and those of a woman—unless indeed, it be that a religious man is bidden to let his "light shine before men that they may glorify his Father in Heaven," while a woman is generally counselled to place *her* Divine light carefully under a bushel!

. . . I hold that whenever Personal and Social Duties seem to come into collision, the Personal Duty must have the precedence. We must not sacrifice our

Truthfulness, and Chastity, and Temperance, in the vain hope of benefiting our neighbours, for these two plain reasons; first, because, as Virtue is the true end of our being, and we can only choose virtue for ourselves and not for another, and can never *make* anybody else virtuous (only in an indirect way *help* him to virtue), it follows that it is absurd to postpone our own virtue to any lesser object. And, secondly, because we can never really benefit anybody by doing wrong on his behalf, and the truest and surest way in which we can serve our fellow men is, not so much to *do* anything for them, as to *be* the very truest, purest, noblest beings we know how. This is I fear, a hard lesson to take to heart, and you will pardon me if, in addressing women, I dwell on it specially because I think it is a matter on which the most generous natured women are most apt to err.

10. James Baldwin Brown, *The Home: In its Relation to Man and to Society*, 2nd ed. (London: James Clarke & Co., 1883), pp. 150-53, 155-56, 174-76.

James Baldwin Brown (1820-84) was a well-known Congregational minister in London from 1843 to 1884 and the author of several books. A "Broad Church Evangelical" whose views were shaped in part through the influence of F. D. Maurice, he was a vocal critic of the theological legacy of a rigid Calvinism. His views on the need for the church to respond to the new intellectual currents of the day quickly marked him as one whose religious orthodoxy was suspect, and he was involved in several theological controversies within his denomination over the course of his career, the last occurring when he was Chair of the Congregational Union in 1878. Brown also associated himself with a number of social movements, especially those that related to the condition of the working classes. But as he believed that the home and family were the basis of a sound moral, religious, and national life, he both exalted the role of women in the home and opposed the activities of those who advocated an extension of women's rights and powers. As such he stands as representative of a group more difficult to characterize than the Burgons of the nineteenth century, for he was a liberal on virtually all issues of the day except for those relating to women. It is the Browns more than the Burgons,

though, who testify to the sustaining power of the traditional understanding of the role
and contributions of women.

We hear much foolish and frothy talk in these days of woman's rights. To me
there is nothing so sacred upon earth as a woman's duties, a woman's life. God
is revealed to us as the Father; it is the one broad, comprehensive word which
describes His parental relation to mankind. But when He would use a plea of
peculiar tenderness and constraining power, the father melts into the mother; "Can
a woman forget her sucking child? . . . Yea, a woman may forget but never
will I forsake thee, saith thy God." We must remember that the father and the
mother are essentially the one parent; just as husband and wife are "one flesh."
The two blend in God. And whenever the Saviour needs an image of peculiar grace,
tenderness, and love, it is the mother's nature which He draws forth and presents as
the fullest image of His own. And if the bearing of another's burden be according to
the mind of Christ, we can understand how it must be so. Is there anything in this
universe within our ken, which may be compared with a mother's willingness to bear
with and suffer for her child? It is the most heavenly image which nature presents to
us of Divine things. A woman's sorrow in her hour of anguish, transmuted into the
purest joy which is known to mortals when the first faint cry of her infant breaks
upon her ear, is the experience which the Saviour selects to set forth that mystery
of holy sorrow in this life, out of which the most glorious joys are to be born in
eternity. (John xvi. 21-2.)

It is wonderful how little we read in the Bible—nay, we read absolutely nothing—
about those rights of persons, sexes, classes, and communities, the assertion or denial
of which has been in all ages the chief spring of the waters of strife in our world.
Men's rights, women's rights, there is not a hint of them in the Bible. The rights
of monarchs, of subjects, of masters, of servants, of nobles, of slaves, find but scant
recognition in Scripture. Even Onesimus, the runaway slave, was remanded to his

master's brotherly love. So much the worse for the Bible, say the prophets of the
"advanced school," as it is called, among us; advanced, no doubt, but towards a
dreary wilderness of negations, in which nothing is known about the sphere out of
which in all ages the purest springs of man's comfort, joy, and hope, have flowed;
. . . The man who wants to lay down a platform of rights on the ground of
which he may urge claims on, and demand service of, his fellow-men, will find no
book so little helpful to him as the Bible; and this is its glory. The Bible is emphatically a book of duties. It throws little light upon what man can claim from
man. What man can do, and is bound to do, for man, it sets forth with matchless
fulness and power. The only class which it pities, is not the class which cannot get
its rights recognised, but the class or the soul which has not found the sphere of its
duties; which has found no ministry to undertake, no burden to lift, no self-denial
to exercise, no sacrifice to offer, no cross to bear for Christ or for mankind. . . .

These few hints will be sufficient to show that I have but slight sympathy with
the tone of that passionate outcry about woman's rights, that fierce complaint of
woman's narrow and poor opportunities, and that imperious demand for a larger
and more prominent part in the public theatre of life, of which, happily, we hear
less in these days than we did when the crusade first began, about a generation ago.
Fierce contentions for rights bring no blessing, but rather the noble self-denying
use of powers. Happily "the woman's question," in our days is passing into an
altogether higher stage of development; not because woman has fully won all that
was contentiously claimed for her, but because women themselves are led to take
a larger and truer view of the essential nobleness and dignity of that part on the
great stage of life which is all their own; and further because the great world has
come to understand that it cannot get on without the blending of the feminine
quality and faculty with the masculine, in all the higher interests and activities of
its life. Women are winning their way to a fair share in the public life and work
of their times, not because by persistent contention they have forced their way into

the citadel and compelled the men to yield the rights which they have claimed; but because society finds out now that it wants them, and that God's ordinance, "neither the man without the woman, nor the woman without the man," in the home, in the State, and in the Church, is right.

. . . The women, because so many are of a sorrowful spirit and are so conscious that their arm is all too weak for the great work which they have to do and the heavy burden which they have to bear, have been in all ages and are still the specially religious element in the community. Maternity and the nurture of children bring them very closely and tenderly into contact with the deepest mysteries of being, and lead them to yearn towards the Being who is in the heart of the mystery that they may be kindled and cherished by His life and His love. Women cannot believe easily, unless they have been much wearied by the "cant" which has so overlaid the Gospel in the Churches, that they are living in a loveless and Fatherless world. "The Father" has naturally a large meaning to a woman's heart. Her nature is a kind of sacred ark in which the idea of the Divine Fatherhood is shrined, and whence its light streams benignly on the self-orphaned world around.

And the women of a sorrowful spirit, for the same and many other reasons, have a deeper insight into spiritual truth, a quicker response to spiritual teaching, and a readier aptitude for spiritual work than falls to the lot of the masculine nature, in any but its highest examples. No doubt the special qualities of the two sexes constantly interpenetrate, and blend happily in the men and the women who stand forth as the elect spirits of their time. There are men who have no little of the delicate feminine fibre in their nature, and women with something of the masculine toughness and tension, and these are probably in either sex the finest human instruments by whom God is in all ages accomplishing His purposes of mercy in our world. But the woman's deep insight into spiritual truth and quick power of apprehension remains her noblest endowment. The women seem to have had fuller comprehension of the scope of Christ's teaching than the wisest of the Apostles. They were the last too at the Cross, and the first at the tomb. There was nothing incredible to them from the first in the glory of the Resurrection day. Their vocation in any age, did they fully understand its greatness, is to keep the inner eye of humanity clear, and open to the higher Divine teachings, while breathing, often with tearful eyes and burdened hearts, the perpetual human intercession into the ear of God. How many tears and prayers rise each night from women of a sorrowful spirit to hallow the atmosphere of our world, and prevail like Hannah's to win a rich blessing for mankind.

CHAPTER 4

WHAT SHOULD WOMEN DO? THE ISSUE OF WORK

A lady, to be such, must be a mere lady, and nothing else. She must not work for profit, or engage in any occupation that money can command, lest she invade the rights of the working classes, who live by their labour. Men in want of employment have pressed their way into nearly all the shopping and retail businesses that in my early years were managed in whole, or in part, by women. The conventional barrier that pronounces it ungenteel to be behind a counter, or serving the public in any mercantile capacity, is greatly extended. The same in household economy. Servants must be up to their offices, which is very well; but ladies, dismissed from the dairy, the confectionary, the store room, the still room, the poultry yard, the kitchen garden, and the orchard, have hardly yet found themselves a sphere equally useful and important in the pursuits of trade and art to which to apply their too abundant leisure.

Thus wrote Margaretta Grey, aunt of Josephine Butler, in her diary in 1853. The problem for women of the mid-nineteenth century was to find an "appropriate sphere" for their activities. It was made more difficult by the economic changes brought by the Industrial Revolution. Options previously available to women in an agricultural economy were reduced, and tasks removed from the home and placed within the factory. The ideal for the woman now included leisure. This was made possible through the work of increasing numbers of domestic servants and factory laborers, and it created opportunities that had never before existed as well as a sense of crisis provoking anger and frustration. Once again, Margaretta Grey, from her diary: "It is time to rise out of this, and for women of principles and natural parts to find themselves something to do."[1]

The two decades from 1850 to 1870 saw significant advances in the awareness of the problems faced by women and in the opportunities available to them in the public world. Some of the developments included the Crimean War activities of Florence Nightingale and her team of nurses, the emergence of religious orders for women in the Church of England, creation of programs for training deaconesses, beginnings of higher education for women, and the recognition in some religious circles of the need for a "ministry of women." At the same time some issues were broached in a public way, such as the legal disabilities faced by women with respect to divorce and property rights and the question of the franchise. Census figures of 1851 and 1861 provided graphic support to those who saw additional problems, by showing that there were more than two million single adult women. Many worked at whatever they could, while others were potentially employable, if only there were something for them to do. At the end of the period Josephine Butler's edited volume, *Woman's Work and Woman's Culture* (1869), represented a new level of public engagement with the issue of work. Add to these items the eruption of voluntary associations which women joined or led, and one has a picture of considerable ferment concerning the "appropriate sphere" for women.

In any consideration of the question of sphere one needs to be aware of these broad developments in mid-century. But the task of this chapter is to focus on the question of work from a religious perspective, giving particular attention to those who sought to be of service to and for the church. What is first apparent is how many women felt called to such service. Considering the possibilities for work was a form of reflection on one's religious vocation. Leaving aside the specifically ministerial dimensions of religious work, the subject of chapter 6, when the perceptions of opportunity and ability coincided, a large number of women understood that God had given both.

Much of the anguish expressed during the century was rooted in the fact that opportunity and ability did not so easily go hand-in-hand. Living on the basis of the prevailing ideal of womanhood meant limiting both to the arenas of home and family. The kinds of available "approved" work as well as social pressure each assured this. Those who were not satisfied with that could easily feel guilty or be made to feel guilty. Elizabeth Fry saw the opportunity but constantly agonized about whether she was able; her sense of vocation was both a source of strength and a burden. Florence Nightingale had confidence in her ability, but was burdened for years by lack of opportunity. When Julia Wightman and Mary Sumner launched their respective programs, it was with the confidence that the need for the work was great and that they as women had particular abilities to meet this need.

Because of the rapidly changing English society, affected in the landscape by industrialization and population growth and in its consciousness by the gradually eroding place of the church in the culture, women had more opportunities for public religious work in mid-century than they had had previously. In this new society the churches' tasks were more complicated and possibilities for response less clear, which made the clergy and the traditional engagements of the church pressed beyond their capacities. But there were women who were both available and capable, a number of people noted; perhaps they would assist in this work.[2] Whether it was demonstrating to the world a truly religious life, supplementing the clergy in a variety of useful tasks, visiting the poor and helping to improve their living conditions, or directly confronting the effects of drink or the emergence of the secular spirit, women could help. To some later in the century, woman's work would be "the saviour of society."[3]

There were, then, in these developments some possibilities of initiative and choice for women. To be sure, they were limited and controlled, determined in part by the expectations of what was "proper" for a woman to do. (Much of the work done by women in factories and mines was not congruent with these expectations, but that did not produce a significant change in them.) The opportunities were often limited to a certain segment of the population—to single women or to married women of the upper classes who had the leisure to take up volunteer work.[4] But even this much helped to correct the sense of having "lost their place" from the previous century, as expressed by people like Margaretta Grey and Florence Nightingale. To them and to others, leisure was a burden and represented having been put aside, either for a life of conventional frivolities or for a thousand daily tasks in home and family that prevented one from developing direction and purpose in life. And when the challenge came, for example, from Nightingale with this complaint, it had a religious foundation:

> Jesus Christ raised women above the condition of mere slaves, mere
> ministers to the passions of the man, raised them by his sympathy, to be
> Ministers of God. He gave them moral activity. But the Age, the World,
> Humanity, must give them the means to exercise this moral activity, must
> give them intellectual cultivation, spheres of action.[5]

She also included the church in the challenge. Her appeal: give us something to do, and show us how to do it! She found her opportunity in spite of the church, and for the rest of her life encouraged women to take advantage of the opportunities that had been opened for them to do the work that needed to be done.

At the same time, the documents show how opposition to greater public work by women continued, how much of this work was perceived to be a threat to existing patterns and relationships, and how cautious advocates had to be with their claims. Frequently the justification for religious and philanthropic work was based on the notion of "women's work for women," that is, the extension of the nurturing and supportive roles in the home into society, there often understood to be limited to other women. Just as frequently the claims to women's special competence for religion and morality became the basis of the advocacy. Thus the activities and the claims often had a double-edged quality to them. Few were able to see the issue in the terms of the stark contrast provided by one commentator who declared, "The truth is, that there is no middle course between a system which shall map out precise duties, not only to each sex, but to every class and to every individual constituting the State, and the system which leaves to all equal freedom to work at what they choose and what they are fit for."[6]

1. Elizabeth Fry, *Observations on the Visiting, Superintending, and Government, of Female Prisoners* (London, 1827), pp. 1-8.

A persistent theme in the nineteenth-century efforts to chart new directions for women's work was the concentration on those activities that women had traditionally done and which they could do better than men. Elizabeth Fry's only published work, which detailed the system pursued by the Ladies' Society with female prisoners, took up this theme in its introduction. She immediately disclaimed any desire to disrupt the existing responsibilities of women, but argued for an enlarged vocation on the basis of Christian charity and the need for improvement in society. Women did their work well in the home; they should be able to make these contributions outside the home, as well. Surely they should help other women who are in need!

Although Fry concentrated on prisons her attention was drawn to all public institutions and to the homes of the poor as well, and she was involved with such activities as programs for home visitation and the improvement of nursing care. She urged that women be put in charge of institutions which dealt with women and that women join forces with one another in their concern to address specific problems. And she thought that women who carried out their Christian vocation in these ways would be more refreshed and stimulated when they returned to their domestic duties. The work she envisioned had a strong patronizing tone to it, where the "pious and benevolent" would aid the "degraded and afflicted;" and the claim she advanced was limited. She did not advocate salaried work, nor did she support the efforts of the American female abolitionists who were refused seating at the Anti-Slavery Convention in London in 1840. Still, the way she viewed the vocation and the responsibilities of women and the proposals she offered for exercising them provided models which were extended considerably by others in later years.

Before . . . I endeavour to develop the system of the British Society, I wish to make a few general remarks, which have long impressed me, respecting my own sex, and the place which I believe it to be their duty and privilege to fill in the scale of society. I rejoice to see the day in which so many women of every rank, instead of spending their time in trifling and unprofitable pursuits, are engaged in works of usefulness and charity. Earnestly is it to be desired that the number of these valuable labourers in the cause of virtue and humanity may be increased, and that all of us may be made sensible of the infinite importance of redeeming the time, of turning our talents to account, and of becoming the faithful, humble, devoted, followers of a crucified Lord, who went about DOING GOOD.

Far be it from me to attempt to persuade women to forsake their right province. My only desire is, that they should *fill that province well*; and, although their calling, in many respects, materially differs from that of the other sex, and is not so exalted an one—yet a minute observation will prove that, if adequately fulfilled, it has nearly, if not quite, an equal influence on society at large.

No person will deny the importance attached to the character and conduct of a woman, in all her domestic and social relations, when she is filling the station of a daughter, a sister, a wife, a mother, or a mistress of a family. But it is a dangerous error to suppose that the duties of females end here. Their gentleness, their natural sympathy with the afflicted, their quickness of discernment, their openness to religious impressions, are points of character (not unusually to be found in our sex) which evidently qualify them, within their own peculiar province, for a far more extensive field of usefulness.

In endeavouring to direct the attention of the female part of society to such objects of Christian charity as they are most calculated to benefit, I may now observe that no persons appear to me to possess so strong a claim on their compassion, and on their pious exertions, as the helpless, the ignorant, the afflicted, or the depraved, of *their own sex*. It is almost needless to remark, that a multitude of such persons may be found in many of our public institutions.

During the last ten years much attention has been successfully bestowed by women on the female inmates of our *prisons*. . . .   But a similar care is evidently required for our hospitals, our lunatic asylums, and our workhouses. It is quite obvious, that there are departments in all such institutions which ought to be under the especial superintendence of females. Were ladies to make a practice of regularly visiting them, a most important check would be obtained on a variety of abuses, which are far too apt to creep into the management of these establishments. Such a practice would be the means, not only of essentially contributing to the welfare of the afflicted sufferers, but of materially aiding those gentlemen, on whom devolves the government or care of the institutions. . . .

While I would direct the attention of my own sex (in whose usefulness I take a very lively interest) to the importance of their visiting and superintending the females in our public institutions, I am far indeed from desiring to discourage them in other and more private walks of Christian charity. Among the most interesting exertions of female benevolence, will ever be numbered the visiting of the poor in their own habitations, the necessary attention to the supply of their temporal and spiritual wants, and, above all, the diligent promotion of the education of their children; but the economical arrangement of time, and more especially a suitable division of labor, will enable the benevolent females of any place or district to accomplish, without material difficulty, *all* their charitable objects. . . .

May the attention of *women* be more and more directed to these labors of love; and may the time quickly arrive, when there shall not exist, in this realm, a single public institution of the kind, in which the degraded or afflicted females who may happen to be its inmates shall not enjoy the *efficacious superintendence* of the pious and benevolent of THEIR OWN SEX!

2. The Journal of Sarah Martin, in *A Brief Sketch of the Life of the Late Miss Sarah Martin* (Yarmouth: C. Barber, 1844), pp. 12-13, 32-33.

> Some women who visited the poor or those in prison came from much more modest backgrounds than Fry or her associates had. One such was Sarah Martin (1791-1843), later called "the Yarmouth prison visitor."[7] Orphaned early and raised by a widowed grandmother, she learned the trade of a dressmaker. She began visiting a female prison in 1819. Because no one else was doing it, she also conducted worship services. At first she read printed sermons, but after several years she gave her own. In addition she helped to establish school programs for workhouse children and to find work for prisoners. A Parliamentary Report in 1835 commented on one of the services held for male prisoners, in which she used the Anglican liturgy and preached her own sermon, "of a purely moral tendency, involving no doctrinal points, and admirably suited to the hearers. . . .   Evening service was read by her afterwards to the female prisoners."[8] No organization was developed or larger concern evidenced as a result of this work; rather, it is simply an illustration of needs being seen and a ministry undertaken where normal pastoral activity was inadequate to the situation.

In August, 1819, I heard of a woman being sent to the gaol for having cruelly beaten her child, and having learned her name, went to the gaol and asked permission to see her, which, on a second application was allowed. When I told the woman, who was surprised at the sight of a stranger, the motive of my visit, her guilt, her need of God's mercy, &c., she burst into tears and thanked me, whilst I read to her the twenty-third chapter of St. Luke. For the first few months, I only made a short visit to read the Scriptures to the prisoners, but desiring more time to instruct them in reading and writing, I soon thought it right to give up a day in a week from dressmaking, by which I earned my living, to serve the prisoners. This regularly given, with many an additional one, was never felt as a pecuniary loss, but was ever followed with abundant satisfaction, for the blessing of God was upon me.

At this time there was no divine worship in the gaol on the Lord's day, nor any respect paid to it, at which I was particularly struck, when in going one Sunday to see a female convict, before her departure for transportation, I found her making a bonnet. I had long desired and recommended the prisoners to form a Sunday service, by one reading to the rest. It was at length adopted; but aware of the instability of a practice in itself good, without any corresponding principle of preservation, and thinking that my presence might exert a beneficial tendency, I joined their Sunday morning worship as a regular hearer. On discovering that their afternoon service had been resigned, I proposed attending on that part of the day also, and it was resumed. After several changes of readers, the office devolved on me. That happy privilege thus graciously opened to me, and embraced from necessity, and in much fear, was acceptable to the prisoners, for God made it so, and also an unspeakable advantage and comfort to myself. I was enabled to continue the two services on Sundays until 1831, when as my strength seemed failing for both, it pleased God that a good minister, who then became resident in our parish, should undertake the afternoon service, which was a timely relief to me. . . .

The manner, in which instruction has been carried forward amongst the prisoners, was as follows: any who could not read I encouraged to learn, whilst others in my absence assisted them. They were taught to write also, whilst such as could write already, copied extracts from books lent to them. Prisoners, who were able to read, committed verses from the holy Scriptures to memory every day, according to their ability or inclination. I, as an example, also committed a few verses to memory to repeat to them every day, and the effect was remarkable; always silencing excuse, when the pride of some prisoners would have prevented their doing it. Many said, at first, "It would be of no use,"—and my reply was, "It is of use to me, and why should it not be so to you? you have not tried it, but I have." Tracts and children's books, and larger books, four or five in number, of which they were very fond, were exchanged in every room daily, whilst any who could read more, were supplied with larger books, all of which were principally procured from the "Religious Tract Society."

Surely the power of God might here be distinctly seen, where a number of persons, differing in temper, although conceited, prejudiced, and ignorant, yet obeyed what was recommended, with the docility of children, and if I left home for a day or two, yet all learned the same, and most of them more in my absence, with the view of giving me pleasure on my return. From the commencement of my labors, to 1832, I read printed sermons on Sundays; and from that time to 1837, wrote my own observations;—but after the appointment of the present governor, when a new system arose, and no attention on my part was required for the preservation of order I was enabled, by the help of God, to address the prisoners without writing before hand, simply from the holy Scriptures.

3. [Florence Nightingale], *The Institution of Kaiserswerth on The Rhine, for the Practical Training of Deaconesses* (London, 1851), pp. 5-11.

In 1852 Florence Nightingale (1820-1910) was asked to help persuade a friend not to leave the Church of England for Catholicism. She wondered if she could do much, for she had experienced only frustration:

The Church of England has for men bishops, archbishops, and a little work. . . .   For women she has—what? I had no taste for theological discoveries. I would have given her my head, my heart, my hand. She would not have them. She did not know what to do with them. She told me to go back and do crochet in my mother's drawing-room; or, if I were tired of that, to marry and look well at the head of my husband's table. You may go to the Sunday School, if you like, she said. But she gave me no training even for that. She gave me neither work to do for her, nor education for it.[9]

Nightingale's formative years were a series of frustrations and thwarted ambitions combined with a strong sense of having been called into God's service. Her mother and sister were as much, if not more, of a block to these interests as the Church of England. She thought of joining a Catholic religious order or of creating a Protestant sisterhood without vows. But when she heard about and later visited Pastor Theodor Fliedner's institution at Kaiserswerth, Germany for the training of deaconesses in 1850, her earlier interests in nursing received a focus and a direction which set a career in motion. Fliedner had drawn some of his ideas from Fry for his modern Protestant revival of the deaconess order. Nightingale was impressed by the program he had established, and the pamphlet she wrote upon her return to England (and published anonymously) called attention not only to the order and discipline of the hospital work and the evidence of Christian commitment manifested by the community, but also to the education received by the deaconesses in training. Women in England lacked sufficient outlets for service and adequate training for the work. By publicizing Fliedner's efforts Nightingale would give them—and herself—a way out.

Additional observation and study at Kaiserswerth and in hospitals in Paris prepared Nightingale to become superintendent of the Harley Street Hospital in London in 1853. A year later she received an invitation from the government to lead an expedition of nurses to aid British forces in the Crimean War. It was an extraordinary request. No female nurses had ever been used by the military, and nursing was not thought to be respectable work for a lady. She returned in 1856 to national honors as "the lady of the lamp" and with interests in reforming the health of the British army and establishing a school for nurses.

Nightingale's commitment to service as an expression of her vocation to God colored her attitude to other issues relating to women. Since she had opened opportunities for women to work as nurses, she was frustrated when others sought new opportunities where the need was not so great. Her advice to women was to avoid special pleading of either extreme, that which claimed "women's rights" to do everything that men did, quite apart from their capacity for it, and that which excluded women from everything that men did: "It does not make a thing good, that it is remarkable that a woman should have been able to do it. Neither does it make a thing bad, which would have been good had a man done it, that it has been done by a woman."[10] What mattered was that there were capable women to do useful work, and what mattered most was that this was God's will and God's work.

There is an old legend that the nineteenth century is to be the "century of woman." Whatever the wisdom, or the foolishness, of our forefathers may have meant by this, English women know but too well that, up to this time, the middle of the century, it has not been theirs. Those who deny, are perhaps even better aware of it, than those who allow it.

And whose fault is this? Not man's. For, in no century, perhaps, has so much freedom, nay, opportunity, been given to woman to cultivate her powers, as best might seem to herself. Man leaves her room and space enough. She is no longer called pedantic, if her powers appear in conversation. The authoress is courted, not shunned. Accordingly, the intellectual development of English women has made extraordinary progress. But, as the human being does not move two feet at once, except he jump, so, while the intellectual foot has made a step in advance, the practical foot has remained behind. Woman stands askew. Her education for action has not kept pace with her education for acquirement. The woman of the eighteenth century was, perhaps, happier, when practice and theory were on a par, than her more cultivated sister of the nineteenth. The latter wishes, but does not know how, to do many things; the former, what she wished, at least *that* she could do.

What then? Shall we have less theory? God forbid. We shall not work better for ignorance. Every increase of knowledge is a benefit, by showing us more of the ways of God. But it was for the increase of "wisdom," even more than of knowledge, that David prayed—for wisdom is the practical application of knowledge.

"Not what we know, but what we do, is our kingdom," and woman, perhaps, feels that she has not found her kingdom. . . .

It has become of late the fashion, both of novel and of sermon writers, to cry up "old maids," to inveigh against regarding marriage as the vocation of all women, to declare that a single life is as happy as a married one, if people would but think so. So is the air as good an element for fish as the water, if they did but know how to live in it. Show us *how* to be single, and we will agree. But hitherto we have not found that young English women have been convinced. And we must confess that, *in the present state of things*, their horror of being "old maids" seems perfectly justified; it is not merely a foolish desire for the pomp and circumstance of marriage—a "life without love, and an activity without an aim" is horrible in idea, and wearisome in reality.

How many good women every one has known, who have married, without caring particularly for their husbands, in order to find—a very natural object—a sphere for their activity (though it might be asked, whether it were not better to take care of the children, who are already in the world, than to bring more into existence, in order to have them to take care of). How many others we know, who are suffering from ill health, merely from having nothing particular to do. "Go and visit the poor," is always said. And the best, those who have the deepest feeling of the importance of this occupation, answer in their souls (if not aloud), "We do not know how. . . . "

To be able to visit *well*, is not a thing which comes by instinct, but, on the contrary, is one of the rarest accomplishments. But, when attained, what a blessing to both visitors and visited!

The want of *necessary* occupation among English girls must have struck every one. How usual it is to see families of five or six daughters at home, in the higher ranks, with no other occupation in life, but a class in a Sunday school. And what is that? A chapter of the Bible is opened at random, and the spiritual doctor with no more idea of her patient's spiritual anatomy than she has plan for improving it, explains at random.

In the middle classes, how many there are who feel themselves burdensome to their fathers, or brothers, but who, not finding husbands, and not having the education to be governesses, do not know what to do with themselves.

Intellectual education is, however, as before said, not what we want to supply. Is intellect enough for the being who was sent here, like her great Master, to "finish" her Father's "work"? There was a woman once, who said that she was the "handmaid of the Lord." She was not the first, nor will she be the last, who has felt that this was really woman's only business on earth.

If, then, there are many women who live unmarried, and many more who pass the third of the usual term of life unmarried, and if intellectual occupation is not meant to be their end in life, what are they to do with that thirst for action, useful action, which every woman feels who is not diseased in mind or body? God planted it there. God, who has created nothing in vain. What were His intentions with regard to "unmarried women and widows?" How did He mean to employ them to satisfy them?

For every want we can always find a divine supply. And accordingly, we see, in the very first times of Christianity, an apostolical institution for the employment of woman's powers directly in the service of God. We find them engaged as "servants of the Church." We read, in the Epistle to the Romans, of a "Deaconess," as in the Acts of the Apostles, of "Deacons." Not only men were employed in the service of the sick and poor, but also women. In the fourth century, St. Chrysostom speaks of forty Deaconesses at Constantinople. We find them in the Western Church as late as the eighth,—in the Eastern, as the twelfth century. When the Waldenses, and the Bohemian and Moravian brothers began to arise out of the night of the middle ages, we find in these communities, formed after the model of the apostolical institutions, the office of Deaconesses, who were called Presbyterae, established in 1457. "Many chose," it is said, "the single state, not because they expected thereby to reach a super-eminent degree of holiness, but that they might be the better able to care for the sick and the young." . . .

We see, therefore, that God has not implanted an impulse in the hearts of women, without preparing a way for them to obey it.

Why did not the institution spread and flourish further? Perhaps this may be sufficiently explained by the fact, that there were no nursery-grounds—preparatory schools for Deaconesses, so that fitness for their office was, so to speak, accidental. This want is now supplied.

In Prussia, the system for the practical training of Deaconesses has spread in all directions.

In Paris, Strasburg, Echallens (in Switzerland), Utrecht, and England, the institution exists. Whether the blessing be greater to the class from which the labourers are taken, or to that among which they labour, it is hard to say. The Institution of Pastor Fliedner, at Kaiserswerth, on the Rhine, near Dusseldorf, is now so well known that the history of its rise will, perhaps, be interesting.

4. Anglican Religious Orders for Women: (A) [Mother Lydia Sellon], "A Few Words to Some of the Women of the Church of God" (London: J. Masters, 1850), pp. 10-11, 17-23; (B) W. M. Colles, "Sisters of Mercy, Sisters of Misery: or, Miss Sellon in the Family" (London: T. Hatchard, 1852), pp. 17-18.

Could women have a genuinely religious vocation? If so, under what organization and in what relationship to the Church ought this vocation best be practiced? These questions exercised a number of Anglicans in mid-century. To many they were made especially significant by the recognition that there were pressing human needs which parish clergy could not meet and a supply of single women who might devote themselves to these tasks. Out of such concerns came the creation of religious orders for women (called "sisterhoods") within the Church of England in the 1840s and, some years later, the restoration of the deaconess order.

Antecedents of these developments stressed a variety of works of mercy that women could perform, including visiting the sick and giving medical assistance, and urged that the Church of England adopt the model provided by the Catholic Sisters of Charity in France.[11] But the specific impulse in the 1840s came from the Tractarians, especially E. B. Pusey (1800-82), who argued that women could come to the same conviction as that which led men into the ministry. At the Church Congress in Oxford (1862) he declared, "To deny the possibility that women can know that they are so called, is to deny the possibility that God could call them." Pusey administered vows for the religious life to the first Anglican sister, Marian Hughes, in 1841; helped to establish the first community of sisters in London four years later; and was closely associated with Priscilla Lydia Sellon (1821-76) in the founding of a sisterhood in Devonport in 1848.

Sellon came to Devonport in response to a public letter from Bishop Phillpotts of Exeter appealing for help in the seacoast towns. She and her small community started schools for orphans, visited the sick, and worked heroically during the cholera epidemic of 1849. The sisterhood was independent of local clergy, but Phillpotts gave his full support and agreed to be the official Visitor. Soon, however, opposition was organized and stories circulated about what really went on there. Fears of Roman Catholic infiltration in Church and kingdom were growing; John Henry Newman's recent defection to Rome, the controversy over the Maynooth grant, and the restoration of the Catholic hierarchy in Britain had made Protestants very nervous. Sellon was accused of imitating Catholic convents, importing Catholic ritual, and assuming excessive authority over the sisters. She rejected all charges and affirmed her loyalty to the Church of England, receiving Phillpotts' support after an episcopal inquiry. But the criticism did not abate, and a flurry of pamphlet opposition in 1852 led Phillpotts to re-consider the evidence and to withdraw as Visitor. One of the pamphlets, by W. M. Colles, curate of Melton Mobray, raised the common accusation of "Romish principles" in the sisterhood, but concentrated more on the destruction of family ties that the "system" allegedly fostered through its separate existence and irrevocable vows. Local feelings frequently ran high, as in the riot of 1857 directed against J. M. Neale and the East Grinstead sisters.

Despite local opposition and uncertain support from clergy and hierarchy, the number of sisterhoods grew; sixty-one had been founded by the end of the century.[12] Their charitable work was widely praised, but their independence and the nature of their religious life continued to be suspect. As late as 1897 the Conference of Bishops was hesitant, declaring about these communities that "more regulation is needed if they are to be worked in through harmony with the general work of the Church as a whole."[13]

(A)   Such are the wrestlings in this present hour of your sufferings; inquiry only the more perplexes you; advice, you know not where to seek it: you doubt every one, you mistrust all, nay your very communion with your soul and God Himself, is interrupted by the fearful strife between the intellect bewildered with strong impressions and the affections. Yes, I say the *affections*, for I will not believe but that every woman's heart is true to her Church—I will not believe but that it would be most bitter to forsake Her in whom she has been cherished with such tenderness, such love, such care; yea, more bitter than death to forsake, to betray, to anathematize Her.

Truly it is very fearful to think that such subjects have been through these last months commonly handled and talked over drawing-room fires, and in mixed societies as carelessly as if on the most every-day topic, that the terms "Romanizing" and "Un-anglican," are passed about with the same freedom as one would talk of Whig, Tory, Conservative, Radical! Thus have men insidiously learned to deceive others and themselves, thus have minds grown into thoughts which they would have shrunk from with terror through careless talk, careless words and alas! careless prayers. . . .

Death, judgment, and eternity are solemn truths, not simply sublime theories; and when the sentence goes forth, "Prepare to meet thy God," our souls, my sisters, will not be the less meet for His appearing, because we have neglected to weigh the conflicting doctrines of divers Churches; because we shrank from controversy; because we pleaded our ignorance, our weakness, our utter inability to sit in judgment upon subjects on which the greatest saints and most learned divines are at issue. Enough for us to receive and cherish the Truth which the Church of our forefathers has transmitted to us; enough for us to ponder over the simple majesty of the Church's Creeds, to teach them to the lambs of the flock, to pray for grace to receive this sublime faith into our hearts, and to show it forth in our lives; enough for us to dwell with awe upon the teaching of Holy Church—teaching given to us in simple words, well fitted to the lips of infant tongues, but words of such high import, that they have ever dwelt in our hearts as we grew to more mature age. . . . Oh! most sweet mystery of mighty Love. Hushed be for ever the din of controversy, the clamour of tongues, the strife of words, the conflict of opinions. *We* may turn from these, my sisters; we have nought to do with these. We may fall prostrate, and adore in silence, and in uninterrupted communings with our Lord, the exceeding beauty of His Love.

But sweet as is the contemplation of the Divine Mysteries, we can only be absorbed therein for a season. Earthly life is a discipline; a discipline to purge us from the corruption of an evil nature. It is also a warfare against the world, the flesh, and the devil; the battle-field wherein the grace of baptism ever strives with the proud will of man. Thus the Church delivers to us the words of Holy Scripture, to be a light unto our feet, and a lamp unto our paths. Blessed heritage which she has preserved for her children! Blessed heritage, imparted so freely to us! teaching us of truths which human reason cannot fathom; truths which make us bold to contend for the faith once delivered to the saints. With our sacramental life cherished by the teaching of the Church in the Creeds, the Catechism, and the Holy Scriptures, what need we more? Why bewilder ourselves? . . . Can you not now try to cast off the perplexities which entangle and envelope you? Can you not live in silence, in prayer, in self-examination, in meditation upon the Holy Word? Can you not in the grace of God seek to do His will? and then will you know of the doctrine. Greatly doth the Church of England reverence the Word of God; greatly doth she teach her children to reverence it. Here we shall find directions for our whole lives; whether in the world, we are taught to live above it, not conforming to its sinful ways and customs, and habits of thought,—not speaking our own words, nor thinking our own thoughts, but to glorify our Lord and Master in all things. Oh! most happy privilege of His children, to be thus suffered to witness for Him, in the midst of a crooked and perverse generation. . . .

I have not sought to argue with you, my sisters. We ought not to live in argument, but in action and in love. Can we picture to ourselves the holy women of old arguing on doctrinal questions, judging contested points of Church divisions, of ancient synods? What is the picture?—"If she have brought up children, if she have lodged strangers, if she have washed the Saints' feet, if she have relieved the afflicted, if she have diligently followed every good work."

And if it be that we are penitents, that the soil is not yet washed from the baptismal robe, that the disease of the heart is yet uncured,—it may be for men to argue for truth, to reason with the learned of the nineteenth century, to preach to the refined sensualist, or the intellectual philosopher as the noble penitent of old from the hill of Mars; but for us, Mary Magdalene of blessed memory has taught us our place; we are to lie at the Feet of our Lord, in silence, in tears, in love; or we may press amid the crowd to touch His garment, and hear the comforting words—Daughter, thy *faith* hath saved thee; go in peace. Life is short enough for penitence; let us not waste it in aught beside.

(B)   The reader of the foregoing pages will observe the way in which this system works to deceive. The Romanizing clergyman instructs his flock in the doctrines and delusions of Popery, and brings some young lady to avail herself of the privilege of private confession and absolution. He thus becomes acquainted with her disposition, the character of her family, and the secrets of her heart and her home. She hears of a Sisterhood, and applies to him, as her spiritual guide, for advice, expressing her desire for this vocation. He complies with her wishes, and, should any difficulty arise, the probability of secession to Rome to satisfy the feelings he has fostered is brought forward, and he represents to the astonished family that going to a Sisterhood for a time is far better than joining the Church of Rome; but the return to her home is put off from day to day, and at last she visits her family for a few weeks, and finally returns to the Sisterhood.

While this state of things is suffered in silence, there can be no natural affection—no obedience to parents—no peace in the family; the destruction of natural affection is considered meritorious, and the disturbance of peace and harmony in the home is the result. The father will be neglected for the spiritual father, whose power is supposed to be from God; the mother will be deserted for the spiritual mother, who usurps her place in her child's affections, and requires entire obedience to her commands; brothers will be disregarded, and their care and kindness practically forgotten; sisters will be forsaken for the "Sisters of Mercy;" the natural ties of God's appointment will be rent asunder—"spiritual ties" not according to his word will be considered binding and eternal: and all this under the pretence of receiving "houses, and brethren, and sisters, and mothers, with persecutions," and of sacrificing self to the service of God.

The Sellon System destroys the social system which the people of England have long enjoyed. Improvement may be desirable, but "destroy it not, for a blessing is in it." We can serve God with our hearts, in our homes. Fathers should not give their money to support monastic institutions. Mothers should not allow their daughters to be the slaves of a self-appointed Mother Superior. This system has no foundation in the Word of God, and nothing less than this authority can require sacrifices such as we have merely attempted to describe in these pages.

Let the families and relatives and connexions of those now entangled in this snare determine that such things shall not be suffered in England. Rome may practise these deceits; the confessional and the convent may find their victims there. England, thank God, knows better; and many of her daughters, as the writer can testify, are true "Sisters of Mercy," ready to visit the fatherless and the widows, the sick and the destitute, the old and the young, while they still do their duty in that state of life to which it has pleased God to call them.

5. R. J. Hayne, "Church Deaconesses. The Revival of the Office of Deaconess Considered" (London: John Henry and James Parker, 1859), pp. 10-14.

To many who opposed sisterhoods, the deaconess order became an attractive alternative. Mrs. Jameson disliked the Catholic trappings of devotion, F. D. Maurice objected to the separateness of sisterhoods, and J. M. Ludlow declared that the cause of evil in Miss Sellon's sisterhood was "that there was no man in the institution."[14] It is not just coincidental that one of the early proposals for reviving the office of deaconess came from R. J. Hayne, vicar of Buckland in Devon, who was close enough to observe Sellon's community. The New Testament examples of female religious work without the ascetic or conventual dimensions of later Catholic piety impressed both Evangelicals and Broad Church people. Fliedner's model of nursing sisters was also important as a precedent, but the title was broadened by Hayne to refer to "women's employment in organized bodies as assistants to the clergy in works of charity." Dean J. S. Howson had also studied the history of deaconesses and stressed the practical dimensions of need for such work and the availability of women to do it. Recognizing that long-standing prejudices against public work for women had declined in the face of the contributions of women like Fry and Nightingale, Howson declared that "no definition is so true . . .   as that her place is *to help*."[15]

The accent on assistance made clear the difference between deaconesses and sisterhoods, where the religious life was primary and works of charity secondary. Vows were discouraged, as the leaders of the deaconess movement sought to combine discipline and freedom within the framework of the Church. There would be training as well as supervision, which would come largely from the clergy. Communities of deaconesses could be organized, but many would do individual parochial work. Yet it was also to be an order of ministry. Bishop Tait of London ordained the first deaconess, Elizabeth Ferard, in 1862; following that, interest spread and deaconess houses were established in other dioceses. Through the efforts of Hugh Price Hughes, his wife, and others, a deaconess order was also accepted by Wesleyan Methodists and English Baptists in 1890.

In this development the Church had provided an alternative to sisterhoods, institutionalized and legitimated women's religious work, and obtained cheap labor as well![16] Still, what was it? Frequently praised in Church assemblies for their contributions and described as "counterparts to the clergy in the other sex,"[17] deaconesses were clearly not clergy and could not move as men did from deacon to priest. Constitutionally neither clergy nor laity, then, they were unrepresented in Church government, as later women's advocates would note.[18] Some thought this modest ambiguity could be re-considered and become the basis for improving the status of women in ministry, until the Lambeth Conference of 1930 in effect said, "thus far and no more" (see chapter 6).

. . . The unpaid labours of the deaconesses would supply, *under the direction of the parish priest*, many a grievous want, and relieve many an over-burdened pastor from no little portion of his anxieties.

It is true that here and there may be found already a few Sisterhoods established for carrying out many, if not all, of the kinds of work enumerated; and most valuable and devoted are their labours. But these Sisterhoods are generally quite local in their character, intended only to supply the wants of a particular institution or particular parish, and more conventual in their rule and arrangements than appears desirable or possible with the freer and more elastic system of work proposed for the deaconesses.

What, then, would seem to be the safe principles on which such an office might be established among ourselves?

1. As servants of the Church, they must act in entire obedience to the authorities of the Church. The constitutions and rules of the Society would, in the first instance,

receive the sanction of the bishop of the diocese; and in no case would they carry out their labours without episcopal permission. They would enter no parish without the express invitation of the incumbent, and would put themselves entirely under his direction in all matters relating to their parochial employment.

2. But how are the devoted and zealous women who may offer for the work to be made capable of conducting it? In order that they may become fitted for their parochial employment, it would be necessary that one central institution should be established, where a certain *period of probation* might be passed; during which, not only the peculiar qualifications of each candidate would be discovered, but the soundness and firmness of the religious principle which induced each to offer herself might be tested; for the success of the Society will depend on its containing no unwilling workers, and as few as possible inefficient ones. . . .

3. But although insisting on this probation as essential, it is not intended to make it preparatory to their taking perpetual vows. Home duties may unexpectedly arise, and claim their services; the hearts, too, of some unstable ones may grow cold and weary, and no longer enable them to labour in a spirit of love; there would, therefore, be full permission to their retiring from the work. The only bond would be an engagement to obey and carry out the rules of the Society for a short period of one or more years, renewable of course at their option.

4. Neither is it intended that there should be any interference with their private property; it would be left entirely in their own hands, at their own free disposal. A certain small payment would be required from them for their necessary expenses; and those whose means allowed of it, might naturally be disposed to pay to the common fund of the Society rather more than enough for their own cost, so as to help a needy sister.

As funds accrued, a suitable building would be purchased for the permanent parent house of the Society; but the migratory character of the members would render all other expensive buildings unnecessary. From the parent house they would be sent out, two or three together, to such places as might require their services, and where, for the time, they would occupy hired accommodation.

5. The close connection with the parochial clergy which their employment would entail, renders it expedient, to say nothing of other reasons, that the superintendence of the Society should be entrusted to a clergyman. The internal government and household management of the parent house would of course be left to a superior: but the rule of the Society would in this fundamental point differ from the general practice of the Sisterhoods, in that the chief government would rest in the hands of a warden or chaplain; and that the members of the Society would *not be subject to female as the chief authority.* The rule would in this respect coincide with that of the Societies of foreign deaconesses.

6. And if it be asked, whether it can be thought within the bounds of expectation, or even hope, that in these days, any community of Christian labourers, men or women, can be organized on such religious principles as to satisfy and conciliate the many conflicting shades of opinion about us, I would answer at once, I believe it to be impossible; and any attempt to meet the opposing sentiments and practices of rival religious sections, by eliminating from our system every point which might be considered objectionable by either, would end in a miserable failure.

. . .   While expressly condemning any attempt at compromise in matters of principle, and therefore of importance, it would be the duty of the Society most carefully to avoid any extravagancies in minor and external circumstances, which might hazard their reputation for sincerity, throw stumbling-blocks in the way of weak brethren, and bring their work and office into disrepute. Confidence is not the growth of a day; but it would only be as confidence in their discretion as well as their zeal became general, that their powers of good would expand into those proportions which the necessities of the times demand, and the excellency of their work ought to secure.

This, then, should be the aim of the Society in these difficult days,—to commend itself to the real lovers of the Lord Jesus by its devotedness to Him, and the activity of its love towards His distressed members; steering as far as possible from the whirlpools of controversy, to sail a peaceful course along the safe and well-marked track of the Church's order; bearing good will to all men in its heart, and seeking to prove itself unto all a handmaid of that Saviour who loved and suffered for all.

Any institution based on these principles surely might fairly claim the confidence and support of at least the sincere members of the Church of England, and could hardly fail, in time, of conciliating the regard of the people at large.

This plan is now most humbly, and with a keen sense of its many imperfections both of idea and statement, laid before the Church. The vastness of the work at this time pressing upon us in evangelizing the estranged masses of our fellow countrymen, is admitted; the usefulness of an order of women specially instituted to assist the clergy in their overwhelming labours by works of charity, is hardly denied. Is not the time come for putting it to the proof, whether earnest and self-devoted women cannot be found to come forward, and agree to such an organization as may best fit them for the work of the primitive and Scriptural deaconesses, and may most certainly ensure their cordial reception as parochial assistants by the clergy?

6. Mrs. Charles W.[ightman], *Haste to the Rescue; or, Work While it is Day* (London: James Nisbet and Co., 1859), pp. 111-14, 134-35.

There were very few women among the nineteenth-century British temperance leaders.[19] One of the most prominent was Julia B. Wightman (1815-98), whose husband was vicar of St. Alkmond's in Shrewsbury. She began by counseling a single individual in 1858, soon expanding her work by holding meetings two evenings a week and forming the St. Alkmond's Total Abstinence Society. At the end of that year she wrote about the effort in *Haste to the Rescue*, which was influential in convincing readers to regard temperance as a religious as well as a social issue. Her book attracted Anglican clergy who had previously disdained the total abstinence pledge and eventually led to the establishment of the Church of England Total Abstinence Society (later, Temperance Society) in 1862. She insisted that her meetings have a religious character to them, using hymns, prayers, scripture readings and exposition, and a reading from another book which illustrated the theme of the biblical text. Members pledged, "I promise, by the help of God, to abstain from all intoxicating drinks, except when ordered by the doctor, or when taken in the Lord's Supper."

For a number of years her poor health prevented active involvement with the cause, but her interest continued to be strong. In 1877 she wrote of the movement,

> It is a holy work and it is a work that has come upon us women specially, owning to the necessity of these evil days, and in which we have a special part to take. . . .   And on whom does the vice of drunkenness press with heavier weight than on the wife, the mother, the daughter? The Church of Christ in Paul's day would have been incomplete without her "Tryphenas" and "Tryphosas," or the "beloved Persis, who laboured much in the Lord," or Phoebe. . . .   This is especially a Christian woman's movement.[20]

But because the Pauline admonitions were regularly used against her, she seldom spoke at her own meetings if a clergyman were present, deferring to him, instead, for an address.[21]

My Dear Friends,—By the help of our God we are come to the close of our first year; and when I look back on the way He has led me in my work amongst you, I am sure I can truly say that His presence has gone with us in every step.

It was on Sunday, the 24th January last, that, with a trembling heart, yet earnest purpose, I asked John Davies, the first man in your list, to allow me to read the Scriptures at his house, with prayer. I fixed on three o'clock, because it did not interfere with the services in our church. I saw, with sorrow, that few women, and still fewer men amongst you, attended public worship; my little meetings were begun in prayerful hope that some might be stirred up to see the importance and the blessing of serving God, and honouring His name, and His day; and blessed be God, I now see, with thankfulness, at least seventy of you attending church and my Sunday readings, shewing, by your earnest and attentive countenances, that you come to worship Him, and to learn to serve Him better.

On Tuesday night, the 26th January, we asssembled for the same purpose at another house. From that time until the present, these *weekly* evening readings have never been omitted; and the attendance, which began by two or three men, and as many women, has swelled as you know, to one hundred and fifty men and thirty women.

Together with the cottage readings, I began at the same time a course of night visits amongst you, in order to become acquainted with the men in our parish. It pained my heart to think that no one from our class of life knew *you*, my brothers. I resolved, therefore, in God's strength, to begin what seemed a strange work for a lady, to go myself at nights, when you return home from your daily work, to learn your habits of thought, to enter into your sorrows, trials, temptations, and to speak kindly to you of Him who is a Brother born for adversity, our blessed Lord, "THE MAN CHRIST JESUS." I bless God I ever did so, for it has taught me to respect and love many amongst you in no common way; and you must allow me to thank you for the hearty and true welcome, and gentle courtesy you have ever shewn me. Some of my happiest moments have been spent amongst you; and it has been a rich reward to me to see the earnest resolve and brave purpose to lead a different life, so nobly carried out by many of you, amidst constant trials and temptations. ALL HONOUR TO YOU, dear friends, for your WILLING teetotalism. If you have been enabled by it to bear manfully the jeers and taunts of those who would delight to see you return to your former courses, or if you have learned that SELF-DISCIPLINE is a necessary part of our Christian soldiership, then your total abstinence has done you good, and you will have to bless God for it to all eternity.

It will be interesting for you to know that one hundred and eighty-seven men have signed this year; of these fifty-eight have broken the pledge, eight have returned to our ranks, and one hundred and twenty-nine have never broken, which makes our total number one hundred and thirty-seven men: to these may be added thirty-four women. During Christmas week, I am thankful to say, we lost only six men, and not one woman; and, what is still more remarkable, on Show-Monday, we did not lose a single member!

In almost every case where a man has broken the pledge, it has been through vexation, not through love of drink, nor often through influence of former companions. Let me beseech you, my dear friends, to come at once to *me* when you are in sorrow, as to one who feels strongly with you, and *do not* fly to the public-house, by which you make matters infinitely worse, inflicting an injury not only on yourselves and all those who have joined our society, but also on me, who am your sincere and hearty friend. . . .

It is to the strictly *devotional* tone of our meetings that I attribute all my success, under God. The way that total abstinence societies are conducted, without any religious element, is most objectionable; and I have felt so strongly on this subject, that I have never allowed any temperance advocate to plead the cause in our room. And when clergymen of ability and piety who have addressed my men, have fallen into the common error of supposing that it was necessary to give a temperance address, or rather, to speak against drunkenness, they have greatly disappointed the people, who expected to have heard some simple and beautiful exposition of Scripture, to comfort and strengthen their hearts by presenting Christ and His love before them as the motive to holy living. More than once has this remark been made by a man, "We didn't want to hear about drunkenness, we know too much about that ourselves, more's the pity—more than any gentleman could tell us." The fact is, there is so much to speak about on other subjects, that drunkenness need never be mentioned unless it happens to come in the portion of Scripture, which is rare; for it seems an insult to their common sense to be always harping upon a sin which they have given up, and are resolved to abstain from, God helping them. And they all know there are plenty of other sins equally dangerous to their eternal interests. They know that a man may be a total abstainer and yet live without God, and thus be lost for ever.

7. "A Poor Woman's Work," *The Victoria Magazine*, III (1864):396-99.

> As the consequences of urban growth in the nineteenth century became clear, many church people sought to respond to the new conditions of industrial poverty and inadequate housing. There were several difficulties. One was that the parish system was not sufficient to the task, there being too many people for the clergy to conduct a meaningful ministry. Another was that vast differences in social class and education made it difficult for the clergy to bridge the gap in ministry. To meet these problems several para-church activities were begun, staffed almost entirely by women. Variously called Bible women, district visitors, or Parochial Mission women, they were often drawn from the lower classes themselves and attempted to make contact with the urban poor who had lost touch with the church. For the most part they were not the more traditional alms-giving activities of the past, but were efforts at education, training for work, and other self-help assistance, together with sympathetic understanding and religious guidance. From scattered beginnings in the 1850s interdenominational philanthropic agencies such as the Charity Organisation Society, founded in 1869, took shape, as well as programs with more limited focus led by people like Octavia Hill and Henrietta Barnett. One contemporary commentator described the work performed by the Bible women by saying, "Nothing can be better adapted than the domestic missions, thus conducted, to assist the Church in her present dearth of labourers, or to prepare the way for her advance, as she is gradually enabled to multiply her ministers so as to meet the requirements of the population."[22]

Whitechapel, Shoreditch, Bethnal Green, Poplar, Rothershithe—who does not know these names? And who, knowing them, does not involuntarily read—condensed, as it were, in the shorthand of those few syllables—the darkest and saddest pages in that great tragedy of want and sin which is ever being enacted at our side? We have all heard these names, and others like them; some of us, perhaps, have seen the courts and alleys to which they belong, either with the astonishment and disgust of an unconcerned passer-by, or with the active sympathy and loving sorrow of a practical worker amongst the poor. But we all know that those grievous histories of crime and suffering, the last scene of which comes before us continually in police courts and prisons, in hospitals, refuges, and penitentiaries, in "deaths by starvation," and suicides from despair—that those histories can be traced, for the most part, to their first origin in the tainted atmosphere, moral and physical, which surrounds the great mass of the London poor.

In these days I think we may fairly say that much is done for the poor everywhere, and not least in London: that much time and thought and money are devoted to their needs: and yet, day by day and year by year, those needs steadily outstrip our utmost efforts to overtake them, and our people die, like the beasts, without help in this present life, or knowledge of the life to come. . . .

Let us transport ourselves in imagination to one of the great eastern, northern, or southern parishes of London, such as I have named in the first words of this article; let us plunge into its crowded courts and squalid streets, and follow one of the figures passing to and fro. It is only a poor woman's; her dress is very plain, almost shabby; she is unmistakeably and really a poor woman, but not less unmistakeably superior to her class in habits of order and cleanliness. She is evidently familiar with this wretched district, and seems by her steady walk and look of quiet energy to be employed on some business in it; but what can she, herself poor, do for all the misery around her?

Ask her how she gets her living, and she will tell you that she is the Parochial Mission Woman of the district, that her wages are eight or perhaps ten shillings per week, and that she is now on her daily rounds. Go with her, and you will see no money given, for her office is specially and distinctively this—*to help the poor to help themselves.* She will rescue a penny here, a halfpenny there, some outcast and vagrant coin—the type, as it were, of its possessor—that would never be found in the company of respectable deposits at the Penny Bank or Provident Club, but would probably slink into the gin shop if not sought for and taken away by her; and in the course of some weeks or months those rescued pence will return to their owner, welcome and unexpected as a gift, in the shape of flannel or calico, or the almost forgotten luxury of a bed. She will bring order and decency into the sick room, and perhaps a little temporary ease to the sufferer himself; for the weary limbs will be moved and the throbbing head supported, and a few words of hope and comfort spoken to the faint heart. She will teach the hardworking widow how best to economise her scanty provisions or eke out her scanty clothing; she will throw open the window and cleanse the room where a whole family lives, eats, and sleeps; she will wash and dress the children whose mother is "down" with fever or consumption; she will listen, not only with warm sympathy but with entire comprehension, to the histories of sorrow, of want, of temptation, which many of those whom she visits will pour into her ears; for is she not herself a poor woman, who has undergone precisely the same sorrows and struggled with precisely the same temptations? And thus those poor suffering ones will feel that she is their friend, one who will serve them and help them (not as the superior can serve and help the inferior, but), heart to heart, and hand to hand, with all the knowledge and energy which spring from personal experience. But this is only the usual work of a Mission Woman's day—in the night she will perhaps be sent for suddenly to a dying baby, or spend the long dark hours in soothing pain or delirium. Once or twice in the week she will help the lady who superintends her district to receive and welcome such of the women as will come to a well warmed and lighted room, there teaching them to sew and cut out, and supplying them with the articles of clothing for which she is constantly gathering their savings. Then to her will come not only the poor for advice and sympathy, but also the clergyman for assistance and information; for she will bring to his knowledge many a case needing relief or consolation, many an unbaptised child or unmarried couple among the swarming thousands whom it is physically impossible that he should himself constantly visit. She is his minister and helper, working under his authority and by his direction, and therefore she introduces no strange and disturbing element into the parochial machinery; rather does she supplement and strengthen all else that is done. Her work is no isolated and irregular effort, wasting some of its strength in the attempt to gain and hold an independent footing; it is linked on to the whole power of our Church, and draws freely upon the experience of the parochial clergy and the varied resources of the whole parochial system. It is done by her simply and quietly; she has no conceited self-confidence and no sanctimonious humility, and yet she is generally found, without much difficulty, by the clergyman himself among his parishioners; for she is only a kindly, energetic, sensible woman, in whom the devotion and unselfishness so often shown by the poor in their intercourse with each other are quickened and elevated by the highest of all motives.

Such is the Parochial Mission Woman—such the work which, I fear, must in many districts languish and die this year, unless it can secure much more abundant support than has yet been given to it. . . .

Let me then earnestly recommend this work as a means by which the burden of the hospital, the refuge, the penitentiary, and the gaol will be lightened. It would be neither wise nor right to expect sudden and radical changes from any such attempt to benefit the poor; but when we see, if only here and there, a drunken wife brought to her right mind, a young girl encouraged to resist the sore temptations which beset her, or rescued at the beginning of her downward course, a room, once comfortless and slovenly, now more nearly realising the English idea of "Home," and the kindly influences of Christian example and sympathy winning their way into hearts which long suffering has left cold and sore—when we see that all this is done, we may hope that the fountain head of the evil has been reached, and that the overwhelming flow of its waters may in time be checked.

8. Josephine E. Butler, "The Education and Employment of Women" (Liverpool: T. Brakell, 1868), pp. 3-5, 22-26.

To his own question, "What shall we do with our girls?," a small-town printer and publisher gave a simple answer in 1884: "We must make them so healthful, so beautiful and so wise, that they will all get good husbands, and have good children, and every blessing that life can give."[23] This was a common judgment in the nineteenth century, based as it was on the assumption that marriage and children were the ends of a woman's life. But the census figures by mid-century showed how unrealistic that judgment was. They revealed three demographic features which commentators took up over the next two decades: females outnumbered males in the birth rate and in the total population (in 1851 the figure was put at over 400,000), 30% of the women never married, and over half worked for their own subsistence. Clearly, the dominant theories of womanhood did not correspond to the realities of women's lives.

Several schemes were proposed over the years to address this problem of "surplus" or "redundant" women, which in turn reflected particular perceptions of womanhood. Some people wanted to encourage more marriages, by permitting military officers to marry and creating land-leasing programs for single men who would promise to marry within six months after taking over the land.[24] W. R. Greg recommended substantial emigration of single women to the colonies and to America, where there was a surplus of men.[25] On the other hand Frances Power Cobbe, recognizing that marriage had become a "Hobson's choice" for women, thought it would be best promoted by helping single women to improve their condition in life, rather than by being forced upon them.[26] Within the Church of England the surplus of single women gave an additional impetus to the revival of the deaconess order, as some anticipated that thousands would take up this religious work.

Another approach was to consider the question of what was "suitable work" for women. The chief interest was to enlarge employment opportunities beyond those of governess, domestic service, sewing, and the recently acceptable vocation of writer. In the face of increasing female employment as miners and factory workers, however, there was some disagreement on this matter.[27] Josephine Butler (1828-1906) argued that philanthropy by itself would not succeed in "redeeming" women; the demand of women in both lower and higher classes was for work. Too many women, she declared, were "people stranded": "Their work is taken out of their hands: their place—they know not where it is. They stretch out their hands idly."[28] Linking employment and education focused more concern on the plight of those who sought entry into such professions as medicine and teaching, but she was also eager for women to break into male-dominated trades such as hairdressing, china painting, and drapery.

Other efforts to call attention to the employment issue had preceded Butler's work. The monthly *Englishwoman's Journal* appeared in 1858, founded by Barbara Bodichon and Bessie Rayner Parkes. In 1859 the Society for the Promotion of Employment of Women was established, and at the same time Emily Faithfull began her all-female Victoria Press. Much of the writing on the subject played down the implied threats to existing wage scales and to the place of women in the family. Further, almost no one took up the question of work for married women, despite the census report that almost 25% of them were gainfully employed.

The economical position of women is one of those subjects on which there exists a "conspiracy of silence." While most people, perhaps, imagine that nearly all women marry and are supported by their husbands, those who know better how women live, or die, have rarely anything to say on the subject. Such social problems as this are certainly painful; they may or may not be insoluble; they must not be ignored.

The phrase "to become a governess" is sometimes used as if it were a satisfactory outlet for any unsupported woman above the rank of housemaid. When we see advertisements in the newspapers, offering "a comfortable home," with no salary, as a sufficient reward for accomplishments of the most varied character, we sometimes wonder at the audacity of employers; but when we learn that such an advertisement offering the situation of nursery governess, *unpaid*, was answered by *three hundred women*, our surprise has in it something of despair.

The truth is, that the facts of society have changed more rapidly than its conventions. Formerly muscles did the business of the world, and the weak were protected by the strong; now brains do the business of the world, and the weak are protected by law. The industrial disabilities of women, unavoidable under the earlier *regime*, have become cruel under the later. There is neither the old necessity of shelter, nor the old certainty of support.

The census of 1861 gave nearly six millions of adult English women, distributed as follows:—

Wives	3,488,952
Widows	756,717
Spinsters over 20	1,537,314
	5,782,983

The census also gives the numbers of women who work for their own subsistence, as follows:—

Wives	838,856
Widows	487,575
Spinsters (above or under 20)	2,110,318
	3,436,749

In the first place, then, it appears that marriage, as a means of subsistence (to say nothing of the indecorum of looking forward to it in this light) is exceedingly precarious in two ways. The proportion of wives to widows and spinsters in 1861 was just about three to two, while of these wives themselves nearly one in four was occupied in other than domestic duties, either as her husband's coadjutor, as in farm-houses and shops, or, of necessity, as his substitute in cases of his desertion, or helplessness, or vice. In the second place, the number of widows and spinsters supporting themselves, which in 1851 was two millions, had increased in 1861 to more than two millions and a half. The rapidity of the increase of this class is painfully significant. Two and a half millions of Englishwomen without husbands, and working for their own subsistence! This is not an accident, it is a new order of things. Of the three and a half millions of women—wives, widows, and spinsters— engaged in other than domestic occupations, it is probable that scarcely a thousand make, without capital, and by their own exertions, one hundred pounds a year. The best paid are housekeepers in large establishments, a few finishing governesses, and professed cooks. 43,964 women are returned as outdoor agricultural labourers—a fact worthy of remembrance when it is said that women are too weak to serve in haberdashers' shops. Women, refused admission to such shops on the pretext that they are not strong enough to lift bales of goods, have been afterwards traced to the occupations of dock porters and coal-heavers. In practice the employments of women are not determined by their lightness, but by their low pay. One newspaper still scoffs at the desire of women to be self-supporting; but starvation is a sufficient answer to sneers. As a favourable symptom of the last few years, I may add that 1822 women are returned as employed by the Post-office. 213 women are returned as telegraph-clerks. It is instructive to note the way in which the salary of these women telegraph-clerks has fallen. When the telegraph companies were first formed, the pay of a female clerk was eight shillings a week, to be increased by a shilling yearly, until it reached fourteen shillings a week. So great, however, has been the competition of women for these situations, that the pay has been reduced to five shillings a week, a sum on which a woman can scarcely live unassisted.

   . . .   There is other work on every side waiting to be done by women,— the work of healers, preachers, physicians, artists, organizers of labour, captains of industry, &c., while on the other hand women are waiting to be prepared for service, and ready to bridge over, as they alone can, many a gulf between class and class which now presents a grave obstacle to social and political progress.

[One] kind of advocacy of the rights of women . . .   is chiefly held by a few women of superior intellect who feel keenly the disadvantages of their class, their feebleness, through want of education, against public opinion, which is taken advantage of by base people, their inability, through want of representation, to defend their weaker members, and the dwarfing of the faculties of the ablest and best among them. These women have associated little with men, or at best, know very little of their inner life, and do not therefore see as clearly as they see their own loss, the equal loss that it is to men, and the injury it involves to their characters, to live dissociated from women: they therefore look forth from their isolation with something of an excusable envy on the freer and happier lot, which includes, they believe, a greater power to do good, and imagine that the only hope for themselves is to push into the ranks of men, to demand the same education, the same opportunities, in order that they may compete with them on their own ground. They have lost the conception of the noblest development possible for both men and women; for assuredly that which men, for the most part, aim at, is not the noblest, and yet that is what such women appear to wish to imitate; they have lost sight of the truth, too, that men and women were made equal indeed, but not alike, and were meant to supplement one another, and that in so doing,—each supplying force which the other lacks,—they are attracted with a far greater amount of impulse to a common center. When St. Chrysostom preached in Constantinople, that "men ought to be pure, and women courageous," he was treated as a dangerous innovator, a perverter of the facts of nature, a changer of customs. I hope that many such innovators will arise, who will show forth in practice the possibility of the attainment of a common standard of excellence for man and woman, not by usurpation on either hand, nor by servile imitation, but by the action of each upon each, by mutual teaching and help. The above misconception, like many other errors, results from men and women living so dissociated as they do in our country; hence comes also all that reserve, and incapacity for understanding each other which has existed between the sexes for so many generations, those false notions about women which are entertained in society, and great injury to the work, and happiness, and dignity of man and woman alike; for it may be truly said that many of the most serious evils in England are but the bitter and various fruit of the sacreligious disjoining of that which God had joined together, the disunion of men and women, theoretically and practically, in all the graver work of life. . . .

I am persuaded that anyone who will candidly and carefully consider the histories of separate communities of men or women, for educational or other purposes, must see that the evils attendant on such a system as they represent outweigh its conveniences. The arrangement is for a given period, but not so the evils which accompany it, for they,—and of this men are not ignorant,—too often leave their effects, I may say their curse, throughout life. The objection rises at once of the difficulty of adopting any other arrangement than the present, which may be called an unnatural one. This objection will be more effectually met by facts than by reasoning, and in time facts will speak for themselves, while up to the present they attest that whenever the experiment of a different system has been tried, the difficulties have been found to be very much less than it was believed they would be, before the trial was made.

To conclude this part of my subject, although I grant that too much stress cannot be laid upon the improvement of the education of women who will be actually the mothers of a future generation, yet I wish, on the one hand, that persons who only look at it from this point of view would take more into account the valuable service our country might command if it but understood the truth about the condition and feelings of its unmarried women, and that a more generous trust were felt in the strength of woman's nature, and the probable direction of its development when granted more expansion, while on the other hand I should like to see a truer conception of the highest possibilities for women than is implied in the attempt to imitate men, and a deeper reverence for the God of nature, whose wisdom is more manifested in variety than in uniformity.

9. Frances Ridley Havergal, *The Ministry of Song*, 2d ed. (London: Christian Book Society, 1871), pp. 2-6.

One of the many nineteenth-century women hymn-writers and translators was Frances Ridley Havergal (1836-79). Others involved in this special religious work include C. F. Alexander, Fanny Crosby, Jemima Luke, and Catherine Winkworth. Havergal was the daughter of an Anglican clergyman, who also wrote hymns and other musical works. She had little interest in public issues. Apart from some children's stories her particular work was a "ministry of song," which expressed in evangelical terms the conviction that a personal religious faith (note the dominant pronoun in her writings) was the answer to every problem. Many of her poems became popular hymns, including "Lord, speak to me," "Jesus, Master, whose I am," and "Take my life and let it be consecrated." The following selection is not a hymn but a foundational poetic argument for the significance of hymnody in religious life. The work of these writers influenced the religious sensibilities of theirs and succeeding generations profoundly, as few other contributions were able to do.

"The Ministry of Song"
In God's great field of labour,
 All work is not the same;
He hath a service for each one
 Who loves His holy name.
And you to whom the secrets
 Of all sweet sounds are known,
Rise up! for He hath called you
 To a mission of your own.
And rightly to fulfil it,
 His grace can make you strong,
Who to your charge hath given
 The Ministry of Song.

Sing to the little children,
 And they will listen well;

Sing grand and holy music,
  For they can feel its spell.
Tell them the tale of Jephthah;
  Then sing them what he said,—
"Deeper and deeper still," and watch
  How the little cheek grows red,
And the little breath comes quicker;
  They will ne'er forget the tale,
Which the song has fastened surely,
  As with a golden nail. . . .

Sing at the cottage bedside;
  They have no music there,
And the voice of praise is silent
  After the voice of prayer.
Sing of the gentle Saviour
  In the simplest hymns you know,
And the pain-dimmed eye will brighten
  As the soothing verses flow.
Better than loudest plaudits
  The murmured thanks of such,
For the King will stoop to crown them
  With His gracious "Inasmuch." . . .

Sing to the tired and anxious;
  It is yours to fling a ray,
Passing indeed, but cheering,
  Across the rugged way.
Sing to God's holy servants,
  Weary with loving toil,
Spent with their faithful labour
  On oft ungrateful soil.
The chalice of your music
  All reverently bear,
For with the blessed angels
  Such ministry you share. . . .

Sing on in grateful gladness!
  Rejoice in this good thing
Which the Lord thy God hath given thee,
  The happy power to sing.
But yield to Him, the Sovereign,
  To whom all gifts belong,

In fullest consecration,
Your ministry of song.
Until His mercy grant you
That resurrection voice,
Whose only ministry shall be
To praise Him and rejoice.

10. Mary E. Sumner, *To Mothers of the Higher Classes* (Winchester: Warren and Son, 1888), pp. 54-60, 62-63.

The Mothers' Union was begun by Mary Sumner (1828-1921) in 1876 in her husband's parish near Winchester, as she sought to respond to a growing sense of moral and religious decline in the country. Her efforts to rouse the interest of mothers in this issue first attracted wider attention when she was called from the audience to speak at the 1885 Church Congress at Portsmouth. In *An Earnest Appeal to Mothers*, published the following year, she declared:

> It is the mothers, above all, that can work the reformation of family life in this country. 'Those who rock the cradles rule the world.' How so? Because the mothers have charge of the children for the first ten years of their lives—those years so all-important to the future of each child. . . .   I firmly believe that the reason for the low tone of so many English women and girls is *that the mothers neglect the moral and religious training of their children.*[29]

Shortly after the Congress meeting the Mothers' Union was established as a diocesan organization in Winchester, and it quickly spread to other dioceses.

By 1888 there was a quarterly journal; in 1891 another publication under the editorship of Charlotte Yonge, *Mothers in Council*, was begun in order to meet the needs of educated women. The Union had three objects: "To uphold the sanctity of marriage; to awaken in mothers a sense of their great responsibility as mothers in the training of their boys and girls (the future fathers and mothers of England); and to organize in every place a band of mothers who will unite in prayer, and seek by their own example to lead their families in purity and holiness of life." A Church of England society, the Union operated under diocesan and parish auspices; by 1903 its membership had surpassed 200,000, and there were 4322 branches in the United Kingdom and the colonies. Besides its affirmation of marriage and its unremitting opposition to the relaxation of divorce laws, the Union took a strong stand against the reduction of the place of religious education in the schools.

[M]ay I earnestly entreat all Mothers, of whatsoever rank they may be, to join hand and heart, to unite together in one strong band, in the great work of awakening in Mothers a deeper sense of their responsibility in the training of their children. "Union gives strength." There are few Mothers so wise and good that it will not be well for them to consider this duty more earnestly and solemnly, and to strive to carry it out more wisely and prayerfully; and there are vast numbers in every grade of life, rich and poor, educated and uneducated, high-born ladies and humble peasants, who think but little, if at all, of their responsibility towards their children.

The "Mother's Union," now started in the Winchester Diocese, and in other Dioceses, is a very simple plan, but it aims at a great reformation. It is above all things a Union for prayer—that is the vital, living part of it. We know the power and strength of Union, and the efficacy of united prayer. "If two of you shall agree on earth as touching anything that they shall ask, it shall be done for them of My Father which is in Heaven." It is impossible for this Mothers' Union to be successful if the lady mothers shrink back and decline to join it and work with it. Already the poorer mothers have asked, "Are we the only class who bring up our children badly? Are there no ladies who fail in their duty and neglect their children?" And so let me entreat the more educated, more influential women to give a helping hand in spreading the principles of the Mothers' Union, each in her own circle, among her equals, and among her poorer neighbours. Those principles I have tried to set forth in this book. God only knows how I pray and hope for success in a movement which, carried on quietly and steadily in every home where it can gain admittance, may work wonderfully for the future of our country, and make each home a centre of pure faith, Christian training, and high-minded chivalry—the cradles of a still nobler race for England than she has hitherto known. This cannot be attained unless many Mothers join us, and unless, as I have already said, the educated Mothers help one another and also their less educated and poorer sisters understand the principles of this Mother's Union, and to carry them out, "bearing one another's burdens, and so fulfilling the law of Christ." They must take the ignorant and weaker Mothers lovingly by the hand, and by prayer and example teach them how to do their duty to their children. "We then that are strong ought to bear the infirmities of the weak." Shall I plead in vain for a widespread support? I think not. If there is one point of contact, one touch of nature, which above all others makes us kin, it is the union of Motherhood. Rank, education, riches, different spheres of life, are outside the human sympathy which exists in Mothers one to the other, for their anxieties and sufferings, hopes and fears, are the same from the Queen to the peasant; and the need of a high standard of life is equally necessary for every one who bears the honoured name of Mother, and who would bring up her children well.

A good Mother, be she rich or poor, shines like a bright light in this dark world. She receives the flame straight from Christ Himself—she reflects His Image. Husband, children, and neighbours rise up and call her blessed. She sheds a benignant influence on all around. This may sound a high ideal, but should it not be our aim? There are many who have wasted their lives and neglected their duties, and are now conscious of it. They are stretching out their hands to God, yearning to retrieve mistakes, and bring back the children who, through their fault in part it may be, have wandered away into the "far country" and given up their principles and their prayers. Let no one despair—let no one doubt the power of God. The tares may become wheat; the prodigal may return; and even this union of Mothers may be the means, not only of awakening many a careless Mother to her high vocation, but it may also, by the strength of united prayer, bring back many a wandering son and daughter to the Bosom of our Saviour.

There is much in the life of a wife and a mother which drives the soul to Christ. . . . A mother who has arrived at this point in the higher life can never rest until she is striving to fulfill all her solemn responsibilities, and trying to lead those around her who as yet do not love God, to know the happiness she herself has found, for the words are true, "No soul goes to Heaven alone."

. . . We aim at this as the true object of Christian education. It can only be attained by means of early home training, by parents united in faith, and love, and purpose. Above all, by the pure, holy, prayerful, Christian MOTHERS who can recognise the greatness of their mission, the sacredness of child life, the consecration of body and soul in Holy Baptism, the force of their own example, the terrible consequences of failure in their duty, the blessedness of success in the pure blameless lives of noble sons and virtuous daughters, the glorious reunion before the Throne of God for Evermore! Mothers such as these can by God's grace purge our land from the evil that defiles it; they can ennoble and purify young lives, sanctify our homes, and teach the heart of this nation that Salvation is a reality, Christianity is a reality, and Eternal Glory is a reality.

11. Maude Petre, *My Way of Faith* (London: J. M. Dent & Sons, Ltd., 1937), pp. 150-54.

Maude D. M. Petre (1863-1942) has been better known for her associations with other prominent Roman Catholics than for her own accomplishments. She was born to wealth and the life of country aristocracy; her father's family had been solidly Catholic since the sixteenth century and was not only loyal to the faith but also vigorously independent regarding ecclesiastical authority. She described her father as "one of the last representatives of Cisalpinism, . . . the English form of Gallicanism." It was a trait she was to continue. The seventh child in a family of eleven, she was educated at home; regarding her own reading she later wrote, "My literature was fairy-tales and lives of the saints." After the untimely death of her parents at the age of nineteen she was faced with a vocational crisis that confronted many Catholic young women: either marry or join a religious order.

In pursuit of a religious vocation she followed the advice of her confessor to go to Rome to study the thought of Thomas Aquinas, which would serve, he thought, to dispel all doubt. It was a very unusual thing for a young woman to do; an aunt told friends that "Maude had gone to Rome to study for the priesthood."[30] Eventually she entered the Sisterhood of the Daughters of Mary, and after several years of service was named Superior of the English and Irish Province, a position she held for more than ten years.

Becoming acquainted with George Tyrrell, a Jesuit, in 1900 at a retreat he conducted for her religious house changed her life, and she entered "the Modernist crisis" in which Tyrrell was a major participant. They supported each other over the next few years in their theological and ecclesiastical struggles. She left her religious order. After Tyrrell's final break with the Society of Jesus he settled in a cottage she had built for him near the house she had bought in the village of Storrington in Sussex. At Tyrrell's death in 1909 she and the French Jesuit Henri Bremond arranged for him to be buried in the local Anglican cemetery, since permission for a Catholic burial had been denied. Petre lived the rest of her life under the stigma of her association with Tyrrell. She was denied communion in her diocese and was asked to take the anti-Modernist oath; she refused. Although she continued to receive the sacrament outside of her diocese, she remained under the ban locally and at death was buried in the same Anglican cemetery as Tyrrell. Among her several works on Catholic Modernism are *Autobiography and Life of George Tyrrell* (1912), *Modernism: Its Failure and its Fruits* (1918), *Von Hügel and Tyrrell* (1937), and *Alfred Loisy, His Religious Significance* (1944).

I was nineteen when my parents died, and the choice of my future life lay yet before me. And here it is necessary, for the full understanding of the Catholic upbringing of our day, to say some words on what is called Vocation.

I do not think that, even in strictly Catholic families, it is any longer taken as quite natural, to consider, from early days, the question of one's call in life—whether to stay in the world, or to enter a religious order. There were families, I think, in which this question was asked far too directly and insistently; families in which the desire to have priests and nuns amongst their offspring led to some moral pressure in that sense. But this was not the rule, though it was quite one of the points of our religious education to put before us the two alternatives.

It is impossible to do justice to this idea of vocation without understanding the conception of life in which it was rooted. I have said enough already to show that life on earth was presented to us as a thing good and desirable in itself, but still more good and desirable from the fact that it was a preparation for a life of yet fuller beauty and perfection. Hence the abiding sense of direction towards a further end than the immediate one; "whether we ate or drank to do all for the glory of God"; the works and interests of life were set towards a greater fulfilment; all things were to be done in the atmosphere of eternity. I do not want to seem to exaggerate. Of course we were not always thinking and feeling in this way; our lives were simple and actual, and religion did not haunt us waking or sleeping. But this was very truly the scheme and philosophy of our life; its main business, which embraced all other business, was that of serving God and saving our soul.

If I be told that religion thus conceived is deadly to the full actuality and happiness of earthly life, I can only reply that it did not seem so to us; in fact, we thought that people who were without this belief were much less happy than ourselves. So that vocation was for us a question outside and beyond that of the choice of a worldly career; it was the question of choice in regard to the form of life that would best carry us forward to our eternal, as distinguished from our temporal, end.

As it interests me above all in all these religious questions to see how far our beliefs and ideals could be applied outside the Church as well as within it, I am asking myself whether the question of vocation could not find a place in life apart from its application to religious life. In sum, the question of vocation was, for us, a question of personal destiny, of our relation to life as a whole, of the disposal of our entire being during our course from birth to death, in order to its highest fulfilment. The question of a worldly career might be as insistent as it was practical, but there was first the greater question as to how we were best to fulfil *ourselves*, fulfil our duty to humanity, and walk nobly through life to its conclusion. It was a question that embraced the secondary one of work and profession, and it is a question which every man and woman might surely ask themselves at the outset of life. It is a choice of destiny and not of profession; not how shall I gain my life, but how shall I use and bestow it.

Well, I, in my turn, faced two alternatives, and thought about marriage and about religious life. As far as I remember I fluctuated considerably. I know that, at one time, I used to dream of the ideal man to whom I would consecrate heart and life. And my word! he *was* ideal—such a man as never walked the earth. He was to be my superior in every respect, and I could indeed have fulfilled, with him, the prescription of "he for God only, she for God through him."

I need not say that I never met him, and that I learned, eventually, the common lesson that one can love a man as much for his needs as for his perfections.

Eventually I made the opposite choice and entered a form of religious community. And it was there, perhaps, that I acquired my sympathy for communism, of which the most perfect form is to be found, to my mind, in religious communities—a communism in which the respect for individual worth is blended with the ideal of consecration to the religious whole.

In the society which I joined I had for superior one of the greatest and wisest women I have ever known—a Frenchwoman. I loved her, and I revered her as I have revered no one else in my life. It would be an amazement to many people did they know what extraordinary powers of direction and government are to be found in many convents. I know well there are sad cases of the reverse, but I know too what such women *can* be. I have always maintained that a woman is more capable of being a great queen than a great prime minister; because a woman, in her method of government, must be free to exercise the personal touch and must not be hampered by criticism. I look back on my association with Emilie Teuliere as one of the privileges of my life, and I only wish I had followed her direction even more closely than I did. She loved me very much; she had her eye on me from the outset of my novitiate as her own probable successor; she told me my faults in a way in which I had never been told them before; she warned me of the dangers incident to my temperament, in particular of the harm I might do by my impulsiveness; she was to us all a model of total disinterestedness, unworldliness, courage, and religious fervour. She was badly treated by certain ecclesiastical superiors, and she was not rebellious, but she knew how to hold her own and feared no one. I owe her much.

Well, after some years of happy subordination, the blow fell, and I was suddenly, when little more than thirty years old, "kicked upstairs," as a Jesuit described his appointment as superior, and put at the head of a religious body of which nearly every member was older than myself.

"Kicked upstairs!" it is a most apt expression! I wonder if I can make many understand that it is possible to feel genuinely humiliated by being made "boss"— not humiliated in the sense of feeling unworthy; not a pious sense of humiliation; but a real feeling of being deprived of one's personal dignity and disguised under ill-suiting garments.

This was what I very truly felt. I accepted but resented being, no longer myself, but just other people's superior. I felt it a kind of spiritual deprivation and outrage, and I can never forget the real horror of those first days and months.

Well, I bore it for more than ten years, during which time I was terribly overworked, and still bear the effects on mind and memory.

As to how I governed it is hardly for me to say, but I think I had the ways of a man rather than a woman; that I interfered, if anything, too little; and gave a very free hand to my subordinate officers.

I had eventually certain joys of office—moments when all gathered round me in love. And I loved them all in return, and have never ceased to do so. I got out of my office when I knew that, during the religious crisis of my life, I should become a danger to them; and I think I may boast that I unsettled no single one of my community by my own change and revolution.

CHAPTER 5

ISSUES AND DEBATES AFFECTING WOMEN

A. EDUCATION

Despite the arguments concerning the need for greater education for women which had been advanced since the late seventeenth century, very little had been done in a concrete way until the mid-nineteenth century. One major hindrance to any development was that education was class-based and widely regarded to be a luxury. Since the state was not directly involved in education until 1870, what schools did exist were sponsored by churches or private individuals and corporations. There were few for any besides the middle and upper classes; and, as the great majority were single-sex schools, there were even fewer for girls.

But the larger problem had to do with the interrelated questions of why female education was necessary, what kind of education should be developed, and what the result of it would be. With certain expectations for the proper roles for women, education does not follow. As one contemporary reviewer wrote concerning several studies on the education of women, their central point seemed to be

> that woman should fulfil her "mission": in other words, that Nature
> having intended every Joan to have her John, she should seek and find
> her true happiness in a delightful round of domestic duties, exactly fitted
> to John's special comfort, and to that of the usual conjugal contingencies.
> The curious part of the argument is that, while it is always taken for
> granted that there is not only a husband in the case, but a pattern one,

whom it will be her privilege to love, honour, and obey, it is as invariably forgotten that there is nothing in this world she is more eager to do. Far from needing pressure or persuasion, the poor lady is as ready to welcome that mirror of manly perfections who is to complete her being, as a duck is to take to the water.[1]

Together with a family-centered perception of "woman's mission" could easily go judgments concerning the intellectual inferiority of women, the kind of subjects that would be "proper" for women to study, and the dangerous effects on society should these boundaries be exceeded and women seek to emulate men. Partly because of the extent of these views, almost no one who participated in the enlargement of educational opportunities for women in the nineteenth century would argue that such education should alter or call into question existing domestic relations; rather, they argued, education would strengthen them. Often a moral argument was employed—that greater education would raise the moral and intellectual character of women, and this in turn would raise the moral level of society. "We shall never have better Men till men have better Mothers," wrote the founder of Bedford College in 1858.[2]

Most of the steps taken to provide more opportunities for women, especially at the secondary and higher education levels, involved overcoming financial difficulties or resistance to the endeavor. The first such institution was Queen's College, Harley Street, opened in 1848 under the primary initiative of F. D. Maurice (1805-72), then professor at King's College, London. It received the support of a number of Church of England leaders, and one of its major purposes was the education of future governesses. This was followed a year later with the establishment of the Ladies' College, Bedford Square, drawing some of its professors from University College, London, and support from the Unitarian community. Because of the sad state of secondary education, students were admitted from the age of twelve to do preparatory work; thus each institution had a mixed character, although the goal of each was higher education. Out of his efforts in developing a college for working men came Maurice's interest in founding a similar institution for working women, which continued for a number of years after its establishment in 1855.

Maurice and Harriet Martineau (1802-76) were, in the early years of the ventures in higher education for women, among their strongest supporters. But their arguments in favor of it reflect significantly different positions. Martineau, well known for some forty years as a journalist and writer of fiction, came from a prominent Unitarian family and gradually moved into free thought; she was a strong abolitionist and supporter of numerous women's causes. In one of her early writings she contended that differences between male and female intellectual achievements were not due to innate differences but to educational discrimination. At the foundation of her interest was a belief in the perfectability of the race through education; and she took the moral argument as it related to women one step further than most people did, by making it a matter of justice in enhancing the capacities of every human being and enabling all persons to pursue any study or any occupation they are capable of doing.

Maurice's background was also Unitarian, but he later joined the Church of England, became a member of the clergy and a university professor. He was identified with what came to be called the Broad Church party, a loose configuration of liberals interested in the relation of the Church to contemporary social issues and of theology to intellectual developments. His support for women's education tended to be based on need; it was not a right, as Martineau would have argued, and it ought not to be open to any possibility. Rather, the nature of women make them peculiarly qualified for the tasks of nurture and instruction; since these are growing needs in society and since people will accept women in these roles, they should be trained for them.

These different perspectives continued to be visible throughout the century, especially in the efforts to attach women's education to the universities. Should women students take university examinations? Should they study the same subjects as men, especially the classics (which would introduce them to the obscenities of Greek and Roman literature)? Should they be educated in the same classes as men? As new opportunities were made available, these questions were considered again and again.[3] In 1865 the Cambridge local examinations were opened to women, followed after a time by Durham, London, and Oxford. In 1869 a college for women was opened at Hitchen, Hertfordshire, under the leadership of Emily Davies, which applied to Cambridge for a relationship; in 1872 it was re-named Girton College and moved to Cambridge a year later. It followed the curriculum of the university exactly, on the principle that women had a right to and capacity for the highest education available to men. Newnham Hall opened in 1875 with a program shaped by what was "suitable" for women; students followed their own course of study and were not bound by a fixed term of residence. In Oxford Lady Margaret Hall (with Church of England support) and Somerville Hall (explicitly non-sectarian) were established in 1879; university examinations were gradually opened to women from 1884 on. Yet even by 1896, when the Oxford University Congregation defeated a proposal to grant degrees to women by 215-140, the question of having women fully integrated into the educational system had clearly not been resolved. Some critics raised constitutional questions concerning university governance, while others supported a separate university for women. The eighteenth-century arguments had thus been followed by the end of nineteenth by definite achievements, but these, too, reflected the deeper continuing conflict over whether women could or should take an equal place alongside men. Harriet Martineau's appeal was not yet realized.

1. Harriet Martineau, *Household Education* (London: Edward Moxon, 1849), pp. 240-45.

I must declare that on no subject is more nonsense talked . . . than on that of female education, when restriction is advocated. In works otherwise really good, we find it taken for granted that girls are not to learn the dead languages and mathematics, because they are not to exercise professions where these attainments are wanted; and a little further on we find it said that the chief reason for boys and young men studying these things is to improve the quality of their minds. I suppose none of us will doubt that everything possible should be done to improve the quality of the mind of every human being. If it is said that the female brain is incapable of studies of an abstract nature,—that is not true: for there are many instances of women who have been good mathematicians, and good classical scholars. The plea is indeed nonsense on the face of it; for the brain which will learn French will learn Greek; the brain which enjoys arithmetic is capable of mathematics. If it is said that women are light-minded and superficial, the obvious answer is that their minds should be the more carefully sobered by grave studies, and the acquisition of exact knowledge. If it is said that their vocation in life does not require these kinds of knowledge,—that is giving up the main plea for the pursuit of them by boys;—that it improves the quality of their minds. If it is said that such studies unfit women for their proper occupations,—that again is untrue. Men do not attend the less to their professional business, their counting-house or their shop, for having their minds enlarged and enriched, and their faculties strengthened by sound and various knowledge; nor do women on that account neglect the work-basket, the market, the dairy and the kitchen. If it be true that women are made for these domestic occupations, then of course they will be fond of them. They will be so fond of what comes most naturally to them that no book-study (if really not congenial to their minds) will draw them off from their homely duties. For my part, I have no hesitation whatever in saying that the most ignorant women I have known have been the worst housekeepers; and that the most learned women I have known have been among the best,—wherever they have been early taught and trained to household business, as every woman ought to be. . . .   One of the best housekeepers I know,—a simple-minded, affectionate-hearted woman, whose table is always fit for a prince to sit down to, whose house is always neat and elegant, and whose small income yields the greatest amount of comfort, is one of the most learned women ever heard of. When she was a little girl, she was sitting sewing in the window-seat while her brother was receiving his first lesson in mathematics from his tutor. She listened, and was delighted with what she heard; and when both left the room, she seized upon the Euclid that lay on the table, ran up to her room, went over the lesson, and laid the volume where it was before. Every day after this, she sat stitching away and listening, in like manner, and going over the lesson afterwards, till one day she let out the secret. Her brother could not answer a question which was put to him two or three times; and, without thinking of anything else, she popped out the answer. The tutor was surprised, and after she had told the simple truth, she was permitted to make what she could of Euclid. Some time after, she spoke confidentially to a friend of the family,—a scientific professor,—asking him, with much hesitation and many blushes, whether he thought it was wrong for a woman to learn Latin. "Certainly not," he said; "provided she does not neglect any duty for it.—But why do you want to learn Latin?" She wanted to study Newton's Principia: and the professor thought this a very good reason. Before she was grown into a woman, she had mastered the Principia of Newton. And now, the great globe on which we live is to her a book in which she reads the choice secrets of nature; and to her the last known wonders of the sky are disclosed: and if there is a home more graced with accomplishments, and more filled with comforts, I do not know such an one. Will anybody say that this woman would have been in any way better without her learning?—while we may confidently say that she would have been much less happy.

As for women not wanting learning, or superior intellectual training, that is more than any one should undertake to say in our day. In former times, it was understood that every woman, (except domestic servants) was maintained by her father, brother or husband; but it is not so now. The footing of women is changed, and it will change more. Formerly, every woman was destined to be married; and it was almost a matter of course that she would be: so that the only occupation thought of for a woman was keeping her husband's house, and being a wife and mother. It is not so now. From a variety of causes, there is less and less marriage among the middle classes of our country; and much of the marriage that there is does not take place till middle life. A multitude of women have to maintain themselves who would never have dreamed of such a thing a hundred years ago. . . . What we have to think of is the necessity,—in all justice, in all honour, in all humanity, in all prudence,—that every girl's faculties should be made the most of, as carefully as boys'. While so many women are no longer sheltered, and protected, and supported in safety from the world (as people used to say) every woman ought to be fitted to take care of herself. Every woman ought to have that justice done to her faculties that she may possess herself in all the strength and clearness of an exercised and enlightened mind, and may have at command, for her subsistence, as much intellectual power and as many resources as education can furnish her with. Let us hear nothing of her being shut out, because she is a woman, from any study that she is capable of pursuing: and if one kind of cultivation is more carefully attended to than another, let it be the discipline and exercise of the reasoning faculties. . . . [T]he more she knows of the value of knowledge and of all other things, the more diligent she will be;—the more sensible of duty,—the more interested in occupations,—the more womanly. This is only coming round to the points we started from; that every human being is to be made as perfect as possible: and that this must be done through the most complete development of all the faculties.

2. F. D. Maurice, "Plan of a Female College, for the Help of the Rich and of the Poor" (Cambridge: Macmillan and Co., 1855), pp. 8-14.

You will not wonder . . . that I should have hailed the suggestion of the ladies whom I consulted, that the proper foundation of a college for working women would be a college in which ladies should learn to teach. It was not that I believed they had more need of this learning than we have. I know the opposite assertion to be true. I believe there is immeasurably more aptitude for teaching in women than in men. I should be very much puzzled if it were otherwise. If the great majority of us have to depend in all our early years for our physical, intellectual, moral life, upon the care and influence of mothers, it would be very strange if powers were not awakened in them which enabled them to fulfil the mighty task. There is no such terrible contradiction in the ways of Providence. The gifts are bestowed, the powers are awakened. The woman receives, not from her husband, not from her physician, not from her spiritual adviser, not from the books which she consults,—all these may help somewhat, if they do not hinder,—but from the Spirit of God Himself, the intuitions into her child's character, the capacity for appreciating its strength and its weakness, the faculty of calling forth the one and sustaining the other, in which lies the mystery of education, apart from which all its rules and measures are utterly vain and ineffectual. God forbid that I should not acknowledge this, or that I should ever urge any Christian mother or Christian woman to expect any substitute for this in schools or colleges. . . .   But we all know that a great part of the influences which are at work upon us in the world are benumbing our faith in this higher guidance; are benumbing, therefore, the energies which we should be putting forth in obedience to it. This is the case with us men; I cannot suppose it is otherwise with women. The motives to distrust and despondency may be different;

different mists may darken or pervert our views of the object which should be before us. But it is mere folly to suppose that the bad influences are not strong enough in each case; just as it is a sin to doubt that there is a way of counteracting and defeating them in each case. That aptitude for teaching which God has bestowed upon women may perish through want of exercise; it may be called forth by exercise. It may be turned into vanity and display; it may be redeemed to the highest and yet the lowliest uses. . . .

Some such reflections as these, I imagine, led my advisers to think that a college where teaching might be exercised in favour of the working class should be connected with a college in which ladies might obtain hints respecting the principles and method of teaching. . . .   If my counsellors were right, a way was indeed opened for a real living communion between the upper and lower classes,—between the lady and the working woman. . . .   There was this hope; and the means to the end seemed scarely less valuable than the end itself. Instead of any departure from the maxims of our ancestors in our attempt to meet the circumstances of this time, we should be going back to them. The principle of the University would be unfolding itself in a new direction. Even the applying it in that direction would be no innovation. For the lady of the old time was the Lady Bountiful; and she would be the Lady Bountiful still, without the least of the airs of one, naturally and unaffectedly distributing what she had received, as an honest stewardess, not as a great saint. She would not claim to be more cultivated than the ladies in Queen Elizabeth's day thought it graceful and comely to be; but she would be saving herself and saving others from any cant and nonsense about the march of intellect and the progress of the species, by acting as if all ought to learn and all ought to teach, without talking or making the least fuss about it, simply because they are living in God's Kingdom upon earth, and are inheritors of His Kingdom in Heaven; and because both are the more glorious for being common. . . .

But then came the question, what is it that the working women need especially to be taught? What is it, therefore, that the ladies should learn to teach them? The very name *working women* indicated that they wanted something else than the lore you impart to children in week-day or Sunday schools. . . . If, then, we want to fit ladies for being teachers of women, it seemed to follow that they must be learning something different in kind from that which they learn in the female colleges which exist at present. All whom I consulted on the subject felt this difference very strongly. If I had pursued the analogy of our Universities more carefully, I might have arrived at the discovery by another road, for our ancestors always recognised a distinction between what they called *Arts*, that is to say, the knowledge which is requisite for the mere scholar, and *Faculties*, that is to say, the knowledge which prepares a man to exercise his profession in life, whatever that may be. . . .   Well, then, female colleges, such as those in Harley Street, or Bedford Square, or Hyde Park, are, I apprehend, professing to teach—in the truest and best sense of the word, in the sense which is most directly opposed to its vile and hateful sense—*Arts*, to those who frequent them, though always with a view to the ultimate exercise of their powers in the world; whereas, in such a college as I am thinking of, the main and direct business would be to cultivate the *Faculties*, that is to say, to fit ladies for engaging in certain tasks which no other persons can perform equally well, or can be so helpful in teaching their countrymen to perform,—the study of Arts not being forgotten in this more advanced and adult education, but pursued in subordination to the other, and for the sake of it.

I hope, by this language, I have guarded myself against the suspicion that I would educate ladies for the kind of tasks which belong to *our* professions. In America some are maintaining that they should take degrees and practise as physicians. I not only do not see my way to such a result; I not only should not wish that any college I was concerned in should be leading to it; but I should think there could be no better reason for founding a college than to remove the slightest craving for such a state of things, by giving a more healthful direction to the minds which might entertain it. The more pains we take to call forth and employ the faculties which belong characteristically to each sex, the less it will be intruding upon the province which, not the conventions of the world, but the will of God, has assigned to the other. This confusion is sure to arise when a notion gains currency that there is no specific work in which women may engage; that what they undertake for the good of their fellow-creatures is a sentimental recreation, not a serious business, to be pursued with just as much settled purpose, just as much in a regular and distinct method, as any business to which we devote ourselves. As long as that opinion prevails in England, till it is vigorously and systematically resisted, some ladies will consider it a great hardship that they are not allowed a free entrance into the College of Physicians and the Inns of Court; and others—taking directly the opposite course, claiming a completely separate work for their sex, insisting that, for the highest and noblest part of them, common domestic duties are earthly and unsatisfactory—will sigh for Romish sisterhoods. We are answerable for the growth of both feelings. As long as we persevere in our frivolous mode of thinking and talking about the duties and occupations of women, we shall foster them, and where we have sown the wind shall reap the whirlwind.

This is not a digression from the subject of which I was speaking. It is an introduction to the topic which presents itself most naturally to our minds at all times, when we think of the works which women have done in the world,—which forces itself upon us at this time more than ever before. Englishmen would not have women surgeons or physicians; they find they must have them as *nurses*.

B. THE DECEASED WIFE'S SISTER BILL

The most striking feature of the debate over parliamentary legislation to permit marriage with a deceased wife's sister is that it lasted so long. First presented as a bill in 1842, the legislation was not passed until 1907. Over the years bills were regularly introduced which passed certain Houses of Commons but were rejected by others; consistently, however, the House of Lords disapproved, with the bishops of the Church of England providing the most solid body of opposition. The issue also found its way into Church Congresses and other ecclesiastical occasions and was the focus of extensive pamphlet warfare, managed on each side by the Marriage Law Reform Association and the Marriage Law Defence Union, respectively.

The debate was confusing because it had both technical and broad dimensions which were handled differently by each side. Church of England law on this matter originated from the prohibitions of Leviticus 18, which had been codified in Archbishop Parker's Table of Prohibited Degrees of Consanguinity or Affinity of 1563 and confirmed in the 99th Canon of the Church in 1603 declaring that such marriages were incestuous and unlawful. There were thirty cases of prohibition, from marriage with one's mother or sister to that with the wife's mother or sister, as well as other immediate relations of the husband and wife. The issue eventually arose in the nineteenth century because any such marriage, despite these prohibitions, was only pronounced void when an action was brought to an ecclesiastical court within the lifetime of the married party. This was particularly important when the matter of inheritance was involved, and inequities occurred simply because some actions had been brought and others had not. As a way of remedying this, a law passed in 1835 (5 and 6 Will. IV, c. LIV) made all future prohibited marriages void from the first, though it legitimized marriages which had taken place before the passage of the act. The hope of those who proposed the bill was that by drawing the line, the problem would no longer arise; but the result was quite the opposite, for it made the issue more serious, and efforts were soon launched to change the law.

Resistance to the proposed change came chiefly from the Church of England clergy, and the arguments were varied and subtle. Biblical authority was the first line of defense; references to God's revealed Word and will filled one tract or speech after another. Proponents of change, including Professor M'Caul of King's College, London, pointed out that Leviticus 18:18 seemed only to prohibit marriage with a wife's sister in the wife's lifetime.[4] But opponents responded that such a marriage after the wife's death contravened the spirit if not the exact letter of Scripture and that the method of analogy or the principle of "the parity of reason" applied to the text demonstrated that these associations are forbidden (e.g., the prohibition against taking your brother's wife—Lev. 18:16—should by inference be extended to a wife's sister also.) From biblical sanctions they moved secondly to an historical argument, referring to the practice of the Church over the centuries and its clear law since the sixteenth; what has been believed wrong and against God's law since the Church's beginning cannot be made right by an act of Parliament! A third argument appealed to logic and to a fear of moral decline: if this break in the Table of Degrees were allowed, it would be difficult to retain the remaining prohibitions. As the years passed the threat of a disturbance in the relationship between church and state was raised, for the passage of a law which was against the law of the Church could endanger the entire connection. But the greatest force in the long struggle came from various aspects of a social argument, in the charge that a new law would lower the sanctity of the marriage bond, assault the peace and happiness of the family, disrupt relations between sisters and between husbands and sisters-in-law, and contribute to a moral decline in the society because of this permission of a kind of incest. It was this dimension that enabled many to label this a "woman's issue." The letter of E. B. Pusey and the "woman's petition" addressed to Parliament around 1880 are representative of these theological, ecclesiastical, and social concerns.

Advocates of change in the law appealed more to the narrower dimensions of the issue. The scriptural argument was dismissed by the vast majority of scholars, who declared that the Levitical prohibition could not be made to apply after the wife's death.[5] Others argued that there were no grounds for extending the prohibitions of marriage beyond those expressly enumerated in Leviticus. On the historical issue it was noted that the early church did not consistently prohibit these marriages; rather, it is found only in two fourth-century provincial councils and in one theologian, St. Basil. That was hardly a uniform tradition! Fears of moral decline were answered by noting that where the law had been changed (some European countries, British colonies, and the United States), no adverse social effects had materialized. Further, some Anglican clergy who supported the change did so on the ground that prohibition operated far more to promote rather than prevent disregard of the law. Thomas Dale, for one, canon of St. Paul's, declared that the law in this case "is observed only by the scrupulous, evaded by the wealthy, and defied or disregarded by the poor."[6] The social benefits of repeal were also noted, in the stability that could come from a step-mother who would treat the children of her sister with care and affection.

Despite the support of several Houses of Commons and the majority of the legal profession, the advocates of repeal were never able to secure popular support for their cause. Bills foundered for years because of a combination of the opposition of bishops, the continuing force of scriptural and canonical arguments against repeal, and the lingering fears of the threats to the family and society if such a bill were passed. For too many people it was inappropriate for Parliament to undercut Church law. Only when the fears subsided and the threats seemed no longer plausible was legislation for repeal finally passed.

3. E. B. Pusey, "A Letter on the Proposed Change in the Laws Prohibiting Marriage Between Those Near of Kin" (Oxford: J. H. Parker, 1842), pp. 16-17.

The repeal of the law would in three ways shake the sacredness of marriage itself. (1) That sacredness depends upon the whole tone of our moral feeling; whatever weakens that feeling undermines that sacredness, even when it does not immediately bear upon the nature of *all* marriage; every thing which lowers marriage any way, affects it altogether; pollution of any sort injures the reverence felt towards the whole institution; a lowered tone about incest cannot consist with a high sense of marriage itself. (2) The way in which the change is proposed to be made adds to this evil, for it implies that marriage is only a civil institution, if incest is to be only what the State declares such, not dependent upon the law of God, or of the Church, or of human nature. If the State claims to make or unmake incest, it has virtually claimed the whole law of marriage as belonging to it. (3) The very principle whereon the sacredness of marriage depends, the unity of those united by it, is involved in this very first case. It is because "they are no more twain, but one flesh," that the wife's sister becomes the sister of the husband. And so, as S. Basil says, "as a man would not take the mother of his wife, nor the daughter of his wife, because neither would he his own mother or his own daughter, so neither the sister of his wife, because neither would he his own sister." Those, then, who deny that the sister is akin to the husband must deny that the husband and wife are really one, and so at once strike at the very root of the holiness and mysteriousness of marriage, and in so doing treat very irreverently our Lord's own words. All this would sadly fall in with the relaxation already made, by which the State has already declared that it regards marriage no longer as a religious ordinance, allowing every one to contract it in his own way, dispensing with the high tone which the solemn service of the Church throws over it, and allowing the carnal to enter it almost "like the brutes which perish."

One can hardly hope that any who have been betrayed into engaging in such a cause should have misgivings, lest they should be unconscious agents of the Enemy in undermining the sacredness of marriage, and preparing the way for the coming of Antichrist, to which so many things now point; but, at least, the very possibility may well make others reconsider more correctly the whole subject, before, upon one inference from one text, they go against the plain declarations of Holy Scripture in that very context, and seek to overthrow the practice of the universal Church in her pure days, and of our own.

If this contamination is, by the blessing of Almighty God, to be averted from the Church, the clergy must prepare themselves to resist it, not as matter of expediency, but on principle, as confounding men's notions of incest, violating the practice of our own and the primitive Church, disturbing the sacredness of marriage, repealing the moral law of God, and preparing the way for every other abomination.

4. "Deceased Wife's Sister Bill. From the Middle-Class Women of England to the House of Commons" (London: Waterlow and Sons, n.d.), pp. 1-8.

The question whether our marriage laws shall be altered or not, is one that will shortly come before the country, possibly for final settlement; and we think that hitherto it has been discussed on an unfair basis, namely, without considering the feelings of those chiefly interested.

We have waited in hopes that some well-known and influential voices would be raised in behalf of the woman's side of the question, which would represent what may be expected to be the practical results of the contemplated change. We have waited in vain, all are silent. Men seem more and more indifferent, and the issue appears to be sinking into a mere *party question.*

Is it possible that, for mere want of thought, a grave domestic evil will be laid upon the country, and that by men who in practice will loath the inroad of confusion, sin and unhappiness that such a bill as this will bring?

The keynote of our position was struck by a speech of Lord Coleridge's, in which he says [House of Lords, 1880]: "Speaking of marriage, besides the man there is the woman, and, in such a matter, it will hardly be disputed that she has equal moral rights with the man. If the vast majority of women in point of number (and especially the majority of refined and educated women in England) are opposed to this measure, if it is abhorrent to their feelings, what right have men, even if all were agreed, to overbear them and disregard their feelings? Such a matter as this is not easy of demonstration. I can only speak as I believe. I scarcely know one amongst my own acquaintances that upholds it."

He says also that, "as a rule, men, most earnest in support of the new measure, have admitted with regret that women as a whole dislike it. It is then not generous, it is not manly, not, in my opinion, just to persevere in it." . . .

Thousands can testify of the joy produced in a family on the announcement of a sister's marriage—"the new brother," the fraternal affection given and received.

This detestable change in the law made, a man takes his wife on her wedding day; she gives up her old home; the members in that home gain no new brother. He becomes, as it were, a connection, but not a relation; brotherly and sisterly union vanishes, his wife's sisters must be to him like any other women, acquaintances only, with whom it might be dangerous to associate in the present easy family fashion. Anyhow, *appearances* must be regarded—"What will the world say?"

Or, if a man may and can disregard this, weigh well the danger to your wife's peace, the new and invidious element of discord that this change in the relationship would introduce into our homes, susceptible to jealousy as all or most women are. And this jealousy is not of necessity a weakness or a sin. It is implanted in their nature. The affection of their husband is their just right, their most valued property. Men are differently constituted in mind as well as body, but they *can* be similarly affected: for what enrages a man more than to have jealous feelings roused towards his wife?

Let us entreat the country at large to open its eyes, and note well how *momentous* is this question at issue!

Let each man look to the interest, the vital happiness of the women of his own household, and from them judge for the sex at large—they number the larger half of the population. If they have not equal rights with men in many matters, surely they have in this. All just rulers of this land—the land of the happiest homes and hearths in all the world—would desire they should be legislated for with due consideration. At present their voice and power in questions of government are so small that the greater part pay no attention to politics at all, holding it a hopeless task, and are not *awake* to the mischief working against them; but again there *are* thousands of our best, our most educated and refined womenkind, who are pained to the quick at the dire prospect, yet feel a shrinking from bringing their fears before the public, and have no means of making themselves heard. *They* know what the change will bring, the discomfort, yea the torture—for righteous jealousy is closely followed by the evil one in his black aspect of envy (the prince of sins). They do not exactly define to themselves whether they are possessed by a right or a wrong passion; they know peace may then be far from their bosoms, yet they fear to be misunderstood if now they lift up their voices to defend a law in truth very precious to them.

We say such women number thousands, could we but get at them. Surely these classes should be especially cared for, and some pains taken to discover their desires on a point so vital to their happiness, by men who prefer to speak personally for their womenkind to letting them stand up for themselves in public. Surely this is a case for them to show a chivalrous spirit on their behalf!

It has been strongly urged by some that, to the very poor and uneducated, this change of law would be a great boon, but this opinion is but little held by men who have real knowledge of the daily life and sentiments of the lower classes.

. . . It is in the upper and lower middle class where the sister comes to help the struggling wife, borne down by care and the anxiety of a large family, with small means and often delicate health—here it is where the wife's sister is so often the good Samaritan, but who, if the law is changed, must henceforth be banished from this sacred intimacy in her sister's home. Well, then, *for* whom and *by* whom is the change desired?

"As a rule, we admit you should be tender to minorities, but this is a case in which you cannot indulge the wishes of the minority without doing a great injustice and inflicting a terrible hardship on the majority. . . . " [Lord Coleridge]

You *do* abolish [sisters-in-law] if this measure is passed. Why are half the maiden maternal aunts to be turned adrift, their occupation with, and active interest in, their sister's children taken from them? For this also will be the effect. Why is the happiness and good of the *many* to be sacrificed to the passions of the *few*? (or happiness of the few, if you think it just to put it so?) Why is the comfort and peace of a thousand households to be thus sacrificed? . . .

We earnestly hope England may never in an evil hour loosen her restrictions with regard to marriage. In America one marriage in every eleven is followed by a divorce, and in Germany, where marriage between uncles and nieces is permitted, all the domestic relations are broken up.

Relax our marriage laws and we open wide the floodgates and know not whither the torrent will carry us. They are not barriers against liberty, but fences against harm—restraints which have contributed in no small degree to the purity and happiness of our family and domestic life, and are an important element in the moral strength of the whole nation. Remove these restraints, relax these laws, for whom? For a few men who have married their dead wife's sister, for a few men who desire to do so, and for some more who will then gain property—in all but a handful—but of whom it might be said "They have bound themselves by an oath that they will neither eat nor drink" till they have gained their point. But these are not the voices to be heeded by a good Government, and would not be listened to as they have been did men *see* the evil there is in the measure, as all thinking women do see it, and even the unthinking would, if the matter was put plainly before them. . . .

Let *special* measures be taken to ascertain our wishes, for it is essentially a *woman's question.*

C. THE CONTAGIOUS DISEASES ACTS

The Contagious Diseases Act was initially passed in 1864 as part of a growing concern over the incidence of prostitution in Victorian society and the spread of venereal disease among the military population. It applied to eleven garrison and port towns and provided that police could bring women suspected of being prostitutes before magistrates, who could order a medical examination and detention in hospital for three months if they were found to have a venereal disease. Additional acts in 1866 and 1869 extended the coverage to seven new towns, provided for periodic medical examinations for a year of anyone suspected of being "a common prostitute", and allowed compulsory detention for up to nine months. A prostitute could also voluntarily have an examination and submit to detention. The legislation did not then make prostitution illegal; in fact, it appeared to assume that military personnel, who were not permitted to marry, were special cases in the society and would routinely resort to prostitutes for sex. When reports came from these towns of some success in reducing not only the incidence of venereal disease but also the number of prostitutes and brothels, interest was expressed to extend the Acts to the rest of the nation. At this point opposition to the Acts, which previously had been minimal, began to grow, received its focus for many years in the person and work of Josephine Butler, and came to prominence as the first major "women's issue" in politics. One M.P. called it "this revolt of the women." "It is quite a new thing," he went on; "what are we to do with such an opposition as this?"[7]

The Ladies National Association for Repeal of the Contagious Diseases Acts, formed in 1869 by Butler and a few other women, quickly became the chief organization of opposition. Its "solemn protest", published in the *Daily News* in December, called attention to the constitutional questions raised by the Acts: violation of personal security by putting the reputation and freedom of women absolutely in the hands of police, provision for compulsory detention without being accused of a crime, and failure to punish the men who also participated in the act of prostitution and carried the disease. Further, the protest claimed that the Acts legalized evil, making it more rather than less accessible to men, and would not succeed in reducing or eliminating the disease; finally, it declared that the conditions of the disease were moral, not physical, making legislation of this sort completely inappropriate. Published widely with signatures from over a hundred women, headed by Harriet Martineau and Florence Nightingale, the protest soon attracted the signatures of two thousand more, together with testimonies of a number of ministers and physicians.[8]

Josephine Butler made much of the constitutional issues, especially the arbitrary accusation of one policeman without additional witness, the absence of trial by jury, the lack of any definition of "common prostitute", and the singling out of one class of women within the society for attention, which put working women and homeless girls as well as prostitutes at risk.[9] But the key to the "great crusade", as she termed it, was the moral argument—not just the treatment of women or the division of women into two distinct classes, but the double standard itself in sexual morality was the deeper issue. She noted that some men joined the cause at the beginning because they were distressed by the cruelty or the illegality of the Acts, but fell away when they realized that it was directed against "the tacit permission—the indisputable right, as some have learned to regard it—granted to men to be impure at all."[10] The C. D. Acts had implicitly legalized prostitution by seeking to control venereal disease, and thus had confirmed in the law the double standard, one for men and another for women.

This appeal to "social purity" received great support from evangelical Nonconformists, especially, as it was couched in the language of God's will, divine law, and the Christianization of society. Leaders of these groups frequently advocated a single-issue politics at the ballot box, as the LNA had done in its opposition to regulationist candidates.[11] There were implications for suffrage in the campaign, also. The law is a great teacher of morality or immorality, Butler declared; how, then, can women be said to make the morals of a country so long as only men make the laws?[12]

Butler's earlier interest in the education and employment of women (see chapter 4) made her sensitive to the economic as well as the moral and constitutional dimensions of prostitution and its control. She recognized that prostitutes were more victims of the system than "fallen women." Many were involved for only a short time or were forced into the life by poverty or the lack of alternative employment. Now the "social purity" theme put the burden of proof on men rather than women. Readily picked up by the churches, it was often at the cost of continuing to view the issue as one of individual morality and ignoring its economic and social implications. Organizations such as the White Cross League (for men only) and The Church Mission to the Fallen (founded in 1880 as an agency for the "redemption" of prostitutes and later to become The Church of England Purity Society) are examples of the religious response. It was also at the cost of re-asserting the notion of the higher morality of women, albeit this time by women for the larger reclamation of society. As Ellice Hopkins, a leader in the social purity movement at the end of the century, exclaimed, "It is this great upward movement, lifting man to a higher level, which is given into the hands of us women, touching as it does, all the great trusts of our womanhood. What are we women going to do in the face of such vast issues for good or evil?"[13]

It is true that there were men on the other side of the debate who defended the double standard as based on the different physical needs of men and women and who accepted prostitution as a necessary, even socially beneficial, reality. But the reason why repeal of the C. D. Acts took so many years was that there was a moral argument advanced for the cause of regulation which many found plausible. Where the repealers attacked causes and based their case on moral principle, the regulationists attacked symptoms and appealed in utilitarian fashion to a social welfare argument. Many of the leaders were themselves social reformers who thought that if it were appropriate for the state to regulate conditions of work within factories, it was also appropriate for it to be concerned about the spread of disease. They were no more in favor of prostitution than the repealers were, but thought their position was the more realistic. William Acton, a physician and advocate of extension of the laws, declared, "Prostitution we cannot prevent, but we can mitigate the misery entailed by it, and can do much if we will to prevent women becoming prostitutes. The evil cannot be done away, but it may be lessened, and that to a very great extent."[14]

Regulationists actively resisted the charge that the C. D. Acts amounted to "state provision for vice"[15] by responding that they were concerned with the people involved. In addition to abating disease, the provisions were intended to deter women from slipping into a life of prostitution and to reclaim as many as possible from that life through instruction and job-training during the period of detention. Yes, they did contribute to a division of women into two classes, said William Barcroft; but the effect was positive in that there was now no easy move from virtue to vice. Some supporters were sensitive to the potentially degrading provisions of the Acts,[16] yet they did not believe that the problem could be dealt with on a voluntary system. Although each side used statistics to support its argument, reports of reduction of disease and solicitation from the affected towns convinced many church people that the laws were having a beneficial effect.[17]

The compulsory dimensions of the Acts were suspended in 1883. Repeal came three years later, but not before a public outcry regarding child prostitution which occurred with W. T. Stead's series on "The Maiden Tribute of Modern Babylon" in 1885, that had been encouraged by Butler.[18] The nation could no longer tolerate the impression that the law sanctioned vice. Yet while the victory of the repealers did make its constitutional mark, the fundamental goal of "social purity" was that much more difficult than the goal of controlling venereal disease. Perhaps the greatest accomplishment in the end was the demonstration that the lobbying power of a women's organization could be a major political force.

5.   Josephine E. Butler, "Social Purity" (London: Morgan and Scott, 1879), pp. 5-10, 12.

The root of the evil is the unequal standard in morality; the false idea that there is one code of morality for men and another for women,—which has prevailed since the beginning, which was proclaimed to be false by Him who spoke as the Son of God, and yet which grew up again after his time in Christian communities, endorsed by the silence of the Church itself, and which has within the last century been publicly proclaimed as an axiom by almost all the governments of the civilized and Christian world.

This unequal standard has more or less coloured and shaped the whole of our social life. Even in lands where a high degree of morality and attachment to domestic life prevails, the measure of the moral strictness of the people is too often the bitterness of their treatment of the erring *woman*, and of her alone. Some will tell me that this is the invariable rule, and that the sternest possible reprobation of the *female* sinner, as being the most deeply culpable, has marked every age and all teaching in which the moral standard was high. No!—not every age, nor all teaching! There stands on the page of history one marked exception; and, so far as I know, one only—that of Christ.

I will ask you the question to-day, therefore, in this connection, "What think ye of Christ?" Come with me into his presence. Let us go with Him into the temple; let us look at Him on the occasion when men rudely thrust into his presence a woman, who with loud-tongued accusation they condemned as an impure and hateful thing. "He that is without sin among you, let him first cast a stone at her." At the close of that interview, He asked, "Woman, where are those thine accusers?" It was a significant question; and we ask it again to-day. Where, and *who*, are they? In what state are *their* consciences? Beginning from the eldest even to the youngest, they went out, scared by the searching presence of Him who admitted not for one moment that God's law of purity should be relaxed for the stronger, while imposed in its utmost severity on the weaker.

Almost as soon as that holy Teacher had ascended into the heavens, Christian society and the Church itself began to be unfaithful to his teaching; and man has too generally continued up to this day to assert, by speech, by customs, by institutions, and by laws, that, in regard to this evil, the woman who errs is irrevocably blighted, while the man is at least excusable. As a floating straw indicates the flow of the tide, so there are certain expressions that have become almost proverbial, and till lately have passed unchallenged in conversation and in literature, plainly revealing the double standard which society has accepted. One of these expressions is, "He is only sowing his wild oats;" another is, that "a reformed profligate makes a good husband." The latter is a sentiment so gross that I would not repeat it, if it were not necessary to do so—as a proof of the extent of the aberration of human judgment in this matter.

Here we are at once brought into contact with the false and misleading idea that the essence of right and wrong is in some way dependent on sex. We never hear it carelessly or complacently asserted of a young woman that "*she* is only sowing her wild oats." This is not a pleasant aspect of the question; but let us deal faithfully with it. It is a fact, that numbers even of moral and religious people have permitted themselves to accept and condone in man what is fiercely condemned in woman.

And do you see the logical necessity involved in this? It is that a large section of female society has to be told off—set aside, so to speak, to minister to the irregularities of the excusable man. That section is doomed to death, hurled to despair; while another section of womanhood is kept strictly and almost forcibly guarded in domestic purity. Thus even good and moral men have so judged in regard to the vice of sexual immorality as to concede in social opinion *all* that the male profligate can desire. This perverse social and public opinion is no small incentive to immorality. It encourages the pernicious belief that men may be profligate when young without serious detriment to their character in after-life. This is not a belief that is borne out by facts. Marriage does not transform a man's nature, nor uproot habits that have grown with his years; the licentious imagination continues its secret blight, though the outward conduct may be restrained. The man continues to be what he was, selfish and unrestrained, though he may be outwardly moral in deference to the opinion of that "society" which, having previously excused his vices, now expects him to be moral. And what of that other being, his partner—his wife—into whose presence he brings the secret consciousness, it may be the hideous morbid fruits, of his former impurity? Can any man, with any pretension to true manliness, contemplate calmly the shame—the cruelty—of the fact that such marriages are not exceptional, especially in the upper classes?

The CONSEQUENCES of sins of impurity far outlast the sin itself, both in individuals and in communities. Worldly and impure men have thought, and still think, they can separate women, as I have said, into two classes,—the protected and refined ladies who are not only to *be good*, but who are, if possible, to *know* nothing except what is good; and those poor outcast daughters of the people whom they purchase with money, and with whom they think they may consort in evil whenever it pleases them to do so, before returning to their own separated and protected homes. They forget that, even if they could by the help of modern impure legislation, leave all the *physical* consequences of their evil deeds behind them, they cannot so leave the moral consequences. The man's whole nature is lowered and injured who acts thus. But the evil does not stop with his own debasement; he transmits a degraded nature to his children. The poison is in his soul. His children inherit the mixed tendencies of their parents—good and bad; and what security has this prosperous man of the world that the one who is to inherit foul blood and warped brain may not be his *daughter*! Have these successful sinners ever thought of Nemesis coming in such a shape as this?

. . . [T]he essence of the great work which we propose to ourselves, is to Christianize public opinion, until, both in theory and practice, it shall recognize the fundamental truth that the essence of right and wrong is in no way dependent upon sex, and shall demand of men precisely the same chastity as it demands of women.

6. W. Barcroft, "The Contagious Diseases Acts. Shall Their Repeal be Permitted? An Appeal to the Common-Sense of Englishmen" London, 1883), pp. 4-10.

[The Contagious Diseases Acts] do not constitute a "regulation of vice." This is a specimen of the easy declamation whose very breath is a good "cry." The Acts do not, in fact, deal with vice in any way, but only with vicious people, and that not in the way of regulation, but of restraint. The distinction, though it may appear subtle, is of the utmost importance, and underlies nearly the whole question, as is evident by the persistent manner in which the curious misnomer above referred to is continually harped upon by the advocates for repeal. The law, in fact, says to the woman, "If you *will* live viciously, we cannot help that. That is purely a moral question, which you must answer to your own conscience; but you shall not be allowed to make your immorality the occasion of spreading far and wide a virulent physical contamination, and from that you must be restrained, as you are from spreading small-pox by compulsory vaccination." This is really the gist of the whole matter, apart from the irrelevant considerations and perfervid language which have been imported into it.

The Acts do not make "provision for vice." . . . There will be found in them nothing to support such an assertion. . . . The reasoning on which it is based has only to be stated to show its weakness. When reduced to a syllogism it is this:

> Sin brings suffering;
> The fear of suffering deters from sin;
> Therefore, suffering must not be prevented
> lest men should sin the more.

It is impossible to conceive a proposition more open to destructive criticism at every point. In the first place, sin is not, in this world, always followed by suffering, particularly not in this case, where, moreover, as I shall presently show, the suffering, when it does follow, often falls upon the innocent as well as the guilty, and upon the hardened offender less than on the casual one. Next, it is untrue that the *chance* of suffering is any effectual deterrent from sin; this is exemplified in the breach of every moral law which we see committed around us. But even supposing that the loose and inaccurate statements cited above were true, they would still form no argument for repeal. On this point I would say, with all the emphasis at my command, "DUTIES ARE OURS, AND CONSEQUENCES ARE GOD'S." It is our duty to heal disease, to alleviate suffering, and to give opportunities to the offender for amendment; and whether or not she makes renewed health the occasion for returning to vice, does not affect our duty one iota.

Of course, the objection I shall be met with is that the Acts are compulsory, and it will be said that we have no right to heal sufferers by compulsion. To this I reply, that unfortunate women are defenceless, abandoned, and too often desperate. . . . If we are justified, as most of us are agreed, in enacting Factory Acts which forcibly restrain women and children from injuring themselves by overwork, how much more are we justified in snatching these defenceless victims of their own abandonment from the consequences just alluded to!

. . . Enough, however, of what the Acts are not; it is time to consider what they are.

They are of immense moral benefit, both deterrent and reclamatory. . . . Take first the preventive effect of the Acts. I suppose no one asserts that innocent girls do at one blow turn into professional courtesans. . . . The social degradation is effected by well-defined gradations. . . . To be seen walking, sitting, flirting, even drinking, with a fashionable stranger or a "well-set-up" guardsman, is accounted no evil, but rather a thing to be proud of; so the moth flies round the candle. But let her once know that to be seen frequenting the company of men at questionable times and places exposes her to be taken note of by the police, to being warned, and possibly summoned; or still more, let any one of these things happen, what a revulsion of feeling must be created! How the flowery, easy descent of Avernus will appear in its true light—the glare of the bottomless pit! . . . Whether the effect produced upon unfallen women by the Acts be as a whole approved of or not, there can be no question that it is highly deterrent.

Again, the preventive action of the Acts is seen as regards "casual prostitution." There is a large class, principally consisting of girls employed in shops, who, while depending for their subsistence upon regular work, do not hesitate to add an occasional sovereign or two to their ordinary income by prostitution, whenever a smarter dress or bonnet, or any other feminine indulgence, is required. To such the

Acts afford the only possible deterrent. . . .

To sum up this part of the subject, the effect of the Acts, though probably it was not aimed at by their authors, is to sharply divide women into two classes— absolutely virtuous, and absolutely abandoned; and while offering the latter unprecedented opportunities of reform, they display to the former a gulf so precipitous that they will shrink from hovering on the brink as they otherwise would.

This brings me to show that the Acts are not only preventive, but reclamatory. . . . First, then, the Acts cause all women who are under a peculiar form of physical suffering to come into hospital, and there remain until cured. And this practically involves the whole class in question, since sooner or later, and in no case with relatively great delay, every abandoned woman is almost certain to suffer in this manner. The Acts provide that no hospital shall be certified for the treatment of these cases unless "adequate provision is made for the moral and religious instruction of the women detained therein;" and if at any subsequent time such instruction is not adequately given, the certificate is to be withdrawn. . . .   The benefit, then, of the Acts is shown in this: 1) that a compulsory season of retirement is imposed upon the women, when, secluded from the associations and patrons of their evil life, from drink, and from excitement of every kind, an opportunity is afforded for the inlet of reclamatory influences, the value of which it would be impossible to exaggerate; 2) that, by the operation of the register of names, a means is afforded to parents and friends of at once tracing their lost ones, and bringing them home again, when, if it were not for the register, precious time might be lost, involving, perhaps, the fate of the girl sought for. Much more might be added on the moral aspect of the subject, but the above is sufficient to indicate the general nature of the claims which the Acts have upon the support of all Christians and philanthropists; and it is difficult to understand how any such persons, having given even superficial attention to the subject, can persuade themselves into agitating for the relegation of these unfortunate women into the condition of unrestrained disease and degradation in which the Acts found them.

D. WIFE-BEATING

In Charles Dickens' *Oliver Twist* (1837) Fagin's evil colleague Bill brutally assaults his wife Nancy and later murders her. And in George Eliot's story, "Janet's Repentance," from *Scenes of Clerical Life* (1857), the prominent lawyer and stalwart defender of the Established Church, Robert Dempster, beats his wife frequently in drunken rages and eventually turns her out of the house. Eliot was careful to note in her story that Janet had done nothing to deserve such cruelty. "An unloving, tyrannous brutal man needs no motive to prompt his cruelty," she declares; "he needs only the perpetual presence of a woman he can call his own." Janet's situation before being turned out admits of no alternative: "She would not admit her wretchedness; she had married him blindly, and she would bear it out to the terrible end, whatever that might be. Better this misery than the blank that lay for her outside her married home." These few literary examples reflect the increased visibility given to the reality of wife-beating in the nineteenth century, evidenced also by greater attention given to such cases by reports in the newspapers. The question, however, was whether anything could or should be done about it.

One dimension of the issue was the relationship of husband and wife according to the law. The eighteenth-century jurist Sir William Blackstone summarized the law in the words, "the husband and wife are one, and the husband is that one." This meant not only complete dependence of the wife on the husband as far as property and income were concerned, but also the full authority of the law for the husband to exercise "moderate chastisement" as punishment or discipline. Blackstone reported that "as he is to answer for her misbehavior, the law thought it reasonable to intrust him with this power of restraining her, by domestic chastisement, in the same moderation that a man is allowed to correct his apprentices or children." He went on to note that while this sanction began to be challenged in the reign of Charles II, "yet the lower rank of people, who were always fond of the old common law, still claim and exert their ancient privilege; and the courts of law will still permit a husband to restrain a wife of her liberty, in case of any gross misbehavior."[19] Periodically the notion that a husband might beat his wife with a rod not bigger than his thumb was revived, though this was debated by judges in England and the United States.[20] The basic claim continued to be honored well into the nineteenth century; in an 1840 case Justice Coleridge said, "There can be no doubt of the general dominion which the law of England attributes to the husband over the wife; 'the husband hath by law power and dominion over his wife, and may keep her by force, within the bounds of duty, and may beat her, but not in a violent and cruel manner.'"[21] But by the Jackson case (1891) the courts had taken a much firmer stand; in that case Lord Evershed, Master of the Rolls, declared bluntly, "An English wife may not by law be insulted or cruelly used by her husband. If he does either the one or the other the court will not let him have her for the purpose of doing it. No English husband has the right to be a brute."[22]

The greater attention of legal opinion and the corresponding legislation concerning the protection of wives from assault by their husbands (1829, 1853, 1878, 1895) only enabled more substantive questions to be asked: why does this go on? and why is the society not outraged by the continuing practice? These were among the questions that led John Stuart Mill to write of "the legal slavery of the woman" in 1869 and Frances Power Cobbe to cry out for help in a letter to the *Spectator* in 1877.[23] Cobbe followed this with the first substantial article on the subject, noting both the basic public indulgence of this kind of assault and the fundamental ambiguity of sentiment in which many men held women: "a wretched alternation of exaggerated and silly homage, and of no less exaggerated and foolish contempt. One moment on a pedestal, the next in the mire; the woman is adored while she gives pleasure, despised the moment she ceases to do so."[24] This was the general ground of the casual attitude toward assaults on wives, supported by political disabilities of women and the general understanding that a man's wife was his property. Specific causes included widespread drunkenness, the corrosive effects of large cities on morality, the crowded home conditions of the working classes, and the extent of anger and cruelty in the society at large. She believed, as did most analysts, that wife-beating was essentially confined to the lower classes, but she refused to moralize against the attackers or to idealize the victims. And although she had no suggestions on how to address the root causes except the wider concern that would be manifest with female suffrage, she did have proposals to deal with the actual brutalities. Flogging, widely advocated at the time, would not work, she argued, because too many women would not bring charges and too many men, if flogged, would seek greater vengeance against their wives. Her proposed legislation had three prominent features: protection of the wife's earnings and property from the husband and his creditors, judicial restraint against the husband's visitation without consent, and custody of any children together with financial support when the husband is released from jail.[25]

The letters in reply to Cobbe's initial protestation indicated a number of additional dimensions to the issue, while continuing to investigate the causes and seek an appropriate response. Was it the fault of the women, or of the demands for work that took women out of the home? Or did it rest in the "irresponsible power" given to the man in the marriage relationship? Did tolerance of wife-beating stem from the general unconcern of the magistrates? And what of the religious sanctions involved? The Rev. F. W. Harper, a Church of England minister, spoke for many when he suggested that concern for the unity of the marriage and for the wife's scriptural obligation to obedience overrode concern for the wife's well-being in that marriage.[26] In Cobbe's later article she commented on this claim and in so doing laid down a challenge for the churches' reflection: "I should have expected that a minister of the Christian religion would have shuddered at the possibility of suggesting such a connection of ideas as these notions involve. Heaven help the poor women of Durham and Lancashire if their clergy lead them to picture a Christ resembling their husbands."[27]

7. Letters to *The Spectator*, December, 1877 - January, 1878.

December 22, 1877:

Sir,—May I beg of you to reprint the following short paragraph from the *Times* of to-day (December 18th)?— "WIFE-BEATERS.—Michael Scully was brought before the magistrates at Blackburn Town Hall yesterday for kicking his wife in a lodging-house in Queen Street, whereby the frontal bone of the forehead had been knocked in. The sufferer has been removed to the infirmary, where her dying depositions have been taken. Alfred Cummins, tailor, Moor Street, was charged with knocking his wife down and kicking her head and face so violently as to deprive her of sight in one eye. Under the Aggravated Assaults Act, the prisoner was sentenced to 12 months' imprisonment. At the Leicester Police-court yesterday William White was charged with assaulting his wife with intent to do her grievous bodily harm. On Saturday night the prisoner went home drunk, and quarrelled with his wife. Ultimately he threw a burning paraffin lamp at her, which broke over her shoulder, and on the neighbours breaking open the door they found the poor creature enveloped in flames from head to foot, the prisoner standing by. She was frightfully injured, and now lies at the infirmary in a very critical condition. The prisoner was remanded."

Having read these three cases, occurring apparently simultaneously—of kicking in one woman's forehead, and another woman's eye, and throwing a burning paraffin lamp at a third—I beg, Sir, to ask solemnly of you and of all my countrymen with *whom* lies the guilt of these never-ceasing, ever-multiplying English "atrocities"? If we, the women of England, possessed constitutional rights, the very first exercise of our power of political pressure would undoubtedly be to compel the attention of our representatives in the Legislature to the prevention of these crimes of wife-beating and wife-murder. Can you, men of England, wholly acquit your consciences, while you tie *our* hands, and never lift your own?

Frances Power Cobbe

December 29, 1877:

Sir,—In the *Spectator* of December 22, Miss Cobbe very properly calls attention to a single paragraph taken from the *Times* of the 18th, in which are recorded three violent assaults by men upon their wives, two of which were likely to end fatally; for very possibly without such special direction we should have passed them over unheeded, our daily papers and our war correspondents making us only too familiar with horrors; and she has done us good service if for a moment she had made us think upon what is really going on about us, at a time, too, when we are inclined to gloss over evils with a show of universal rejoicing and large-heartedness. Yes it is right that we should be forced to think over the condition of our women, but whether the questions Miss Cobbe puts to her countrymen suggest the true remedy is the point I wish to consider. She makes it an entirely political question, and at once—perhaps necessarily—becomes unjust; for surely men feel no less keenly than women these vile outrages, which disgrace men and women alike; and Miss Cobbe's questions, put with such unsparing severity, and attributing to men alone the responsibility, will not, or need not, make them wince; for if, as Miss Cobbe, I think, elsewhere allows, men's and women's interests are really one, and their true relation towards each other that of alliance, not conflict, all our remedial measures should be guided by this idea; but to bring political passions into our homes and amongst our women is to strengthen conflict and aggravate their condition, for if men and women are to stand towards each other in the position of rivals and competitors, there can be but one result,—hopeless struggle and inevitable defeat for our women; this is appointed to women by Nature, if woman abandons her true position, which is to be the helpmate of man and the mother of the race. And now I come to my true point and real remedy,—a man must have a decent and a real home, and a wife or daughters there supplying his real home wants, not labouring in a factory or elsewhere to add to his money earnings. . . .   Our crime and our brutality and our disgraceful infant mortality have their origin in the want of homes for our men and women, and the consequent temptation of the tavern; and to redress this we must withdraw our women from the labour market, refusing her, too, a political arena, but placing her where Nature intended, where her power would indeed become her heaviest responsibility, rather than the want of it or of "constitutional rights" her wrong.

F.

January 5, 1878:

Sir,—Permit me to remind your courteous correspondent "F." that his proposed remedy for wife-atrocities,—namely, "to withdraw woman from the labour market, refusing her, too, a political arena, but placing her where nature intended," &c., has been already tried on a very large scale, and with results the reverse of satisfactory. If the women in those countries where the "withdrawing" system has prevailed for some thousands of years—India, China, and Turkey, to wit—have been less often kicked to death than their Western sisters, it has been, I fear, only because slippers were less convenient instruments for the purpose than hobnailed shoes, and the sack or the bowstring accomplished the same end, without fatigue to the muscles of their masters.

Endeavouring to bring my first letter within the narrowest limits, I was, perhaps, guilty of passing too rapidly, and without indicating the intermediate steps of my argument, from the evil of wife-beating to the remedy of the political enfranchisement of women. I am, however, entirely prepared to maintain each of those inter-mediate steps:—

1. That one of the chief causes of outrages on women is the deconsideration and contempt wherewith they are regarded by the lower class of men.

2. That those contemptuous sentiments are largely due to the position of women under the law.

3. That the concession of political rights to qualified women would, indirectly, but very efficiently, tend to educate men better to respect their sex.

4. That that concession would also directly lead to some serious and probably successful efforts to put down the crimes of wife-beating and wife-murder, which are now the disgrace of our country. . . .

In the days of *Uncle Tom's Cabin*, we can many of us recall how the Southern slaveholders—their English advocates used to assure us that *if* the Negroes were now and then cruelly treated, it was all the fault of the Abolitionists, who disturbed their minds and produced ill-blood—and that if these troublers could all be hanged, with John Brown, the state of the slaves would thenceforward become quite paradisiacal. The *Spectator* did not attach much faith to such promises in those days nor do I now look for the relief of the miseries of women from extinguishing the woman-suffragists, and returning, as "F." would have us, to the *status quo ante*.

Permit me, in your great kindness to add two words more in rejoinder to your own remarks. You say that the form of woman suffrage which I advocate (namely, the extension of the franchise to women possessing the property qualification, and to them alone) is "illogical." Surely it is not *our Bill* which is illogical, but the *law*, as it stands, which, while professedly basing representation on the tenure of property, refuses representation to a seventh part of the property-holders in the kingdom. I am aware that you apply the term because, like most of our opponents, you persist in assuming that we *ought* to ask for votes for wives as well as for spinsters and widows. Whether it be fair or expedient that wives should be deprived of property by the common law is a question which I am not concerned to argue. It is not we spinsters or widows who have deprived them of it. But we do question the "logic" of refusing to A. and B., who possess property, those rights which on constitutional principles belong thereto, *because* C. has been deprived of both her property and her rights together.

Frances Power Cobbe

January 5, 1878:

Sir,—As the remarks of your correspondent "F." on "Wife-Beating" may serve to mislead some whose knowledge of the conditions of women in our lower-class homes is as slight as his own appears to be, permit me to ask if women, as he insists, are to be prohibited by law from "labouring in factories or elsewhere," what is to become of those with idle, sickly, or drinking husbands, thousands of whom must see their children starve, or to go out themselves to earn their bread by factory or field work, charing, washing, or the like? I would ask "F." also to solve the problem how, in a single close and dingy room, in which cooking, washing, and all domestic operations must needs be carried on, a woman with three or four young children, and a sickly infant in her arms, herself perhaps feeble and sickly too, shall make his "home" at all times so attractive to a tired, a selfish, or a brutal husband as to compete successfully with the warmth and glitter and garish comfort of the gin-palace or public-house. It is difficult, also to see with "F.", how the fact of Members of Parliament finding themselves committed to defend and promote the interests of women—as would be the case, did the latter possess the suffrage—could place either in the position of "rivals and competitors," or involve women in "hopeless struggle and inevitable defeat."

"F." may rest assured that even the possession of the suffrage will not prevent woman from being the "mother of the race;" nature will take care of that. But she is certainly more likely to be the true "helpmate" of man, if encouraged to supplement his comparative indifference and ignorance by her own larger knowledge of the wrongs and keener concern for the welfare of her suffering sisters. "F." himself has to confess that even the publicity of the *Times* failed to draw his attention to the most frightful outrages on women, until a *woman's* hand pointed them out to him.

Lastly, may I say, from personal knowledge of many of these wretched "homes," that it is not the lazy or unfaithful wife, not the termagant or virago, who is the most frequent victim in such cases? The drunken or brutal coward vents his rage where he can do it with impunity. We have it on the authority of the *Birmingham Daily Post* that in the colliery districts it is an increasing custom for men to maltreat and attack their wives when they are about to become "the mothers of the race." Has "F.'s" chivalrous helpfulness made him acquainted yet with this mode of wife-torture, as practised on "our women" in these degraded homes, by the brutes who claim to own them?

The true and only remedy for this state of things is to raise the relative status of women in every class, to give to the weak and poor that social strength which is the result of union, and to bring the cultivated and industrious among them into *collective* alliance with able and manly helpers, who will see to it that the affairs and interests of women receive their due share of Parliamentary attention. What the franchise has done already for the oppressed and down-trodden of the working-classes, what we may trust it will presently do for the agricultural labourer, that we may equally hope it would accomplish in promoting the welfare and elevation of women, and through them, of the entire community.

A Working Gentlewoman

January 12, 1878:

Sir,—My experience as a magistrate, and my reading of police reports, convince me that Miss Cobbe is right in asserting that men have no such sense as she has of the evil of wife-beating and other forms of cruelty to women. Gentlemen do not beat their own wives, but they rarely show or feel much indignation at the cruelty of the lower classes towards either women or children. I do not remember having ever known or read of the *full* penalty being inflicted for the most cruel treatment of a wife; oftenest magistrates are content with the sham punishment of binding over to keep the peace. Brutality is a large element in the character of most Englishmen, and not less in gentlemen than in boors; only the latter show it by their acts, and the former by their indifference to those acts. The Englishmen who read with complacency how those "real gentlemen," the Turks, dispose of wounded Russian prisoners by lighting fires upon their stomachs, are not likely to be much moved by the injuries inflicted on a wife with a paraffin lamp. And if all we hear of "Society" being on the side of the Turks is true, it is from men with an innate sympathy with brutality that our legislators and administrators of the law are chiefly taken.

Edward Strachey

January 19,1878:

Sir,—Will you allow a woman to enter a protest against the severe, and as I think, unjust sentence pronounced on his countrymen by Sir Edward Strachey, in his letter to you last Saturday, that "brutality is a large element in the character of most Englishmen, gentlemen as well as boors"? So far from this being true, I believe, on the contrary, that there is in Englishmen an unusually large element of generous compassion and even tenderness for the weak and helpless; and I would point, as a proof of this, to the fact that, wielding, as they do, absolute power over their wives, the instances of its abuse quoted by Miss Cobbe are, thank God, the exceptions, and not the rule. The real source of the evil is the corrupting influence of irresponsible power in itself. The Englishman is absolute master over the women of his family. He may and does, as I have too often seen, make their home a hell, but no one can or will interfere with him. His religion, if he has any, does not check him, for he believes that it gives a divine sanction to his authority. The law does not check him, so long as he stops short of physical violence threatening life, and then but very leniently, unless he actually takes life. "Society" does not check him, so long as he observes the external decencies of the class he belongs to. Public opinion does not check him, for it holds his wife to be his property, and that he has a right to do as he wills with his own. I shall never forget the horrified amazement with which I listened, when a gentleman whom I knew to be himself incapable of cruelty told me that on one occasion, seeing a man cruelly beating a woman, he was rushing to the rescue, but on hearing from a bystander that the woman was the man's wife, he passed on, thinking it best not to interfere, and two gentlemen who were also listening agreed that they should have done the same! Can we wonder that so tremendous a power as this, placed in the hands of men of all kinds, from the highest gentlemen to the lowest ruffian in the land, is misused, and produces oppression, misery, and crime? Shall we not rather wonder that the misuse is not a hundredfold greater, and admire the generosity and self-restraint which alone prevent it?

It is, however, another question, and one requiring the greatest consideration from all lovers of their country, whether this is a healthy or desirable state of things; . . . whether the first principles of well-ordered liberty, that every duty is the co-relative of a right, and every right, be it of high or low, rich or poor, weak or strong, is under the equal and supreme guardianship of the law, can be violated with impunity only in the relations between the sexes, which give all the rights to the men, and all the duties to the women? . . .

Maria G. Grey

January 26, 1878:

Sir,—"I would rather," in the "Fortunes of Nigel," says Richie Moniplies, when George Heriot was for saving him from his master's wrath, "I would rather stand by a lick from his baton, than it suld e'er be said a stranger came between us." May I commend the consideration of that sentiment to the lady who, in last week's *Spectator*, expressed her horror at English gentlemen's non-intervention between man and wife?

"What sort of a lion do you mean to be, if you should turn into one?" . . . Yet, Martial notwithstanding, I make bold to believe that if ever I should turn into a wife, I shall choose to be beaten by my husband to any extent (short of being slain outright), rather than "it suld e're be said a stranger came between us."

As to an Englishman's "religion," it sets no limits either to the wife's obedience or to the husband's devotion and self-sacrifice. "As the Church is subject unto Christ, so let the wives be to their own husbands *in everything*." "That this man may love his wife, even as Christ also loved the Church, and *gave himself for it*." What Christ is to the Church, what the Church is to Christ,—such are the English Prayer-book's ideals for relations matrimonial.

F. W. Harper

E. WOMEN'S SUFFRAGE

Debate over women's suffrage in Great Britain took place between 1866 and 1918. In that first year John Stuart Mill, M.P., presented a petition to Parliament asking for the enfranchisement of women householders, signed by 1499 women; and committees of women were organized in London and Manchester to advocate the suffrage cause. In the course of debate on the Reform Bill of 1867 Mill proposed an amendment to substitute "persons" for "men," thereby including women in its provisions; it was defeated by 196 to 73. Over the next fifty years the issue was

addressed in Parliament, journals of opinion, organizations established to defend
one side or the other, and in public occasions of advocacy and resistance. The effects
of the First World War on the national consciousness contributed significantly to
the inclusion of women's suffrage in the Reform Bill of 1918, which gave the vote to
married women, women householders, and women university graduates age thirty
or older. A decade later, when it was apparent that the change had produced no
disastrous consequences for family or society, the age was lowered to twenty-one,
finally making the qualifications for voting equal for men and women.[28]

During this period a number of inequities suffered by women were modified,
removed, or addressed through greater public attention—such as laws concerning
divorce and the control of married women's property, opportunities for education
and employment, and laws on the punishment of domestic violence. With the
Education Act of 1870 women could vote for and be elected to local school boards;
later in the century they were able to be elected as Poor Law Guardians and to
vote in municipal elections, and from 1907 they could stand for election to local
government offices. At the beginning of the national debate suffrage advocates used
the existence of political and social disabilities to argue that an all-male electorate
or legislature could not be counted on to correct the injustices of the law toward
women. But by the end of the century the anti-suffrage forces were able to counter
that the existing machinery had done the job quite well![29]

One might have thought that removal of inequities, expansion of opportunities
for service, and greater participation at many levels of public life would soon lead
to an extension of the parliamentary franchise to women. A number of suffrage
leaders certainly thought so. But that question became a special burden, the final
breakthrough into an uncharted world that called up all the fears and threats of
what might happen to family and society, all the perceptions of woman's special
dignity and mission, and all the views of proper relationships between men and

women in private and public life that had characterized more than two centuries of discussion and advocacy. A complicating factor was that government was not understood to be "democratic." Extension of manhood suffrage took place in stages in the nineteenth century by broadening the property qualifications; the franchise was a privilege rather than a right possessed by the citizen. Thus when suffragists pointed to the only remaining disability for the vote—that of sex, the notion of a "right" of female citizens did not attract much support. In many cases among the Antis, lingering fears of what "democracy" might lead to were simply transferred from males to females.

The arguments ranged from practical assessments to expression of principles. Antis claimed that most women were ignorant of politics and did not want the vote. Suffragists countered that the same observation could be made of many men, but was not used to prevent their voting; no one would be compelled to register or vote.[30] Male opponents often asserted that women were unduly influenced by priests and other authority figures, that home and family would suffer if women were distracted by politics or if political differences intruded into domestic life, and that the laws of nature and divine revelation had established an essential and absolute inequality between men and women which would make it unsuitable for women to participate in politics.[31] Female opponents tended to appeal to the separate spheres of men and women, while at the same time urging the full development of female capacities and education. The 1889 "Appeal", signed by 104 prominent women and by a later list of two thousand, declared, "We believe that their work for the State, and their responsibilities towards it, must always differ essentially from those of men, and that therefore their share in the working of the State machinery should be different from that assigned to men."[32] Further, the wide influence for good possessed by women in home and society might be blunted should they enter the arena of partisan politics. And the opportunities for additional work are great. As one writer put it, "Do not the poor, the sick, the sad, and the erring, call loudly for woman's care, her energies, and her sympathy? The cry has gone up since the recent mission in London, not merely for money, but for helpers, for workers. Surely the woman of leisure, the woman craving for employment, has her answer here."[33]

Most of the early proposals for female suffrage excluded married women because they were already represented by their husbands and in order to preserve the peace of the home. But to the basic arguments of the Antis Samuel Smith (1836-1906), Liberal M.P. and an active philanthropist, added the legitimate concern that only a limited extension of suffrage could not be maintained. The real alternatives, he thought, were to include all women or none.

The suffragist case called attention first to the situation of single women and widows who, when householders, were ratepayers and taxpayers but were not represented by anyone. They had no husbands to vote for them and, often, no families to command their energies; many had to work rather than devote their time to charity. The ideal simply did not fit them, and it ought not restrict their participation in public affairs.[34] In addition, it was argued that special grievances and disabilities suffered by women, fostered either through injustices in the law or by virtue of political and economic dependence on men, existed because women were denied the franchise and could only be adequately addressed when it was open to them. This was part of the case made by R. J. Campbell (1867-1956), prominent minister of the Congregationalist City Temple in London from 1903 to 1915, in a tract published by the Women's Freedom League. By the early twentieth century much of the suffragist case was based on the claim that the vote was a recognition and symbol of responsible citizenship—a claim which made the individual rather than the family or the economic unit the most basic ingredient of the state.

Even the "separate spheres" argument was used on the suffrage side. To the assertion that women would be sullied by descent into the dirty world of politics came the reply that politics needed women to raise it out of the dirt. Early in the debate Francis W. Newman declared that philanthropy would unite with politics when women received the vote and that this would leaven the whole society. Other advocates noted the modest inconsistency between the claims to separate spheres and to all-male representation. M. M. Dilke wrote that suffragists "wish women to vote because they are different from men, and because no alteration of laws, or customs, or social habits will make them the same as men."[35]

The churches, representing a wide spectrum of opinion, for the most part tried to ignore the debate. At the least, they could not easily take sides. When one parish church held a service which supported suffrage, the bishop of Liverpool responded, "It is the duty of the Church of England to proclaim the great principles of truth, and righteousness, and Christian love, and not to descend into the arena of party politics."[36] That did not prevent numerous sermons being preached against suffrage. But the charge that the suffrage cause was hostile to religion was simply false, for a number of church people were involved from the beginning. Active organization within the churches did not come until late, however, with the creation of the Church League for Women's Suffrage in 1909, followed shortly by the Free Church League and the Catholic Women's Suffrage Society. These societies engaged in recruitment, lobbying, and educational activities as they sought to show that the aims of the women's movement, broadly conceived, and the specific issue of female suffrage, were consistent with the teachings of Christ and the basic principles of the Christian ethic.

8. "Mr. Samuel Smith, M.P., and Women's Suffrage" (London, 1891).

I premise by observing that the movement for women's suffrage springs out of a sincere desire to raise the status of the sex, and to redress woman's wrongs, real or supposed. It is advocated by many men of warm sympathies and earnest philanthropy; and if it be a mistake, as I consider it to be, it proceeds from excess of tenderness for the weaker sex. Let me here make the confession that in the earlier stages of the movement I somewhat sympathised with it, mainly on two grounds—first, that women were subject to some injustices which men seemed unwilling to remedy; and secondly, it seemed that the inclusion of women householders was all that was aimed at; in other words, that an addition of some 800,000 women would be made to an electoral roll of say 6,000,000 of men, all those women being single or widows, all ratepayers and discharging the duties of heads of households, and therefore presumably, fairly well qualified to take a part in public life. They have the vote already for local affairs, such as town and county councils, school boards, &c., and it seemed to me that perhaps some good would arise from the extension to them of the parliamentary franchise. My opinion has changed since then, for the two following reasons:—First, the injustices which women suffered have been remedied one after another, the C. D. Acts have been abolished, the Married Women's Property Act and the Guardianship of Children Act have given to wives and mothers reasonable control over their property and children. Parliament of late years has shown itself most willing to remove any wrongs under which women labour, and to legislate for their welfare as far as it is practicable to do so. . . .

But the second consideration weighs with me more, namely, the question of limiting the franchise to women householders. Twenty years ago no one dreamed of going further than this, but the whole situation has altered since then. The British Constitution has been broadened again and again by the inclusion of large classes of electors, and it is clear to those who can read the signs of the times, that this country is going the way of all other countries, namely, to the goal of manhood suffrage. I know that many are opposed to this. I agree with them that household suffrage is a sounder basis for government than manhood suffrage; and I do not wish to see so extreme an extension; but one cannot shut one's eyes to the signs of the times, it is as certain to come as that the night follows the day. We cannot keep this island

on a different basis to the surrounding nations, our own colonies and the United
States. The first political party which thinks it can make capital out of it will go
for it; and with manhood suffrage will come womanhood suffrage, if we accept the
principle of the Bill now before Parliament, namely, identical qualifications for men
and women. . . .

Let us consider what are the qualifications of our future rulers. Let us say that
there are eleven millions of adult women in the United Kingdom by the present
census. What are their qualifications? How many have ever read a political speech,
or know anything of the critical and difficult problems of government? Let any one
investigate the ordinary reading and intellectual pabulum of maid-servants, shop
and factory girls, working men's wives, &c. These will constitute nine-tenths of the
ultimate female electors. I make bold to say that he will find not one in twenty
ever reads a political speech or article, or has the slightest knowledge or concern
for the staple questions that occupy Parliament. Nine women out of ten care less
for principles than for persons; they reverence their clergyman, their priest, their
political chief; they ascribe to him all kinds of imaginary virtues, and see no defects.
. . . Among our dense population the man who would carry the day with the
poorer women would be the man or woman (for undoubtedly women would then
sit in Parliament) who would promise the wildest Socialistic legislation—such, for
instance, as a fixed compulsory eight hours day for all kinds of work, and a fixed
wage guaranteed by the State: one who would promise to build comfortable homes
for all the poor, and to supplement their wages by grants from the State. . . .

This question is often argued on the ground of the rare and exceptional political
woman. We admit there are highly gifted ladies who can address large audiences
as well as any man; but in conferring the franchise we have to consider the average
woman as contrasted with the average man. The average man in a free country
naturally takes to politics; but the average woman does not. Some argue that

because there are many ignorant male electors we should not be afraid to emancipate ignorant female electors. They say that the ship of State can be navigated fairly well with a considerable deck cargo of male ignorance on board; why not with female ignorance as well? A ship of five thousand tons may carry a deck cargo of five hundred tons in addition, and though very perilous, it may ride through the storm; but put on a deck cargo of five thousand tons and it will certainly founder. We have six millions of male electors, of whom say five millions are fairly intelligent, and perhaps one million ignorant; but under manhood and womanhood suffrage our electoral body would consist of about twenty-one millions, nearly eleven millions being women, of whom ten millions at least are absolutely ignorant of politics, and perhaps two or three millions of the men. No ship of State could avoid being capsized with such a cargo. It is said that the franchise itself educates men, and therefore it would educate women. That is a question of degree; most men rapidly and easily take to politics, most women will never do so, because the Creator has made them different.

Let me glance for a moment at what may be termed the religious argument. It is allowed by all that Christianity has wonderfully raised the condition of women. Contrast the women of England and America with the women of Mahomedan, Hindoo, or Buddhist countries; the superiority of our civilisation is indisputable. Yet it is undoubted that the framework of human society as laid down in the Bible gives to men the place of authority and power. Woman was created to be "a helpmeet" for man; the wife was appointed to be subject to her husband. "The husband is head of the wife, as Christ is head of the Church." Such passages may be quoted by scores. They rebut the idea that Christianity affirms absolute equality between the sexes. It does nothing of the kind, and I allege that much of the present movement to attain absolute equality springs from the denial of the authority of Revelation. Of course there are many exceptions to this statement. Some of the leaders in this movement are among the best of women, but I think, all the same, that they are mistaken in their interpretation of the Scriptures.

This too lengthy letter must be brought to a close by glancing at the social effects of the change. . . . Is it not a fact well known to all that the dirtiest election work is often deputed to women; that they are allowed to deceive and intimidate voters in ways that men could not do without punishment? If there is anything certain, it is that "political women," as they are called, are usually bitter partisans, and their intrusion into political life has added to its acrimony, not lessened it. Women feel far more keenly than men; they take matters in a more personal way, and they provoke enmities where men would laugh and shake hands next day. The reason is that woman has a finer and more highly-strung constitution than man; she was never meant for this rough and dirty work, and her very virtues turn to vices when she is pushed into man's place.

But all the evils we now experience are a trifle to what we must endure were all women to have votes. None need take part in politics now, unless they are inclined; but then every one will be pressed to do so whether they will or not. Incessant canvassing will force every woman to declare herself on one side or another. The wife will often be brought up to the poll by her friends, while the husband goes the contrary way; the peace and quietness of home will be exchanged for a turbulent, excited life, out of which will spring innumerable scandals. . . . Ask any medical man what will be the effect on the children of the future of this nervous excitement on the part of the mothers. Already it is well known that a sad physical deterioration of the children is the penalty of a mother exhausting her nervous powers in public life. No physiological fact is more certain than that febrile excitement in a mother is ruinous to the unborn babe, and nearly all great men are children of mothers who have led wholesome, quiet lives. Nothing is more certain than that we shall have an enfeebled race just as we draw the mothers aside from the sacred duties which God and nature have assigned them.

9. (A) R. J. Campbell, "Women's Suffrage and the Social Evil" (London, 1907); (B) "Why the Church League Exists," *Church League for Women's Suffrage Monthly Paper*, June, 1913, p. 228.

(A)   Of all the objections that have been offered to the demand for the enfranchisement of women, there is not one which appeals to any higher motive than selfishness. In all previous movements of a similar kind, there has been a considerable amount of honest and well-founded distrust of the probable effects of any sweeping measure of reform. Broad-minded statesmen might, and did, dread the advent to political power of a large and comparatively uneducated working class. As Robert Lowe said, after the establishment of household suffrage, they had now to set to work to educate their masters. But in regard to the enfranchisement of women the case is entirely different. No one pretends, or could pretend, that the granting of their just demands would mean the inrush of unreasoning animalism into affairs of State; so with a frankness unrivalled in the history of political movements, opponents of Women's Suffrage fall back on appeals to sheer brute selfishness which, as often as not, they hardly take the trouble to disguise. This is the meaning of all the talk about the unsexing of women by political activities, and the constant insistence that their proper sphere is the home. What is really at the bottom of the opposition is the fear that if the vote be granted it will mean a long step in the direction of bringing to an end the present economic and social dependence of women upon men. Man likes female subservience and dreads female competition. . . .

But this is just the very point at issue in the present campaign, and it is the clear perception of this which turns the Suffragist agitation into a moral movement, claiming the sanctions of civic righteousness and justice on its side. We British people have an almost unlimited capacity for shutting our eyes to facts until a situation becomes too intolerable to permit of self-deception. We have been assuring ourselves for generations that the women of this country were the respected equals and companions of their male protectors in whose chivalrous devotion lay their true security. Unfortunately the facts do not bear out this poetic way of looking at the question of the relations of the sexes. . . .

Let me mention only one aspect of the problem in which the disparity in the relative economic position of the sexes operates disastrously without our apparently being aware of it. You will forgive me, I am sure, for doing a little plain speaking on this point; I refer to the nauseous problem of prostitution. Opponents of Women's Suffrage profess to be terribly anxious to safeguard the integrity of family life, but modern civilization is having to pay a terrible price for this desirable thing. In every great city of the western world there exists a class of women who live by hiring themselves to men with whom their only bond is that of lust and lucre. In London alone it is estimated that the number of these women amounts to scores of thousands. Everybody knows this, and, in polite society, pretends not to know it. Where has this class come from, and why does it exist? The answer is that for untold centuries the woman has been not only the dependent, but more or less the private property of the man. Broadly speaking, the man owns all there is to own; he used to own the woman out and out; now he only owns her indirectly as it were. Man is woman's capitalist. Women have little or no access to the sources of productive employment, and therefore they have to remain in a position of dependence. At the best this position of dependence makes the woman to some extent the inferior of the man; at the worst she becomes his victim. This is where prostitution comes from; it has an economic root. . . .   But for the economic dependence of one sex upon the other it could not exist for an hour.

In stating this one hard moral and economic fact I have deliberately chosen one of the more prominent evils for the remedying of which a radical change is called for in the political status of women. If this terrible evil, with all its vicious accompaniments, is to be abolished it is the women themselves who will have to do it. And it will not be done by moral appeals, for while these appeals are being made the conditions are continuing unchecked which produce fresh victims. All honour to those who are devoting time and energy to rescuing a few from the crowded ranks of ill-fame; but we all know well enough that the impression made on the appalling total is but small. We shall have to go one better than Social Purity organizations.

What is wanted is such a representation of women in the Legislature as shall secure to them a living wage on the same terms as to men. There are far-reaching economic problems here upon which I hardly dare to touch at present, but we may as well recognize plainly that to give women political power is the best way to secure to them in the long run such an economic status as will lift them clear out of their present position of reputable and disreputable dependence upon men. It may seem an utterly unpractical thing to say that the housewife deserves her wage just as much as the husband, and that it ought to be secured to her independently of his favour or caprice, but this change will surely come. Women know too well the hardship of the present state of things not to be able to recognize the remedy when once it is put into their hands. Moreover, to educate women and then deny them a living is damnable. . . .   Governments never lead in the direction of administrative reform; they are always driven. Give women the vote and the pace will be accelerated in the direction of those great social changes which are already on the horizon, and which mean ultimately the abolition of pauperism, unemployment, and prodigal waste of life and energy among the lower classes. No one knows where poverty pinches better than the working man's wife; it is she who has the making of the family budget; she can tell you best what the difference will be if the loaf becomes a farthing dearer. Every year we are interfering more and more with the venerated maxim that an Englishman's house is his castle. Whether we will or no we are being driven to care more thoroughly for the welfare of child life, not only in schooling, but in feeding, clothing, and housing. Is there any sensible reason why the mothers of England, to whose hands is committed the principal care of the children in their early days, should not have a direct share in legislation which is having increasingly to do with the making and maintenance of the home?

And, apart even from marriage and the family, we are having to face one new and portentous fact—the emergence of the woman who is being fully equipped to take her place in professional or commercial life along side of the man. Woman is demanding a career, not merely an existence. She is the proved equal of the man in any field of service where physical strength is not a *sine qua non.* This problem is not going to decrease; it is going to become larger. You can no more prevent the intrusion of women into fields of activity hitherto reserved for men, than labour was able to prevent the invention of machinery. What are you going to do about it? Barring them out is no good, although it has been tried, with every species of intolerance, from the Universities downward. You will have to face a new economic situation. You will have to reconcile yourself to the replacement of male by female labour wherever it happens to be cheaper, and then you will have to ask whether it is good for the body politic, or even possible, to prohibit such labour; if it cannot be prohibited, it will have to be represented in Parliament like all other labour.

There is no need for sex competition. Enlightened self-interest ought to bid us welcome every improvement in the status of women. If they have shown themselves capable of taking their place in our industrial and public life, we ought to see to it that the principle of comradeship is extended still further. If the new industrialism means—and it does mean—the employment of a vastly increased number of highly trained and intelligent women, it will be to the interest of the whole nation to see that these women are fully represented in the councils of State. Let there be no barriers of sex privilege. If we are comrades in the home, comrades in the school, comrades in the office and the workshop, let us be comrades at the hustings too. We need the woman's point of view in all questions affecting the national well-being. Let the men of England request it as a measure of wise patriotism; do not let us concede it in any grudging or half-hearted manner. Honour, prudence, and fair play unite to bid us take this enlightened course. The hour is not far distant when we and our descendants will wonder that such a battle ever needed to be fought, and we shall vie with each other in respect and admiration for the brave women who are fighting the battle of their sex against such heavy odds of bigotry and prejudice today.

(B)   The Church League for Women's Suffrage exists primarily owing to our recognition of the truth, that women's demand for enfranchisement is a demand which is in harmony with the teaching of our Master, the granting of which is essential to the perfecting of his kingdom. In our view the subjection of one sex to another in any department of life is in contradiction to the whole ethic of Christianity. We feel constrained to labour for women's enfranchisement for just the same reasons as those which impel us to promote such causes as temperance and social purity. Without meaning in any way to reflect upon the sincerity and piety of those who differ from us, we assert quite definitely that we are suffragists because we are Christians, and we feel it to be our duty to emphasize this assertion by banding ourselves together in the Church League.

Furthermore we recognize in the women's movement, one of the greatest forces of our time. We believe that its final triumph is assured. But great forces are not always forces which make for righteousness. In every century, in every department of life, liberty is only too prone to degenerate into licence. How can we ensure that the influence of the women's movement shall operate to righteous ends? How can we hope to win the liberty for women which we desire and avert the licence which we dread? The dread of that licence holds many back from joining in the movement at all. To us, on the contrary, the recognized danger is an incentive to more earnest co-operation. We do not believe for one moment that the movement can be controlled from without; we are sure that it can be influenced from within.

If the struggle for justice and freedom be left to those who have not learned that the only true freedom is to be found in the service of Christ, we foresee unspeakable disaster. The Christian Church is powerless to resist the movement if it would. It is potent, if it will, to influence its character and results. But it must make its position plain. In our League we seek to rally the forces of the Church for this task.

Again, in the Church League we find opportunity for that corporate communion, that fellowship before the throne of Grace, which would otherwise be lacking to us. We value such opportunities as means to our own strengthening and refreshment in a struggle which has proved arduous beyond any of a like kind, which has brought with it misconception and calumny. And we believe quite simply in the power of prayer. We know of no way in which we can more effectively further our cause than by our practical recognition of the truth that the help that is done upon earth, God doeth it Himself.

Finally, we band ourselves together as Church people for the honour of our Church. We find the conviction widespread that the Church is indifferent or hostile to the demand of women—a demand which has been made with growing insistence for half a century—for wider opportunities for self-realization and service. We believe that such an estimate of the attitude of the Church is not really warranted by facts. The debt of women to the Church of Christ can hardly be overestimated. But we cannot disguise from ourselves that the charge is not wholly without foundation.
. . . And in the sphere of so-called "secular" politics, the Church as a whole has taken no effective step to demand justice for women. If our Church League can do something, and it has already done much, to make it clear that Church people do really care for justice, we may yet be recognized, in quarters whence we are now looked upon askance, as having striven, and not in vain, to retain for the Church the love and allegiance of many who have proved in the past its most loyal and devoted servants.

CHAPTER 6

THE QUESTION OF THE MINISTRY OF WOMEN

Q. Who are they that more especially employ women to preach?

A. Those who call themselves "Bible Christians."

Q. Is not this a very strange thing?

A. It is indeed a very strange thing, that any person professing to be a "Bible Christian" should be the very one to do that which is so plainly contrary to the Bible.[1]

A widespread set of assumptions in the late nineteenth century continued to make the "ministry of women"—in its more narrow sense of regular preaching or having pastoral responsibilities in a congregation—"a very strange thing." Except for the Quakers and the newly-established Salvation Army (see selections 1 and 2), the subject attracted little interest in the churches. Wesleyan Methodists, who had had many active women preachers in Wesley's later years, would have none of it. Even the "offshoot" groups such as the Primitive Methodists and Bible Christian Methodists, which had a prominent place for women in the ministry in their early years, now had almost none in their itinerancies, even though the rules of the Conferences had not been changed. More elaborate church organization, a regular pool of male candidates, and even greater expectations for ministerial education had all worked against encouraging women to become ministers.

To be sure, there were thousands of women serving as local preachers and class leaders in Methodist groups and as Sunday School teachers and parish visitors across the other denominations, plus countless others engaging in charitable and philanthropic works that were thought to be an appropriate part of the church's ministry. By the end of the century women were also being sent out in substantial numbers as missionaries; in 1918, for example, the *Congregational Year Book*'s list of English missionaries working under the auspices of the London Missionary Society showed that almost one-third (89 of 275) were women.[2] This was a new outlet for their religious work, but still they were not ordained.

In different denominations the issue took different shapes: admission to the itinerancy, public teaching to a mixed audience, appointment to pastoral charge, or ordination to the priesthood. Yet at its root it was the same: would everything else in church and society be open to women, but the church's public ministry and its attendant authority be denied them? When the Anglican feminist Edith Picton-Turberville addressed this question in 1916, she noted wryly how many people had been indignant over the recent discussion in the Church of England of whether God's grace was confined to the channels of Apostolic Succession (the so-called "Kikuyu controversy"). But then she asked, "Are we not face to face with the fact that almost every man and every woman holds a similar doctrine when they hold that full blessings conveyed by the ministry of the Church can be conveyed by man alone, and that in this ministry women can have no share? This belief is held not by 99 out of every hundred, but by 999 out of every thousand, and most tenaciously by those in the Christian ministry."[3] Even though her figures were impressionistic and would not fully apply across the denominational spectrum, a broader point could be made here as well: namely, that the question of women in ministry is not solved simply by the admission of women to ministerial work. Wesleyans, Primitive Methodists, and even Quakers could testify to that.

The debate, when it was taken up, went to-and-fro. Traditionally, the first source of authority was the biblical, especially Pauline, injunctions against women assuming authority over men or engaging in public teaching and preaching. Certainly many people in the several denominations thought that this was enough to settle the issue. But developments in the nineteenth century made this a less than invincible argument. For one thing, the Evangelical impulses from Wesley to Hugh Bourne and beyond had brought both interpretive modifications of the absolute prohibition and additional criteria for authenticating a person's call to preach. These modifications, including searching the text for positive statements of women's roles (such as Joel 2:28, Acts 2:18, and Galatians 3:28), were also expanded by independent women evangelists in mid-century. Secondly, advances in biblical criticism encouraged people to think of the cultural and historical context in which the biblical injunctions appeared. Should first-century prohibitions apply universally? If the Bible and Christian tradition support limitation of ministry to males, they supported slavery as well; and the latter was certainly not thought justifiable. One could set the injunctions against the teachings of Jesus or, more broadly, the fundamental affirmations of the faith. Thus, for more people than before it was not absolutely crucial whether the Bible prohibited women's involvement or whether there were women "ministers" (albeit as prophetesses, judges, deaconesses, etc.) to be found in its pages; the cultural situation called forth new expressions of faithfulness to the gospel. It is not for nothing, then, that the biblical argument took a secondary place in the cases presented by J. Hiles Hitchen (selection 3) and others, to be supplemented by other arguments.

Those other arguments took up the issue of "woman's sphere" and questions of expediency. Perceptions of an appropriate "sphere" had been challenged on several fronts, although it must be said that the challenges were often on behalf of single women only—in education, in the professions of medicine and law, and in the realms of politics and public affairs. Even with its appeals to the divine ordering of society, could the church be the only exception? The claim that personal equality before God is consistent with administrative subordination in church and society (i.e., that Galatians 3:28 does not mandate transformation of human relationships) was increasingly implausible to those women who participated in one or more of the other challenges. The principle of complementarity, namely, that as women and men are different, so they have different but equally important spheres of activity, was used on both sides of the debate—but as in suffrage, so also on the issue of ministry, it was employed more on the side of keeping women out.[4]

Questions of expediency contained a host of fears. Would women ministers be accepted by congregations, by either men or women? Would they split the churches? Could they function in positions of authority over men? Would the present pastoral activities currently done by women, that is, in largely voluntary work, be undercut by the opportunity for regular positions in ministry? The uncertain effects of such a change certainly delayed its coming. Many thought that it would simply be a capitulation of the churches to secular pressure, as if there had been no debate within these churches at all. Others, like the Anglican theologian B. H. Streeter, wanted to move forward cautiously. The Church of England could not have women as principal officers until there had been considerable change in the society at large, he wrote; though the Church should be ahead of public opinion, "in a matter of this kind it cannot be too far ahead."[5]

When some churches moved to ordain women and place them in pastoral charges, they did so because the old arguments against it had lost credibility and because their people were ready for it. In the period before 1925 there were very few. The Unitarian and Free Christian Churches were pioneers in opening the ministry to women; the first women prepared by theological training for ministry in the denomination was Gertrude von Petzold, educated at Manchester College, Oxford (1901-04). Congregationalists ordained Constance Todd Coltman, who had been educated at Mansfield College, Oxford, in 1917, and she served with her husband as joint assistant ministers at the King's Weigh House Church, London. The first Baptist woman minister was Maria L. Taylor (1922). Presbyterians had formal barriers against women holding offices in the churches. For some of the Methodist bodies, the recently established deaconess order was sufficient for woman's ministry.

Because much of the Anglican discussion in the nineteenth century had been confined to the role of sisterhoods and deaconesses, the more specific debate over women and the priesthood did not begin in earnest until external pressures brought it within the Church. Two particular controversies can provide a context for the debate. In 1916 the Bishop of London announced that he was prepared to license specially chosen women to preach in churches during the forthcoming National Mission. This evoked such a storm of protest across the Church that he was compelled to withdraw the suggestion. And in 1922 the bishops of the Convocation of Canterbury proposed a resolution that would permit women to speak in churches under conditions laid down by the local bishop; these occasions would be other than the regular and appointed services and were intended "normally" for congregations of women and children. The clergy delegates objected to the word "normally." When the bishops responded that the word simply meant a bishop's discretion, the clergy still refused to support the resolution, with the mover of the amendment saying that this might be the thin end of the wedge.[6]

In the Church of England the question had particular complications, largely in the symbolic weight attached to the term "priesthood" (see selections 5 and 7). As Streeter noted, "Tradition, though it can be quoted in favour of the recognition of women as prophetesses, cannot be quoted for their admission as priests."[7] He proposed extended discussion and activity on a number of questions before addressing this one, including matters of church government, the functions appropriate to the sexes within the religious community, and the meaning of priesthood. Even that modest encouragement was seen as a further delaying tactic by those who believed the Church to be the final representative of the old order with respect to women's participation. To them the deaconess order was still a position of inferiority. In 1928 Canon Charles Raven tried to appeal to the Church as an organism rather than an organization, which grows through the operation of the Spirit of Christ upon it and in relation to fresh tasks that appear. Thus, he argued, "to develop its ministerial system by admitting women to the priesthood would only be to continue the process by which the whole of the institutional structure of the Church has come into being."[8] But the appeal made little impact.

For the advocates of women in ministry in this period, then, the advances were distinctly modest. The relative weight of opposing arguments had shifted, and wider social and political changes with respect to women made more people open to the prospect of women ministers. Despite the modest gains, there were intimations that even this step would not be enough, intimations that a further theological reconstruction was needed, which addressed questions from the nature of God to implications for church life, sexual roles, and the contributions of women. Frances Power Cobbe had suggested the need but had not pursued it. Hatty Baker, Secretary of the Free Church League for Women's Suffrage, wrote in 1911, "It is impossible to think truly of God without seeing womanly-manly attributes. . . .   We surely need a woman as well as a man to interpret the heart of our Mother-Father God."[9] But these comments were seldom more than intimations. Without support in the Church of England and with only a few women in ministry or other leadership positions of other churches, there was little incentive to take up the task. Even the presence of women in ministry did not greatly alter the picture of that being "a very strange thing."

1. Joseph John Gurney, "On the Ministry of Women," in *Observations on The Religious Peculiarities of the Society of Friends*, 2nd American ed. (Philadelphia: Nathan Kite, 1832), pp. 194-96, 203-205.

Although various Methodist societies had attracted some attention in the early nineteenth century for their employment of women ministers, the Society of Friends continued to be the group that was best known for its encouragement of women in the ministry. In fact, women ministers outnumbered the men.[10] For Joseph John Gurney (1788-1847), Elizabeth Fry's younger brother, this was a matter of some concern, but it did not alter his support for them. Yet even among the Quakers there was opposition. William Sturge later recalled the 1830s controversy which led one quietist minister, Ann Jones, to rebuke an audience of evangelicals with the words, "I know that some of you despise women's preaching. I care not for that."[11] The quietists represented the mystical strain within Quakerism, emphasizing the free work of the Holy Spirit and looking with suspicion on any human construct, such as doctrinal statements or even teachings from the scriptures. Evangelicals gradually came to dominate in the Society, having interest in such issues as the nature of the atonement and the authority of the Bible, the latter making some of them less supportive of women ministers.

One of the most influential evangelical Quakers in the first half of the century, a well-known philanthropist and religious writer, Gurney's defense of women in ministry was based primarily upon the biblical evidence.[12] One should note, however, that Gurney's support was limited to the public preaching and praying of women, to that sanctioned by the Apostle Paul, and that he opposed the emerging woman's rights movement and the seating of female delegates to the Anti-Slavery Convention in London in 1840. He had declared before that event, "I do not approve of ladies speaking in public, even in the anti-slavery cause, except under the immediate influences of the Holy Spirit. *Then*, and then only, all is safe. Should *my* dear ladies have to speak in *this* way, I shall have no objection."[13] Still, Gurney was a consistent supporter of his sister's work. Clearly, Quaker women had opportunities for ministry that few women had in the early nineteenth century; but without any involvement in the Society's governance or much support for involvement in public issues of the day, this was a rather thin reed for building a larger movement. That would come from other sources.

While, by the bulk of the Christian world, the public preaching and praying of women is strictly excluded, and it is even considered as an indisputable doctrine, that the duties which peculiarly appertain to their character and station in society, and the offices of the Christian ministry, are absolutely incompatible; Friends believe it right, freely and *equally* to allow the ministry of both sexes. . . .   Since we conceive, on the one hand, that all true ministry is uttered under the immediate influence of the Spirit of Christ; and since, on the other hand, we confess that the wind bloweth where it listeth—we cannot reasonably do otherwise than make way for the exercise of the gift by those persons, of every description, whom the Spirit may direct into the service, and whom the Great Head of the church may be pleased to appoint as his instruments, for the performance of his own work. It is, indeed, declared that "the spirits of the prophets are subject to the prophets," and hence it may be inferred that in the conduct of our gifts, we ought not to neglect the dictates of a sound and enlightened discretion: but we believe that we must not limit the Holy One of Israel, or oppose to the counsels of infinite wisdom our own fallible and unauthorized determinations. We dare not say to the modest and pious female, "Thou shalt not declare the word of the Lord," when we believe that, from an infinitely higher authority, there is issued a directly opposite injunction, "Thou shalt go to all that I shall send thee, and whatsoever I command thee, thou shalt speak." . . .

Nor is there any thing either astonishing or novel in this particular direction of the gifts of the Spirit. Nothing astonishing, because there is no respect of persons with God; the soul of the woman, in his sight, is as the soul of the man, and both are alike susceptible of the extraordinary as well as of the general influences of his Spirit. Nothing novel, because, in the sacred records of antiquity, there are found numerous examples of women as well as of men, who were impelled to speak to others on matters of religion, by the direct and immediate visitations of Holy Ghost.

[Here begins an extended discussion of the scriptural passages relating to women and their roles, leading to the following conclusion on the basis of the apparently conflicting passages in the letters of Paul.]

. . .   It appears then that the allowance of the public preaching and praying of women, in the Society of Friends, necessarily results from their principles respecting the character of all true ministry—that we dare not in this respect, more than in any other, limit the Holy One of Israel in the exercise of his own prerogatives—that our practice in reference to the present subject is justified by the records of Scripture, respecting the effusions of the Spirit of God in times of old—that even under the legal dispensation, many female servants of the Lord were called to the exercise of prophetical gifts—that of the gospel times, the common participation of those gifts by men and women, was a decisive characteristic—and that the injunctions of the apostle Paul against the public speaking and teaching of women, can only be understood (himself being witness) of speaking and teaching which were not inspired—which were not *prophesying*.

Such are the general sentiments entertained in the Society of Friends respecting the ministry of women—a subject which suggests in conclusion one or two reflections of a practical nature.

When the apostle Paul said, "I suffer not women to teach," he added "nor to usurp authority over the man;" I Tim. ii.12. Had the women in the church of Ephesus, after receiving this injunction, assumed the office of pastors; had they attempted that description of public teaching which was immediately connected with the government of the church; they would have been guilty of infringing the apostle's precept, and would have usurped an improper authority over their brethren: but as long as their ministry was the result of the immediate influence of the Holy Spirit, and consisted in the orderly exercise of the prophetic gift; so long must they have been free from any imputation of that nature. Women who speak in public assemblies for worship under such an influence, assume thereby no *personal authority* over others. They do not speak in their own name. They are the instruments through which divine instruction is communicated to the people; but they are only the instruments; and the doctrine which they preach derives its true weight and importance, not so much from the persons by whom it is uttered, as from that Being in whom it originates, and by whose Spirit it is prompted.—This remark is not only in accordance with the principles which obviously appertain to the present subject, but is confirmed, as many of my readers will be aware, by our own experience: for we well know that there are no women, among us, more generally distinguished for modesty, gentleness, order, and a right submission to their brethren, than those who have been called by their divine Master into the exercise of the Christian ministry.

Lastly, I may venture to direct the attention of my friends to a fact which I deem to be worthy of the consideration of the Society; namely, that during the earlier periods of the history of Friends, the work of the ministry devolved much more generally and extensively upon the men, than upon the women. If, in the present day, a similar result from our religious principles does not take place; if, on the contrary, the ministry of the women is found rather to preponderate in the Society over that of the men; such a circumstance can by no means be deemed a favourable sign. Justified, as Friends appear to be, by the doctrine of Scripture, and by the powerful operations of the Spirit of Truth, in equally admitting the ministry of both sexes; it is far indeed from being an indication of life and soundness in the body at large, when the stronger sex withdraws from the battles of the Lord, and leaves them to be fought by those whose physical weakness and delicacy have an obvious *tendency* to render them less fit for the combat. Were we of that stronger sex less devoted than we now are to secular objects—were we less prone to a worldly spirit, and more diligent in seeking *"first* the kingdom of God and his righteousness"— there can be little doubt that we should be called forth in greater numbers into the arduous duties of the ministry of the gospel; nor would the burthen of the word be found to rest, in so large a proportion as it now does, on our mothers, our sisters, and our daughters.

2. Catherine Booth, "Female Ministry; or, Woman's Right to Preach the Gospel," in *Papers on Practical Religion* (London: S. W. Partridge & Co., 1878), pp. 95-97, 110-12, 117-18, 121-23.

When Dr. Herbert and Mrs. Phoebe Palmer, visiting American revivalists, were holding services in Newcastle in 1859, an Independent minister from the area, the Rev. A. A. Rees, spoke out against the public ministry of women and published his remarks in a pamphlet. At the time Catherine Booth (1829-90) and her husband William were living nearby in Gateshead, where he was minister of a Methodist New Connexion congregation. She responded to Rees with her own vigorous defense, "Female Ministry," which included views that she had been advocating for some six years in correspondence with her family's minister and again with her husband prior to their marriage.[14]

In that earlier correspondence she had argued against the view that held woman to be intellectually and morally inferior to man, affirming their natural equality in God's creation and the irrelevance of gender in the gospel. She disclaimed any interest in altering the domestic and social position of women, but appealed to the benefits to society of "women's exaltation to her proper position mentally and spiritually."[15] In the pamphlet she extended this argument, contending that women's abilities are as high as men's, that in the church there is no more a woman's sphere than a man's sphere, that the witness of scripture taken as a whole is not against female preaching, and that many women have in the past century or so taught and preached with great results—she named such examples as Mary Fletcher, Sarah Mallet, Mary Taft, Elizabeth Fry, and Julia B. Wightman. While accepting the absolute authority of the Bible, she brought another authority to bear on the issue, as she noted in a letter to a New Connexion minister to whom she had sent her pamphlet: "How can it be that the promptings of the Holy Spirit and the precepts of the Word should be in such direct antagonism as Mr. Rees makes it appear? . . .   I cannot but think that the error lies in the interpretation and application of two isolated passages in Paul's writings."[16]

The Booths had each come out of Wesleyan Methodism, being expelled for sympathies with the "Reformers" in the Wesleyan crisis of 1848. They met in the context of this reform movement; he was interested in conducting evangelical meetings and soon became a traveling evangelist for the New Connexion. They were married in 1855. The Conference recalled him from revival work in 1857 and gave him a specific appointment; when in 1861 it continued to deny him appointment as a traveling evangelist, he resigned. She took her own admonitions to heart and began public preaching in 1860. After becoming independent of the denomination in the following year, they worked side-by-side conducting revivals in Cornwall.[17] They founded the East London Mission in 1864 and the Christian Revival Association a year later, with a permanent tent erected in Whitechapel. Eventually a military structure and titles were adopted in 1877 and the name of the operation changed to the Salvation Army. In the organization the fruits of her early concern became evident, as all rank, authority, and duties were open equally to women and men. In the Booths' vision the religious reclamation of the urban poor was pre-eminent, although their enterprises carried a number of implications for broader social reform. And because of her taking up the cause of female ministry, many women, frequently ridiculed by the society at large,[18] were recruited to this work.

The first and most common objection urged against the public exercises of women, is, that they are unnatural and unfeminine. Many labour under a very great but common mistake, viz., that of confounding nature with custom. Use, or custom, makes things appear to us natural, which, in reality, are very unnatural; while, on the other hand, novelty and rarity make very natural things appear strange and contrary to nature. So universally has this power of custom been felt and admitted, that it has given birth to the proverb, "Use is second nature." Making allowance for the novelty of the thing, we cannot discover anything either unnatural or immodest in a Christian woman, becomingly attired, appearing on a platform or in a pulpit. By *nature* she seems fitted to grace either. God has given to woman a graceful form and attitude, winning manners, persuasive speech, and, above all, a finely-toned emotional nature, all of which appear to us eminent *natural* qualifications for public speaking. We admit that want of mental culture, the trammels of custom, the force of prejudice, and one-sided interpretations of scripture, have hitherto almost excluded her from this sphere; but, before such a sphere is pronounced to be unnatural, it must be proved either that woman has not the *ability* to teach or to preach, or that the possession and exercise of this ability unnaturalizes her in other respects; that so soon as she presumes to step on the platform or into the pulpit she loses the delicacy and grace of the female character. Whereas, we have numerous instances of her retaining all that is most esteemed in her sex, and faithfully discharging the duties peculiar to her own sphere, and at the same time taking her place with many of our most useful speakers and writers. Why should woman be confined exclusively to the kitchen and the distaff, any more than man to the field and workshop? Did not God, and has not nature, assigned to man *his* sphere of labour, "to till the ground, and to dress it"? And, if exemption is claimed from this kind of toil for a portion of the male sex, on the ground of their possessing ability for intellectual and moral pursuits, we must be allowed to claim the same privilege for woman; nor can we see the exception more *unnatural* in the one case than in the other, or why God in this solitary instance has endowed a being with powers which He never intended her to employ.

There seems to be a great deal of unnecessary fear of women occupying any position which involves publicity, lest she should be rendered unfeminine by the indulgence of ambition or vanity; but why should woman any more than man be charged with ambition when impelled to use her talents for the good of her race? Moreover, as a labourer in the GOSPEL her position is much higher than in any other public capacity; she is at once shielded from all coarse and unrefined influences and associations; her very vocation tending to exalt and refine all the tenderest and most womanly instincts of her nature. As a matter of fact it is well known to those who have had opportunities of observing the private character and deportment of women engaged in preaching the gospel, that they have been amongst the most amiable, self-sacrificing, and unobtrusive of their sex. . . .

Whether the Church will allow women to speak in *her* assemblies can only be a question of time; common sense, public opinion, and the blessed results of female agency will force her to give us an honest and impartial rendering of the solitary text on which she grounds her prohibitions. Then, when the true light shines and God's words take the place of man's traditions, the Doctor of Divinity who shall teach that Paul commands woman to be silent when God's Spirit urges her to speak, will be regarded much the same as we should regard an astronomer who should teach that the sun is the earth's satellite. . . .

As to the obligation devolving on woman to labour for her Master, I presume there will be no controversy. The particular sphere in which each individual shall do this must be dictated by the teachings of the Holy Spirit and the gifts with which God has endowed her. If she have the necessary gifts, and feels herself called by the Spirit to preach, there is not a single word in the whole book of God to restrain her, but many, very many to urge and encourage her. God says she SHALL do so, and Paul prescribed the manner in which she shall do it, and Phebe, Junia, Philip's four daughters, and many other women actually did preach and speak in the primitive Churches. If this had not been the case, there would have been less freedom under the new than under the old dispensation. A greater paucity of gifts and agencies under the Spirit than under the law. Fewer labourers when more work to be done. Instead of the destruction of caste and division between the priesthood and the people, and the setting up of a spiritual kingdom in which all true believers were "kings and priests unto God," the division would have been more stringent and the disabilities of the common people greater. Whereas we are told again and again in effect, that in "Christ Jesus there is neither bond nor free, male nor female, but ye are all one in Christ Jesus." . . .

As we have before observed, the text, Corinthians xiv. 34, 35, is the *only one* in the whole book of God which even by a false translation can be made prohibitory of female speaking in the Church; how comes it then, that by this one isolated passage, which, according to our best Greek authorities, is wrongly rendered and wrongly applied, woman's lips have been sealed for centuries, and the "testimony of Jesus, which is the spirit of prophecy," silenced, when bestowed on her? How is it that this solitary text has been allowed to stand unexamined and unexplained, nay, that learned commentators who have *known* its true meaning as perfectly as either Robinson, Bloomfield, Greenfield, Scott, Parkhurst, or Locke have upheld the delusion, and enforced it as a divine precept binding on all female disciples through all time? Surely there must have been some unfaithfulness, "craftiness," and "handling of the word of life deceitfully" somewhere. Surely the love of caste and unscriptural jealousy for a separated priesthood has had something to do with this anomaly. By this course divines and commentators have involved themselves in all sorts of inconsistencies and contradictions; and worse, they have nullified some of the most precious promises of God's word. They have set the most explicit predictions of prophecy at variance with apostolic injunctions, and the most immediate and wonderful operations of the Holy Ghost in direct opposition "to positive, explicit, and universal rules."

Notwithstanding, however, all this opposition to female ministry on the part of those deemed authorities in the Church, there have been some in all ages in whom the Holy Ghost has wrought so mightily, that at the sacrifice of reputation and all things most dear, they have been compelled to come out as witnesses for Jesus and ambassadors of His Gospel. As a rule, these women have been amongst the most devoted and self-denying of the Lord's people, giving indisputable evidence by the purity and beauty of their lives that they were led by the Spirit of God. Now, if the word of God forbids female ministry, we would ask how it happens that so many of the most devoted handmaidens of the Lord have felt themselves constrained by the Holy Ghost to exercise it? Surely there must be some mistake somewhere, for the word and the Spirit cannot contradict each other. Either the word does not condemn women preaching, or these confessedly holy women have been deceived. Will anyone venture to assert that such women as Mrs. Elizabeth Fry, Mrs. Fletcher of Madeley, and Mrs. Smith, have been deceived with respect to their call to deliver the Gospel messages to their fellow-creatures? If not, then God does not call and qualify women to preach, and His word, rightly understood, cannot forbid what His Spirit enjoins. . . . A few examples of the blessing which has attended the ministrations of females, may help to throw some light on this matter of a Divine call. . . .

We have endeavoured in the foregoing pages to establish, what we sincerely believe, that woman has a *right* to teach. Here the whole question hinges. If she has the *right*, she has it independently of any man-made restrictions which do not equally refer to the opposite sex. If she has the right, and possesses the necessary qualifications, we maintain that, where the law of expediency does not prevent, she is at liberty to exercise it without any further pretensions to inspiration than those put forth by the male sex. If, on the other hand, it can be proved that she has *not* the right, but that imperative silence is imposed upon her by the word of God, we cannot see who has authority to relax or make exceptions to the law.

If commentators had dealt with the Bible on other subjects as they have dealt with it on this, taking isolated passages, separated from their explanatory connections, and insisting on a literal interpretation of the words of our version, what errors and contradictions would have been forced upon the acceptance of the Church, and what terrible results would have accrued to the world. . . . Judging from the blessed results which have almost invariably followed the ministrations of women in the cause of Christ, we fear it will be found, in the great day of account, that a mistaken and unjustifiable application of the passage, "Let your women keep silence in the Churches," has resulted in more loss to the Church, evil to the world, and dishonour to God, than any of the errors we have already referred to.

And feeling, as we have long felt, that this is a subject of vast importance to the interests of Christ's kingdom and the glory of God, we would most earnestly commend its consideration to those who have influence in the Churches. We think it a matter worthy of their consideration whether God intended woman to bury her talents and influence as she now does? And whether the circumscribed sphere of woman's religious labours may not have something to do with the comparative non-success of the gospel in these latter days.

3. J. Hiles Hitchens, "Preaching Women," *The Congregationalist*, XV (1886):719-26.

By the 1880s the context for considering the ministry of women had changed. Revival preaching was almost a thing of the past, as were the "ranter preachers" of the more free-wheeling Methodist days. Although the Salvation Army was organized, its "Hallelujah lasses" could be dismissed as odd. With the suffrage campaign growing, reform activities of women such as Josephine Butler more visible, and political participation through school boards and other local opportunities more widespread, the issue became rooted in the broader question of the place of women in society. Few were clamoring for women's access to the pulpit; but if women were speaking in public on religious and moral themes, some asked, what next would they seek?

In this general discussion such words as "good taste," "influence," "unseemliness," and "sphere" recur frequently. Margaret Lonsdale thought that "platform women" lowered the standard of womanhood before the rest of the world because they "are descending from their firm pedestal . . .   and are anxiously engaged in climbing up a ladder." And to what end? They are leaving behind acknowledged sovereignty for an uncertain future; "their power may be increasing . . . , but in their proper sphere, a small, it may be only a home circle, their once all-powerful influence is waning."[19] Two Congregationalist ministers took up the debate. J. Hiles Hitchen appealed to Christianity's role in the improvement of the condition of women and wanted to focus attention on the question of sphere. Assessment of scriptural evidence was important to his argument, but beneath this was the broader claim, "Woman's modesty is her crown." George Reaney's reply offered three points of rebuttal. First, he declared that women should be the better judges of the ideals of womanhood. With respect to scripture he argued that Christians must have liberty to decide matters of discipline rather than be bound by first-century perceptions and that "circumstances do alter cases." Finally, he contended that the examples of many public women in the century laid to rest the fear of unseemliness. In a postscript to this debate the editor of *The Congregationalist* agreed with Reaney that scripture could not be used as a permanent prohibition, but thought the issue had to be settled on the basis of expediency—in part, then, on whether people would accept this role for women. His conclusion recalled Lonsdale's and others' fears of the uncertain future: Would women gain in real influence by such a development?

Since the light of Christianity has fallen upon the world there has been a remarkable improvement in the condition of woman. Once she was enslaved, depreciated, and shunned. Once it was declared that "if the world were only free from women, men would not be without the converse of the gods." Even Chrysostom is said to have pronounced woman to be "a necessary evil, a natural temptation, a desirable calamity, a domestic peril, a deadly fascination, and a painted ill." The Hebrew women were secluded from the men, having their own special apartments, so that only the daughters of the humble orders quitted their houses, and then mainly to fetch water or watch the flocks. When they went up to the synagogue they were divided from the men by a partition five or six feet high. . . . But where the Scriptures have been accepted as the will of heaven how altered is the domestic institution! An Italian artist once sketched a woman chained by the ankles to a rock, but portrayed a fountain which sent forth a jet of water, drop after drop of which fell on the links of the chain, and wore them away. Woman was thus fastened to the demoralizing rock of slavery and sin, but the religion of the Scriptures has gradually worn away the infamous fetters, and she today occupies an honoured and dominant position among us.

Not content, however, with the privileges already secured, there is a class of females in this land eagerly pressing forward for what is denominated "women's rights." They demand an entrance into the professions hitherto held almost exclusively by the sterner sex. They have obtained a place in university examinations, and to their credit have shone brilliantly. They have commenced the practice of medicine, in which art they can be of unspeakable service to their own sex. They have not yet figured among the gentlemen of the long robe, nor have they secured seats in the council of legislature. But they have asserted their right to the platform and the preacher's throne. Their voices are now frequently heard addressing promiscuous assemblies upon religious themes.

We are not about to discuss the much debated query of the relative mental capabilities or moral strength of man and woman. Our intention is to deal simply with the question of *sphere*, in which a woman's abilities, great or small, should be exercised. We believe that a woman steps aside from the position appointed her by the Divine Ruler when she enters upon the arduous task of addressing mixed multitudes of men and women.

Woman's nature indicates that she is constitutionally adapted to, and designed for, retirement. With intellectual faculties less productive than receptive; with delicate nervous susceptibilities; with feelings giving birth to thoughts, rather than thought being the parent of feeling; with exquisite sensibility to pain and poverty; with a clinging dependence upon the sterner sex; with blushing modesty and shrinking gentleness; with a voice tremulous with tears, and a fragile physical organism unfitted for the rude, harsh, and prolonged labours of the world, she is specially suited to the sacred duties of home, and unsuited for the excitement and fatigue of the public arena. All the mental and physical strength with which God has endowed her may well be employed in forming the characters, soothing the tempers, banishing the anxieties, and anticipating the necessities of those beneath the domestic roof. Should she have energy for a wider sphere of labour she will find it in the chambers of the poor and sick and dying, where the gentle word of sympathy will be as a balm to the wounded heart; or in the Sabbath school, the Dorcas society, the mother's meeting, and the many other forms of service among her own sex. But let her not come forth as a public mentor to men. The very instincts of humanity protest against a female shaking off her claim to the attention and care of the man, and vaulting to the assumed platform of man's level. Would any such aspirant feel content to be treated by men as an equal?—that is, as men treat their fellow-men?

But it will be said there are cases mentioned in the Scriptures in which females were employed by God for important purposes. We shall be pointed to Miriam, Deborah, Huldah, Noadiah, and Anna, and told that there were prophetesses in ancient times, and that this fact justifies pious women *now* speaking for Christ to mixed assemblies. It must, however, first be shown that these females spoke in public. Of this there is no record whatever in the Scriptures. The word "prophetess" does not necessitate that the person so denominated should be a public speaker. . . . Thus there is no evidence that the prophetesses of Scripture were preachers or public teachers to promiscuous assemblies—no proof that on any single occasion either of them addressed a mixed congregation. If, however, it could be shown that the prophetesses did stand forth on one or more occasions to publish the word and will of God to whomsoever would listen—*that* would not justify women doing so in these times. Those females who aspire to the position of public speakers upon religious themes should evince the qualifications the prophetesses of old possessed. They should give proof that they are directly inspired by God—that for some definite purpose and time Heaven has breathed into their minds important truths which they are Divinely deputed to disclose.

There were attempts in the direction of female preaching in the Apostle's time. He alludes to the *then* growing custom, but does so to denounce it. No words can be stronger than those of the Apostle Paul when he prohibits females speaking in the assemblies of the Church. In I Corinthians xiv. 34, he says, "Let your women keep silence in the churches; for it is not permitted unto them to speak;" . . . "[I]n the churches" must not be accepted according to the modern practice of terming a building a "church," but as meaning the assemblies of the avowed followers of Christ whenever met together for religious observances. . . . The word here rendered "to speak" is very suggestive. It is the most comprehensive term the Apostle could have chosen. He does not say that the woman shall not *preach* or *teach,* but she shall not *speak.* . . . He selects one [term] that will cover *all* speaking, whether in prayer, preaching, or asking questions, and says, it is not permitted unto women *to speak.* Surely no rule can be more positive, more comprehensive, or more explicit than this. Its universality is also shown by the plural *ekklesias*—churches. The rule does not apply to the one church at Corinth, but to the churches generally. . . . Paul advising Timothy on the mode of conducting public worship, says, I Timothy ii. 11, 12, "Let the woman learn in silence, with all subjection. But I suffer not a woman to teach." . . . So that the Apostle gives Timothy a general rule for all cases and times, and says the woman's duty is to learn, not to teach in public, and her attitude is that of silent subjection, not voluble usurpation of authority.

To evade these strict injunctions it may be said that changes occur in the habits and manners of people with the lapse of years; that many things customary in Paul's time are not customary now, and *vice versa*; that circumstances alter cases, and hence the prohibition is *not* binding. But such an objection strikes at the very root of Scripture precepts. Who is to determine what is and what is not subject to alteration in its application to our social life and ecclesiastical practice? Adopting such a lax method of interpreting the contents of the Holy Book, one man will dispose of one duty and another of another till the volume is robbed of its applicability to the state of modern society, and will cease to be a guide to any man's steps. Was not the Apostle as much inspired when he penned the words we have quoted above as when he penned other portions of his Epistles? If he *was*, then they are as binding upon us as other directions. If he was *not*, let it be shown that such was the case, and to what exact extent. We fail to find any internal or external evidence which can help us to make any distinction as to the authoritative force between these and other of his writings.

Moreover, the Apostle himself presents reasons for enjoining the prohibitions given, which reasons are universal and perpetual in their application. . . . Here are three reasons, namely, the priority of man's creation, the pliancy of the feminine character, and the propriety of modesty in women. *All these three reasons still exist, and exist in all lands.* That man was first spoken into existence and made lord of the lower creation before woman was given him as his helpmeet will always remain a fact, to remind humanity that woman is not to usurp authority. That woman was the first to fall, and then by her example and entreaties induced the man to sin also, is likewise a fact which will ever remain as a sad indication of the feebleness of will which characterized her. Nor, let us hope, will it ever cease to be an acknowledged fact in society that modesty is proper and desirable in the female sex. Woman's modesty is her crown. Every husband would rather have his wife quietly shine in the "little royalty of home" than unblushingly neglect that nearest and dearest of all spheres of work, and self-complacently illumine the minds of an indiscriminate audience. Whilst this is so, the reason assigned by the Apostle for woman's silence in the public gatherings of the Church will continue to exist. Let her exert her influence for good upon those who are under the domestic roof, and "learn first to show piety at home;" let her engage in sick visitation, Sabbath-school tuition, Zenana missions, and any other method of usefulness where she has to deal with her own sex; but let her eschew the pulpit and the platform where she is brought into unseemly rivalry with, or indecorous authority over, men. We do not deny that there are devout and intelligent women whose public ministrations are greatly appreciated and widely useful. But such should be regarded as exceptional cases, and by no means an encouragement to the development of such a practice. That there have been pious and serviceable nuns does not justify every religious female becoming a recluse, nor demonstrate that the vow of perpetual chastity is right. It will scarcely be affirmed that because the French heroine, Joan of Arc, clad herself in armour, and conducted the troops victoriously, therefore it is a proper thing for women to be warriors. Indeed, it is probable that the excellent women who have devoted so much energy to public preaching would have been—and some may yet be—far more honoured of God and man if they confined their ministrations to their own sisterhood. We contend that public addresses by women to promiscuous gatherings are offensive to good taste, opposed to feminine characteristics, and antagonistic to Scriptural directions.

4. George Sale Reaney, "Preaching Women," *The Congregationalist*, XV (1886):844-49.

It is always a rather difficult task for men to discuss the true sphere of women. Many men have many ideas as to what the woman, the wife, the mother, the daughter, and sister ought to do and be. The truest conception of womanhood can only be possessed by women. Dr. Hitchens has an ideal of his own, and in its negative side it may be summed up in the phrase, half contemptuous and half fearful—Preaching women. This ideal seems to present itself to Dr. Hitchens' mind as something more than ideal. Scripture seems to ring with the command from end to end, "Thou shalt not preach." The spectacle of a pulpit with a woman in it evidently greatly exercises our friend's mind. A male minister, orating to empty pews from year to year, does not move his mind; but the moment a Christian lady, cultivated, modest, and full of tender and earnest love of souls, enters the pulpit and begins a ministry that is fruitful with good, then he flies to questionable Scripture expositions and exaggerated moralizings for consolation. Dr. Hitchens' whole idea is that woman is too tender, sensitive, and gentle to speak to men and women about Him who was in character both woman and man. For the domestic duties, for the sick chamber, for the Sabbath school, and the mothers' meeting, she is well fitted; but to say a word to men and women about home life, purity, good temper, watchful care of each other, and chivalrous honour, with deep faith in Christ and noble living—for that, because she is a woman, she is utterly unfit.

She may become a hospital nurse, and discharge the most delicate duties for men as well as women; she may follow the path of war and mingle with its horrible scenes; she may visit the lowest haunts of vice as a sister of mercy; but the moment her congregation enlarges and the men come in with their wives and daughters, then she is bound, by everything that is scriptural, womanly, and in good taste, to leave the pulpit, disperse her congregation, and end her work. This extraordinary position is justified by some rather prejudiced references to Holy Writ. Challenged by the fact that women did take a very prominent part not only in the domestic, but the judicial, military, and prophetic incidents of the life of Israel, Dr. Hitchens endeavours to escape the difficulty by an attempt to reduce the character of those notable women to the feeble type, "tremulous with tears and of fragile organism," with which he sets out. But we can but think that the attempt fails. Miriam was surely something more than a leader of women in music and song. Was she not one of the three whom God by Micah says He sent before His people? Did she hide her blushing face in her tent when with Aaron she rebuked Moses because he had married an Ethiopian woman? Miriam was punished, but we cannot think of her as a timid, nervous creature, but rather as a woman of strong character, and one suited in many senses to be in counsel with her brother, and a leader of the people.

. . . Was Deborah the timid, blushing type of woman of whom Dr. Hitchens seems so much in love? The references to Huldah, Noadiah, and Anna are, I think, equally insufficient in a true appreciation of the publicity and greatness of the work they did—a publicity and greatness that in no sense spoilt their womanhood or marred the beauty, devotion, and splendid bravery of all but one of them. The time may come when in the motherhood and wifehood of our land we may need women who shall combine strength with tenderness, and high public spirit with true and gentle love.

But Dr. Hitchens' main argument is based upon Paul's very energetic dealing with what, I suppose, Dr. Hitchens would call the preaching women in the Church at Corinth. . . . Paul may have insisted that women should be utterly dumb in the Christian assemblies. The reference to Timothy is quite conclusive, I admit, if the rule laid down by Paul is to be absolute, universal, and final. I venture to think that there must be some liberty left to the Christian Church in these matters of discipline. What is the use of the guidance of the Holy Spirit if we are bound hand and foot to the letter of all Paul's injunctions and arguments? Is it not generally admitted that for a Greek woman to be in any sense educated carried with it a "shamefulness" that can only be hinted at in the pages of a family magazine? Was Paul quite in ignorance of these things? But did not Paul say something in regard to women in the public assemblies on which all our mothers and wives ought at once with eager earnestness to get some exposition from Dr. Hitchens? Are we quite sure that the modern "covering" worn by women in our churches is quite up to the orthodox shape and size used by the women in Paul's day? It may be that the apostle might, if he were with us, rule that many of the Christian women are not only barefaced, but bareheaded. Will Dr. Hitchens give some little attention to this? for this too may be a "shame" upon our womanhood, and the only truly apostolic female headgear a "cowl" or a hood somewhat after the fashion that babies wear.

When Paul wrote the Christian faith had not freed the women from the thraldom of man's passions and jealousy. It took many centuries to accomplish this. Can Dr. Hitchens ask us to accept his exposition of Paul's decision as to preaching women in the first century as binding upon all womanhood for all time? Can any of us imagine Paul *then* giving his consent to Christian girls studying at the public schools, taking degrees in medicine, nursing in public hospitals, and visiting the poorest parts of Corinth and Rome, and ministering alike to men and women in their sorrow, sickness, and sin? Circumstances do alter cases, and in the "household of God" some discretion is surely left to those who are the children of that home. It is more than unjust to say that the womanhood of the Christian Church is to be ruled in matters of personal service by regulations laid down by Paul at a time when the position of women *in* the Church was largely conditioned by her place in the heathen world. The gospel has changed these things, and to say that they are just as they were when Paul wrote to Corinth can only be consistent when Dr. Hitchens sets to work to wash other people's feet.

But a further argument is adduced by Dr. Hitchens, and that is the unseemliness of preaching women. Here, I need scarcely say, he touches upon very delicate ground. . . . I will put what is a very good test case. For many years there is one Church in which the public ministry of women has been sanctioned with the fullest approval of some of the most cautious and grave of men. The Quakers have long been celebrated for their preaching women. What has been the effect upon the "women" of that Church? Can Dr. Hitchens tell me of any women more given to home duties, any whose characters are more uniformly grave, gentle, courteous, and in the fullest sense beautiful in the highest sense of Christian womanhood? May I go further? Are the women ministers of the Society of Friends any exception to the high type of the women of that Christian community? Now, if Dr. Hitchens' essay were true, we ought to find amongst the Quakers many women with little modesty and less grace. The contrary is true. Dr. Hitchens' references to the lack of all this in the character of preaching women is as true and generous as the contemptible sneer at the "feebleness" of Eve. Why did not he remember the much more contemptible feebleness of Adam in being led by the nose by such a miserable creature? Why did he not let a little of his scorn out upon the cowardice of Adam when he laid all the blame upon the woman? What right has Dr. Hitchens to point such a suggestive insult as this? "Nor, let us hope, will it ever cease to be an acknowledged

fact in society that modesty is proper and desirable in the female sex." Will he
tell me whether that is lacking in Mrs. Josephine Butler, Mrs. Ormistan Chant,
Mrs. Lucas, and a score of others I could mention? Immodesty! Why does not
my friend attack the immodesty of dress which he must often witness in West-End
drawing-rooms and amongst the very well-dressed women of society? What right,
too, has Dr. Hitchens to print this? "Every husband would rather have his wife
quietly shine in the 'little royalty of home' than unblushingly neglect the nearest
and dearest of all spheres of work, and self-complacently illumine the minds of an
indiscriminate audience." How dare Dr. Hitchens make so widespread a charge
against women whom he cannot know either in the pulpit or in their homes! The
qualification made a little lower down does not take the sting out of a bit of rhetoric
that has added nothing to the force of Dr. Hitchens' argument, but has somewhat
spoilt its otherwise gentlemanly tone. Dr. Hitchens is somewhat affrighted with the
prospect of a great army of women preachers. He need not fear, women so gifted
are not the many in our Churches. Is it not a mistake to make the pathway of
their service more difficult by raising the cry unwomanly? The whole essay should
lead its author further. He ought to send it to the Queen, with the most respectful
request that she will abdicate and get the Salic law passed, for ever barring the
throne from any woman.

5. Arnold Pinchard, "Women and the Priesthood" (London, 1916).

Some historians have argued that the Tractarian support of sisterhoods provided
the most radical religious response to the question of the vocation of women in Victorian
society.[20] Within the Church of England at that time the public ministry of women—
in the more technical sense—was not an issue. But when it became a matter for
consideration it was soon obvious that the Anglo-Catholic successors to the Tractarians
had very definite limits to their understanding of the place of women in the Church, and
these did not include ordination to the priesthood! The English Church Union, founded
in 1859, promoted the high church cause by its attention to sacramental theology,

defense of ritual and ritualists, and interest in Catholic validation of Anglican orders. In due course it opposed women priests. Arnold Pinchard, who wrote the following tract when vicar of St. Jude's, Birmingham, became Secretary of the organization in 1920. His argument focused the Anglo-Catholic opposition on the connections between theology, biology, and history. Because of certain absolute differences between male and female, the male has been given (by God in creation) a priority of initiative and decision. Because solely masculine terms are used for God (even though God is of no sex), because Jesus Christ was male, and because he chose only males to govern the Church, Pinchard concluded that God's will is to exclude women from governance of the Church. Their model should be the Virgin Mary, who provides the ideal of exalted womanhood. The argument had no need of the Pauline injunctions, so it could not be debated through exegesis. Being based in a form of determinism, it was difficult to debate at all.

The question is occasionally asked as to why women cannot be admitted to the sacred ministry of the Catholic Church. At the moment of writing, the question is being debated with considerable warmth, even in church newspapers. It may perhaps, therefore, be just as well to see how one may arrive at an intelligent and reasonable answer to the question.

There is, of course, a priesthood of the laity, which belongs just as much to women as it does to men. All women who are members of the mystical Body of Christ, are kings and priests before God, in just the same sense that men are: and no doubt women might do (and indeed do already) a great deal more in the minor councils of the Church than they did in the past, and perhaps they will do even more in the future. But we are dealing now with the one simple question, as to whether women should or could be admitted to the sacred ministry of the Catholic Church; whether it is a feasible proposition that women should ever be ordained as priests or consecrated as bishops.

It seems that there are four or five fundamental and important facts, which have to be considered carefully before it is possible to answer this question in a final and decisive manner. Let us state these facts in order:

1. The nature of the spirit of man, and the likeness and the difference between male and female nature in human experience.

2. The fact that in Holy Scripture God is always spoken of as though he were of the male sex; that masculine descriptive terms are aways used by the Holy Ghost in speaking of the Godhead.

3. The fact that, when the Everlasting Son took human nature from the womb of the Blessed Virgin, his Mother, he took *male* human nature.

4. The fact that Our Lord Jesus Christ is shown to have deliberately excluded women from the government of the Church, by and in the fact that he excluded the Mother of God from any such position.

5. The fact of the Assumption of the Blessed Virgin St Mary, after her death, to her proper place in heaven.

1. All human beings are essentially and eternally spirits. They belong to the family of God and of the angels. . . .

The fact that one spirit-soul has to make its way in a male body, and another in a female body, towards the day of deliverance and of perfection, is a fact of the very greatest importance; and any attempt to minimise the necessary difference which this means between one human being and another is both dangerous and wrong. But it is very important also to remember that these conditions of male and female nature are a purely temporal and transitory accommodation to necessity, ordained by God for the present conditions of human life. They involve, of course, primarily, a physical difference: but, so close and intimate is the relation between spirit and body, that the physical difference always carries with it other differences— temperamental, mental, and moral—which are as obvious to anybody who takes the trouble to consider them as they are inevitable, and which must always be taken into account in considering questions of this sort.

Now these differences between men and women are closely related to and accord with the purpose which governs the physical difference. The very qualities which you require in a mother are those which belong specially to womanhood, as considered in comparison with manhood. Consequently, however much some people may endeavour to ignore or to deny the fact, there are certain things which women do far better than men, and some things which are only and exclusively to be done by women. On the other hand, there are some things which men do far better than women, and some which are exclusively and rightly to be done only by men. Between these extremes there lies an enormous range of activity, physical and intellectual, which is equally open to men and women alike. . . .

Perhaps it is wrong to use the word 'superiority,' yet it is difficult to know quite what word to use. Perhaps one should call it, not so much a 'superiority,' as a Priority of Initiative and of Decision, which belongs to the male sex, but does not detract in any kind of way from the essential equality of the one sex with the other in the general conduct of life.

It seems that this priority of initiative and decision is a part of the Divine intention in creation. It seems to be closely related to all the physical facts which dominate the case; to carry with it a special responsibility in the partnership of men and women; to involve the endurance and the deliberate acceptance by the male of certain risks, dangers and labours, which women, for obvious reasons, ought not and cannot be called upon to endure. And further, it seems to carry with it a kind of final responsibility for guidance and decision in difficulties and differences that must inevitably arise in the imperfect conduct of life under present conditions. . . .

The man is not necessarily either better, or wiser, because of it. It is a useful accommodation to inevitable circumstances in the practical conduct of daily life, which does not touch the question of the equality of the one sex with the other, any more than the same kind of thing touches the fact of the equality of God the Father, God the Son, and God the Holy Ghost, in the life of the Blessed Trinity.

In the life of the Blessed Trinity, which, of course, is the ideal, perfect life, presented to us for our contemplation, you will find the same kind of thing. We believe that, in that undivided unity of the Blessed Trinity, the Father is equal to the Son and the Son is equal to the Father, in the truest sense of the word. Yet it remains that the Father is father, and the Son, son. It remains that there belongs to God the Father, in the Blessed Trinity, just that kind of priority of initiative and of decision in the conduct of the Divine life, which belongs to the male, as differentiated from the female, in the conduct of this human life of ours. That illustrates what is meant when one says that the fact of this priority of initiative and decision, which belongs to men, does not infringe upon or diminish anything from the reality and truth of the equality that subsists, and ought to be recognised as subsisting, between men and women in the conduct of the affairs of life.

2. Now consider the second fact. Why is God always spoken of in Holy Scripture in masculine terms?—have you ever asked yourself that question? God is no more male than he is female, and one would have thought that some neutral term might have been used by the Holy Ghost in speaking about God. But it is not so. Always masculine terms are used about God. There is no reason that we know for it, at the first glance, though we shall perhaps see one directly.

3. Again, in this connection one must inevitably ask why the Everlasting Son, who is neither male nor female but pure Spirit, when he took flesh from the womb of the Blessed Virgin and was made Man, did also specifically assume male human nature. There must be some reason why the Incarnate is necessarily and properly of the male sex. Why should not such an one as the Blessed Virgin St Mary, conceived without sin by the intervention and interposition of Divine grace, in her spotless and

unsullied purity and with her immeasurable capacity for self-sacrifice and love—why should not such an one as she have bled upon the Cross and risen from the dead, and have been the vehicle for the redemption and salvation of mankind? Why is the Christ necessarily not a woman? . . . Since God took this way and, in his Divine wisdom, did assume the male sex in the Incarnation, we may be perfectly certain that it was absolutely necessary, and that there were, and still are, the very best of reasons for the adoption of this course.

As has been said, we may not be able to see or understand all the reasons at present. With a little care, we may find one reason, at any rate, which very closely affects the question which is before us. God, of course, has no sex—he is neither male nor female, but pure Spirit. It follows, then, that the sex of the Incarnate and the deliberate application to himself, by God, of masculine descriptive terms, while they imply nothing at all about the essential nature of God, do, nevertheless, imply that there is something very important in the fundamental difference which God, in creation, has caused to be in the nature of men and women and in their relations with one another.

When God would reveal something about himself to men, it is necessary that he should do so in the terms of human language, life and experience. . . . Now the fact in humanity, and the only fact that we know of, which can possibly govern this use of masculine language and this deliberate adoption of the male sex by the Incarnate, is that very thing of which we have been speaking, namely, the endowment in creation of the male sex with this priority of initiative and decision which, by the Divine decree, governs the relations of male and female for purposes of the practical conduct of life in time. It appears then that a right conception of the true relation of God to the Universe and of the Incarnate to the human family is conveyed to the mind of man by the use of masculine descriptive terms applied to God, and by the adoption of the male sex by the Incarnate. And this both verifies the idea that a Priority of Initiative and Decision does belong to the male sex and by this Divine recognition of it emphasizes and confirms its importance.

4. On these considerations, it will not be altogether a matter for surprise to find that, in his provision for the work of the Church in the world, Our Lord Jesus Christ placed the government in the hands and under the control of men, as such; and that for the same reason he deliberately excluded women from the priesthood of his Church. It may be doubted whether one is justified in using so strong a phrase, as to say that he deliberately excluded women from this position; but let us remember that Our Lord was perfectly free to choose and to do as he thought right and wise. If he had thought fit to open the priesthood to women, he had, what would seem to us, an exceptionally good opportunity. No one could have been more considerate of or have set a higher value upon the spiritual powers and the love and devotion of women than he. Nevertheless, with the choice open to him, and valuing as he did the services of women, he deliberately excluded from the government of his Church the one woman who, of all others, would, one imagines, have been best capable of such service, had it been at all desirable in the will and wisdom of God that any woman should be called upon to undertake that responsibility and to do that particular kind of work. . . .

5. If anyone were to suggest that this deliberate exclusion of women from one particular kind of work and activity in Christ's Church implies, or could imply, anything disparaging to womanhood, he would be suggesting an idea that is quite impossible of acceptance. When one remembers the love and consideration that the Perfect Son, even in his last hour of agony, always manifested towards his Perfect Mother, it is impossible to suppose that he would have done, or allowed to be done, anything which would be derogatory to the dignity of womanhood in her. But, further, there are two considerations which must be taken into account, and which more than counterbalance the fact of the exclusion of women from the priesthood.

There is, first of all, the extraordinary honour which is conferred upon womanhood by the fact that Blessed Mary is, for all eternity, Mother of God; and, secondly, the fact of her elevation to the highest place that heaven affords to any member of the human family, under the Incarnate himself.

6. "Women and the Priesthood" (London: League of the Church Militant, n.d.).

> Anglican activities on behalf of an increased role for women in the Church emerged naturally out of the suffrage movement. When partial suffrage for women was achieved in 1918 the Church League for Women's Suffrage was brought to an end. In that work an interest in the ordination of women had grown steadily, but it seemed appropriate to seek other opportunities for advocacy than those which had been directed along political lines. Thus a new organization, The League of the Church Militant, was established in 1919 with a new goal, "working primarily for the admission of women to Holy Orders." It was in turn succeeded by the broader, interdenominational Society for the Ministry of Women in 1929, whose stated ambition was "to secure equal opportunities for women with men in the service of the Church." The League's hopes were stated very optimistically in a public letter to the press in 1928: "Since the League started its work of education and propaganda, thought on women's service in the Church has advanced so rapidly that it was felt that ordination to the priesthood must inevitably follow in due time, and that the best way that women of this and future generations could further this cause was by prayer for its fulfillment and by preparing themselves mentally and spiritually to meet those opportunities and responsibilities of service in the Church that may open up to them in the future."[21] A number of leaflets and pamphlets advocated its position, of which the following anonymously-authored document is a good example.

It is the conviction of the members of the League of the Church Militant that the time has come when it is necessary to do more than say that, apart from the apparent witness of catholic custom, they can discern no reason why women should be excluded from the priesthood. They believe it to be incumbent upon them to urge that what threatens to be the last remaining sex disability should be removed, and that the Church should call to its sacred ministry those women as well as men who believe they are inwardly moved to undertake the priestly office, under such disciplinary regulations as it may judge best for the edification of its members.

They feel that as matters now stand the Chuch is perpetuating at the very innermost shrine of its ordered life a tradition, partly Jewish, partly pagan, which the rest of the world has in theory abandoned or is on the eve of abandoning, a tradition which is the fruitful source of much which is amiss in sex relationships, which is wholly inconsistent with the Catholic faith—the tradition of the inferiority of women. One of our Bishops has recently told us, whilst repudiating the thought that women are inferior in nature to men, that women are subordinate to men, that to man belongs a permanent and essential headship, and that this truth has been embodied in the refusal of the Church to call women to the priesthood. Very well. We repudiate "subordination" just as earnestly as we repudiate "inferiority"; we deny that upon man there is conferred according to the divine intention a permanent and essential headship. Can it be a matter of wonder that we feel bound to call in question a restriction which is openly set forth as witnessing in the ordered life of the Church to a principle which with all our hearts we believe to be a hoary falsehood, fraught with pernicious consequences to the society which accepts it and necessarily antagonistic to the foundation principles of the Catholic faith?

For that we take to be the essence of the whole matter. If "the priesthood for men only" were a claim advanced solely on grounds of practical convenience, if it had all along been admitted that women were capable of the priesthood and their exclusion from it had been justified on grounds of expediency alone, then, though we should have denied the expediency and felt that the Church was rejecting much needed service and that women were being improperly debarred from work to which they believed the Holy Spirit was calling them, we should have admitted that there was much to be said on both sides, and our challenge to the Church to reconsider its ways would have been made in milder tones than it is to-day. For to-day we have no care to dissemble our indignation that one of the most liberal-minded prelates in England should stand forth as the exponent of views which involve acceptance of the doctrine of male domination (but perhaps "headship" no more involves "domination" than essential and permanent "subordination" implies "inferiority"!) and that the voice of authority on all sides should be loud in asserting that there are fundamental reasons which render women unfit to minister at the altar.

But though we are indignant we are not disloyal. We shall promote no schism. We shall not counsel our members to withdraw from altars at which they are forbidden to minister nor urge them to refuse to contribute to the maintenance of a ministry in which they may not share. We shall not seek to organise parliamentary pressure to further the cause we have at heart. We shall make our appeal to the Church. We shall rely on the truth and the truth will prevail.

And though indignant we are not unreasonable. We are perfectly aware that no Bishop can rightly ordain women to the priesthood on his own individual responsibility. If any are disposed to argue that not even the whole Anglican Communion could rightly decide on such a step without the concurrent assent of the rest of Christendom, we shall give attentive hearing to such arguments even if we should ultimately come to reject them as inadequate. We are conscious that there are many difficult questions which must be determined before any woman can be ordained a priest. Is a vocation to the ministry compatible in the case of a woman with a vocation to matrimony? If not, must women priests be vowed to celibacy, and, if so, at what age should such vows be accepted? These are only some of the problems which will call for solution, which would make precipitate action unthinkable. But we do desire a speedy acknowledgment on the part of the Church that woman is capable of the priesthood and that any hesitation about throwing open the priesthood to women is due to reasons of ecumenical statesmanship or domestic convenience, not to reasons of principle. When that has been explicitly affirmed and accepted we should hope to be able to show that the practical difficulties were not insuperable.

There are those who believe that women are capable of the priesthood and desire that they should serve in the priesthood, but are yet persuaded that the time is not ripe for such a change. In a sense we agree with them. The time will not be ripe for such a change until our Church as a whole feels that it is guided to make it by the Spirit of God, and at present our Church is conscious of no such guidance. But the guidance of the Holy Spirit is rarely if ever vouchsafed in the first instance to the Church as a whole. One here, one there, becomes conscious of a new aspect of divine truth and proclaims what his eyes have seen. At first his words seem as idle tales, his vision is ridiculed; but the very opposition he encounters makes his testimony more insistent, and by and by all perceive the truth and wonder that it was ever hidden from them. In the spiritual world the dawn will never come if the heralds of the dawn hold their peace.

7. A. E. Oldroyd, "The Place of Women in the Church" (London, 1917).

The involvement of women in the suffrage movement eventually provoked questions concerning their exclusion from decision-making in the Church of England. But besides these political spin-offs, it was the increasing participation of women in the life of church and society that collided with principles held by such people as A. E. Oldroyd, vicar of St. James, West Hampstead. Some bishops, including Talbot and Gore early in the twentieth century, favored inclusion of women in the Councils of the Church of England; the Life and Liberty movement, founded in 1917, had a greater place for women as one of its foci for Church reform. "Democracy" was in the air. But it still needed to be debated, as Oldroyd, Bishop Henson, and others claimed, whether democracy was an appropriate foundation for the Church. Can progress, that is, greater realization of the truth, come first to the world and then to the Church? It should be noted that Oldroyd, whose strongest complaints were directed against women's participation in the Church and based on tradition, scripture, and biology, was also not very pleased with the greater involvement of lay men in the Church.

A combination of external pressures and fears that women would leave the Church if a greater voice were denied them ultimately defeated Oldroyd's argument. Each advance followed the changing status of women in politics. In 1905 only women who could vote in local elections were permitted to vote for parish council representatives. In 1914 all lay women could vote for and be elected to parish council offices, but not for regional councils above them. After national suffrage passed, the Church followed suit with equal rights for lay women in 1919. To those who objected to the concepts of equality and rights, this was a bitter blow. In this process the burden of proof had shifted, for the Church was no longer a political "kingdom" and had become at least a fully representative community (save for the ministry), if not a democracy.

The claim that "women may occupy any position and exercise any function in the Church that men do" has come to the fore too rapidly and asserted itself too widely to be a natural outcome of Church life; the demands made, the names of the leaders, the time, place, phraseology, and manner of the agitation, all combine to prove that the movement is rather an overflow from the political into the ecclesiastical sphere, than a legitimate development within the Church.

As in the political sphere the initial franchise is avowedly only a step to further advances, so in the ecclesiastical sphere, while some women's societies carefully print the words "laymen" and "laywomen" in their official version of the above claim, nevertheless writers and speakers associated with them state quite frankly that their demand includes the admission of women to the Diaconate, to the Priesthood, and to the Episcopate, on the same terms as men, and as frankly state their reasons for the demand, viz., that women have gifts for that work equally with men, "and that the teaching of Christ recognizes no distinction of nationality, class, or sex."

With the question of "Holy Orders" we do not intend to deal, except incidentally, in this paper; we confine our attention chiefly to the lesser demand, that laywomen, equally with laymen, shall be "permitted to vote for and serve as representatives on all *Lay Assemblies* of the Church, and that all other offices in the Church to which *laymen* are admitted shall be open also to laywomen, e.g., the office of *lay reader* (which carries with it permission to preach), of server, etc."

Now, two features stand out very prominently in the literature of this women's movement in the Church: first, the frequent use of the words, "*democracy*" and "*equality*"; and, secondly, that the examples of women ministers quoted as precedents are often taken from the annals of ancient heretical sects, or modern "Free Churches." While one writer indeed boldly states that for three hundred and fifty years after Christ women exercised the priesthood, and for eight hundred years served at the altar, she fails to state whether they were heathen or Christian priestesses, and when we look for proof, it is perforce admitted that the general claim is clean contrary to the Catholic tradition of the Church for two thousand years.

But surely we have the right to demand that professing *Churchwomen* shall consider this question from the standpoint of Church principles, and not from that of political expediency or modern undenominationalism. Most of their arguments begin at the wrong end, and seem more concerned with the supposed grievances of women than with God's revelation and the faith and practice of the Church.

Before jumping to a sudden and superficial decision on this vexed and complicated question, it would seem necessary to consider three preliminary questions: (1) Is the Church of Christ essentially democratic in its organization? (2) What position may "laymen" rightly hold in the councils and offices of the Church? (3) Is it right, seemly, and expedient that women should publicly exercise all the functions that a layman may rightly perform?

(1) Our Blessed Lord's declaration, "My kingdom is not of this world," seems to carry with it two deductions (a) that the Church is a kingdom, and not a democracy; (b) that its authority, constitution, and organization is not of the same character

as that of earthly kingdoms, for its constitution and authority come from above, from its only Head and King, Jesus Christ, God's Son, and not from below, not even from the *laos*, still less from the *daemos*.

The Catholic Church has ever taught that "the fullness of the grace of God can flow *freely* only through one channel, the channel of Apostolic Succession from Jesus Christ; not through all men, but through some men." As it is with sacramental grace, so is it with the teaching of the Faith. It is not a question as to whether one man is as clever as another, or whether women are as clever and as eloquent as men; it is a question of the revelation of the truth and the interpretation of that revelation by the Church which alone has authority to do so. Whereas the arguments used in the present agitation must, if logically applied, destroy the Apostolic Succession, and place the cleverness of private judgment above the divinely ordered guidance of the Church Catholic.

. . . [T]he Church is not of the world, but called out of the world: not a *daemos* at all, but a *laos*. No one can become a baptized member of the Church, one of the *laos*, without explicitly renouncing the world and adopting a standard differing from that of the *daemos*. It is the business of the Church to Christianize the world, not of the world to democratize the Church. The kingdoms of this world are to become the Kingdom of God and His Christ, and not *vice versa*. How can there be such a thing as a democratic Church? It is a flat contradiction of terms; the more democratic and the less Church of the Lord, till once more the people and not Christ reigns. A voluntary society may be organized on what is called "democratic lines," but such a society cannot be a Church. The voice of the people is by no means the voice of God in matters of Faith and practice, and the constitution and authority of the Church do not depend on the suffrages of the people.

(2) What place may a "layman" occupy in the Church? . . .   That laymen were sometimes present at Church Councils is admitted; that they were constituent

members with a vote is not proved; that the consent of the laity was necessary before any decision, or canon, or usage became ecumenical, is a simple truism. But that is a very different thing to giving the laity a legal and preponderating vote in the decisions of the Church on matters of Faith and practice. . . .

So with regard to the offices in the Church which a layman may lawfully occupy: no licence from any individual Bishop can properly delegate to a layman that which is reserved to the clergy, *e.g.* to ministerially present the alms of the people at the Altar, as some do, or to pronounce the absolution and benediction, as others do, or to stand up (while the rest of the laity kneel) during the recitation of the prayers. Thus the layman has already intruded where he ought not to be, and it is not advisable that Eve should follow Adam.

There is much criticism of clerical preaching, but it is safe to say that if the present system of preaching by selected laymen is widened to include more of it, and by women as well as by men, there will be a great outcry from the laity against it when the glamour of novelty is worn off (cf. the local preachers on Wesleyan plans).

(3) Can women lawfully fulfil any function within the Church which laymen lawfully execute? Here we trench on that other word which is so frequently heard in this discussion, viz. *"equality."*

Just as the phrase, "Government of the people by the people for the people," is a fine platform phrase, but in reality nowhere exists—for the democracy simply elects one or more individuals who do the ruling, and so create a monarchy (rule by one, whatever he is called) or an aristocracy (rule by a council supposed to be of the best), and behind both alike the shade of a Cromwell or a Napoleon is always waiting for the democracy-in-a-muddle to welcome a Dictator—so the word *"equality"* has a fine flavour in this form, but simply does not exist outside the equality of Persons in the ever-Blessed Trinity. In organisms (as distinct from manufactured articles) no two of any species whatever are equal, and to talk about equality between men and women is really quite nonsense, because it nowhere exists.

The whole discussion has started from a wrong basis; there are no rights, either of men or women, as distinct from duties. The question is really one of *function*, not of right; and no one can for a moment maintain that the function of a woman is the same as that of a man . . . The oft-quoted text, "In Christ Jesus there is neither Jew nor Gentile, male nor female, bond nor free," cannot by any stretch of imagination be made to cover the abolition of the differences of nationality, or sex, or class; for that is simply and, as a fact, impossible.

Moreover, many things which may, as a matter of logic, be as *lawful* for a woman as for a man, are not *expedient*; and many more simply won't work, and any attempt to force nature spells disaster to the woman; *e.g.* the Deaconess cannot receive and exercise exactly the same powers as the Deacon, unless she abrogates her sex and abstains from marriage; but if she is to be released from the obligation of the Diaconate on her marriage, then she must not claim Holy Order, for that confers indelible character. Whereas no such disability attaches to the married Deacon as to the married Deaconess. For this reason even the younger widows were to be refused and not "taken into the number." . . .

Again, with regard to official ministering in the congregation, it may be that a woman is spiritually as qualified as a *layman*, but nevertheless it is not seemly that she should minister publicly in a mixed congregation, nor that she should fulfil the duties of a server at the Altar; and it is curious that those who advocate this are the same who demand women-confessors for women-penitents, and for just this very reason. While, with regard to the highest offices, it is safe to say that the highest office of womanhood is motherhood, and the highest office of manhood is Priesthood; and that the two offices are not interchangeable. A woman is *incapable* of the Priesthood, even as a man is incapable of motherhood. . . . .

In conclusion, we who care for and believe in the Catholic Church more than the ever-shifting opinions and cults of Modernism, feel it our duty to ask our fellow-Churchmen and Churchwomen, "sharers together of the grace of God," to consider this question from the standpoint of the Catholic Faith, and not from that of modern politics, "that our prayers be not hindered" by secular wrangles, and that the whole body of the faithful may be edified and built up as "the Body of Christ," and not as a modern, up-to-date republic of the world.

8. A. Maude Royden, "The Ministry of Women" (London: League of the Church Militant, Leaflet No. 8, n.d.)

Described by one contemporary source as the "world's greatest woman preacher,"[22] A. Maude Royden (1876-1956) was both a leader and a victim in the efforts to enhance opportunities for the ministry of women. Born in Liverpool to a family of means she was educated at the Cheltenham College for Young Ladies and Lady Margaret Hall, Oxford. She worked for a time at a settlement house in Liverpool and then became "unpaid curate" to the Rev. Hudson Shaw, whom she had first met in 1901.[23] She became the first woman lecturer in the University Extension program directed by Oxford, but was soon deeply involved in the suffrage movement, traveling extensively and speaking almost daily. An early leader in the Church League for Women's Suffrage, she delivered its May Mission Speeches in 1910; and for two years (1913-14) she was editor of *The Common Cause*, the weekly organ of the National Union of Women's Suffrage Societies.

In 1917 Royden was invited by Joseph Fort Newton, an American minister who had been brought to the City Temple (Congregational) in London, to become his assistant.[24] She had never preached before. But she accepted the invitation and soon was preaching three times a month and engaging in other pastoral activities. When Newton left the City Temple in 1919 Royden did also, forming a year later an independent congregation with the Rev. Percy Dearmer which met first in the Kensington Town Hall and later found a home in the Guildhouse, Eccleston Square. Services were held on Sunday afternoons and evenings, so as not to conflict with other churches' morning worship. In this work she established a radio ministry and traveled on preaching and lecture tours to the United States, Australia and New Zealand, India, and China. She resigned in 1936 to devote herself fully to the cause of world peace.

Royden described herself as "a soul naturally Anglican,"[25] who refused to be identified with any one party within the Church but wanted something of all of them. As such she could not be ordained, and she did not seek ordination in another church. Nonetheless she devoted considerable energies to the issue of female ministry in the Church of England, writing, lecturing, and debating on behalf of the cause. She herself became an issue on more than one occasion. An original member of the Life and Liberty Council led by William Temple, she was forced to resign in October, 1917, when at a Council meeting at Cuddesdon College the principal refused her permission to sleep in the college on the ground that she had offended the Church by participating in christenings at the City Temple. In 1919 the bishop of London prohibited her from preaching from the pulpit at the Good Friday service in Hudson Shaw's parish; the service was then held in the parish hall. Four years later Shaw defied the bishop, and Royden conducted the Good Friday service in the church. Her arguments in the tract, "The Ministry of Women," thus are rooted in strong personal engagement and sense of religious vocation.

When women have won their victory nearly all along the line, even in the matter of government, it seems at first sight strange that the Church should hold out against them. I discount the easy but deceptive retort that "organised religion" is always conservative, for one has only to look at the history of Christianity to see that organised religion has often been a revolutionary force in order to realise that it may easily become so again. I seek the explanation in something deeper than the easily assumed perversity of religious people; and then it does not seem so difficult to understand why the *spiritual* equality of the sexes should be harder to admit than their political, social, or even economic equality.

The spiritual nature of Man is the last, highest product of his evolution; religion, after all, the deepest and most unconquerable of his interests. Naturally therefore, in whatever other matter he may admit equality with those he has been accustomed to regard as his inferiors, in this matter his reluctance will be greater than all.

The belief that the race we belong to is one of peculiar spiritual achievement is a very old one. . . . The belief in a spiritual class is no less enduring, and has left its mark very deep on history. Not Christians only, but priests of all religions have sought to arrogate to themselves a peculiar relation to God. . . . Of the same nature is the pride of sex. As women have claimed and won advance after advance within the Church, the nature of the opposition becomes clearer and clearer. To-day it has been forced to define itself, and that it should have done so is itself a victory for women. There are, I believe, few men who will continue to hold a view which has been defined in all its native ugliness as some of our opponents have now defined it.

The advance of feminism within the Church of England has already been very great. When the question of women missionaries was first raised, the great principle that women might preach the gospel was at once established. People, knowing only of the decision, and being perfectly accustomed to the idea of women missionaries, have forgotten how the battle raged, and with what earnestness and sincerity religious people pointed out that our Lord had only sent out men, chosen men apostles, and never even suggested that women could preach. St. Paul's familiar figure was at once brought forward, accompanied by St. Peter, and the author of the Epistle to St. Timothy. In fact the controversy followed lines now exquisitely familiar, and reached its cheerfully inevitable end in the defeat of the opponents of women missionaries.

More recently, women have been invited to preach to Church Congress meetings, to National Mission meetings, at conferences and in retreats. Great care was taken however, to insure that such "preaching" was always to be called "speaking," such sermons to be described as "addresses," and such meetings never to be held in consecrated buildings. For reasons difficult to apprehend, it is held that the

Almighty attaches enormous importance to the difference between a *sermon* and an *address*, and that He is unmoved by a speech delivered in a hall or schoolroom, which would arouse His indignation if heard in a church.

It is however, obvious that such distinctions cannot really be maintained. It is true that St. Paul said that women should not speak "in church." Whatever he meant—and I am not scholar enough to decide a point on which scholars disagree and St. Paul himself seems in doubt—but whatever he meant, he *cannot* have meant that women must not speak in consecrated buildings, because at the time of his writing, consecrated buildings did not exist. Christian people as we all know quite well if we stop and think, met mostly in each other's houses, but did not meet in what we call "churches," for the simple reason that they had not built any churches to meet in.

If therefore, when St. Paul said women were not to speak "in church" he really meant to lay down an eternal principle, he must have meant that they were not to speak *in the assembly of the faithful* and no assurances that they were not "preaching sermons" but only "making speeches," and that these were delivered in a hall, and not in a consecrated building, would have mollified him in the least. Frankly, we have ignored St. Paul on this point, when women were allowed to speak at Church Congresses, National Missions or Pilgrimages, and it is useless now to make a point about "consecrated buildings" which St. Paul never made because he could not.

It is here, however, that the real nature of the opposition defines itself. The ministry of the Church is, in fact, to be reserved for men because of some inherent superiority in their sex. As it was with the Jews as a race, and with priests as a class, so it is with men as a sex: it is claimed that they stand in a special relation to God, and through them alone is God mediated to the world.

Man, we are told, has a "headship" over women. He is nearer to the divine. "No one," said a distinguished writer the other day, "ever thought of God as a woman." As a matter of fact, any student of comparative religion can tell us of some most ancient beliefs in which God was always represented as a woman. But we are not now dealing with facts: we speak of something much more intractable—of prejudices; and it is a deeply-rooted prejudice in the minds of many that if God is not exactly a man, He is at least much more like a man than a woman! . . .

Now I believe that the average and normal man probably thinks that men have, on the whole, more strength, more judgment and more knowledge of affairs than women. They are often inclined to concede to women a certain superiority, rather than a defect, in spiritual or religious gifts. But *on the whole,* as I say, they would probably say that men were, taking them all round, the superior sex, just as in their hearts, most Englishmen think that Englishmen are the superior race. But such men—and I believe that they are in the great majority—would never dream of denying that any given woman might have gifts quite equal to those of men, or of fencing her out of a position she was qualified to fill *merely* because she was a woman. Of course most of us are slow to welcome any change in long established custom. Of course, in any given question, professional jealousy, class jealousy, or actual fear of competition may come in. But stating the matter broadly, I simply do not believe that the average man really thinks that he is nearer God than his mother, or that he is more fit to speak in a consecrated building than she. Women, have, I believe, nothing to fear from his opposition to her in the Church.

But there is another type of man, from whom opposition comes, and it is he who is the real enemy. Such a man—self-described years ago by a distinguished doctor of medicine—literally cannot work with women without extreme difficulty. He suffers from an obsession of sex so great that the mere spectacle of a woman at the altar or within the sanctuary appears to him "a source of scandal and even of danger." Lest my hearers should suppose that I exaggerate, let me add that I quote the actual words of an opponent. In the nature of women however saintly there seems to him to be something so essentially earthy and corrupt that it really and deeply shocks him to think of her celebrating the Holy Communion. In conception, motherhood, child-birth, and all that leads up to and follows from it, he discovers an element of uncleanness, which makes the priesthood for women impossible. I do not speak of physical incapacity, for this is a perfectly simple matter quite easy to discuss—let me add, quite easy to exaggerate—in the light of day. But the imagined disability to which I refer is something which our opponents assure us they cannot bring themselves to discuss at all—it is too profound, too mysterious, too fundamental to be put into words; but its nature may be dimly guessed by the conclusion drawn by those who are able to understand it—namely, that women may speak, but not in a consecrated place; may come inside a church, but not inside the sanctuary rails; may be members of the Church, but not "in holy orders."

This ancient superstition about the uncleanness of a sex dies hard even in the twentieth century. One finds it not only in the strange and often cruel "tabus" of primitive religions, but among the superstitions of uneducated and unthinking people everywhere. One finds it, also, among the educated and the civilized, and modern psychology is teaching us the reason, and tracing out the cause of this obsession. It is the man whose nature has been in some way repressed but not controlled, who suffers from what in the jargon of psychology we call a "complex," to whom the presence of women is so disturbing, and association with them in work so impossible. To him, as to some of the most famous of medieval ascetics, the mere presence of a woman is a possible source of danger. Is he likely to trace the cause of his difficulty to himself? Most certainly not. It is the woman who is in the wrong! . . .

It is this belief that stands to-day between women and the establishment of their equality with men in the Church and every ministry of the Church; and it is this belief alone. I do not now discuss the question whether women should wait to press their claims for this or that branch of the ministry till some more convenient season, till the question of reunion has been settled, or till the Bishops can make their peace with the English Church Union, or decide whether women are "normally" fit to address men or not. I want at this time rather to emphasize that the sole reason for excluding women from *spiritual* office is the belief that they suffer from a *spiritual* inferiority. Those therefore who hold that, at whatever point women may fall below men, it is un-Christian and untrue to give them an inferior *spiritual* status, those to whom the physical nature of woman is as holy as that of a man, those who would shrink with disgust from the idea that she is in some strange way a degree further from the divine, ought now to claim with us the recognition of the Church for her. It is useless to quote St. Paul to us against our Master Christ. He Himself warned us to try every teacher by one standard only, and that is the one to which we appeal. Was St. Paul most like Christ when he affirmed that the head of the woman was the man, or when he said that in Christ there was neither Jew nor Greek, male or female, bond nor free? Was the Church of England more or less Christian when, at the Reformation, she affirmed the use and value of a priestly class, but refused to allow that God could only be mediated to the laity by a priest, or that any priest had the right to stand between man and God? To that same spirit women appeal to-day, with the same conviction that in affirming their complete spiritual equality with men, they are appealing past even the greatest of His Apostles, to the spirit and teaching of their Master Christ.

9. *Report of the Lambeth Conference, 1920* (London: SPCK, 1920), pp. 97-101.

It was almost sixty years after the restoration of deaconesses before the Church of England gave serious official attention to the question of the ministry of women. A Lambeth Conference committee in 1897 expressed gratitude for the revival of the office, and another in 1908 had suggested that it was premature to set official directions for it. The Archbishop's committee appointed in 1917 frankly admitted that "there has been little or no official recognition of women's work in the Church. It has too generally been assumed that women's work should be gratuitous, and that they could have no defined status in the organisation of diocese or parish."[26] This report provided an historical and theological background for addressing the issues at the Lambeth Conference of 1920.

In addition to showing awareness of the changing position of women in modern society and concern for the Church's failure to acknowledge the work of women, the Lambeth Report went on to underscore the equality of women with men in the Councils of the Church, affirm the place of deaconesses in the Church's ministry, and declare that the same opportunities for speaking and leading in prayer should be given to laywomen as to laymen. The order of deaconesses was the only order of ministry which could be recommended for women; but the affirmation that it was an order of ministry and the recognition of the historical and social context which shapes the Church's thinking each led some to be hopeful that further gains—now with respect to the priesthood for women—would be forthcoming. Renewed activities took place and a new set of literature appeared prior to the Lambeth Conference of 1930.[27] That was not persuasive, however; the 1930 Report stated that it could not encourage "in any way those who press for the Priesthood of Women," for it saw in the order of deaconesses both scope and need "for the exercise of women's ministry within the commissioned Orders of the Church of such a kind as to satisfy the highest aspirations."[28] While this judgment did not bring the cause of ordination of women to the full ministry in the Church to an end, it was a severe blow from which the cause did not quickly recover.

In our belief, . . .   St. Paul asserted the spiritual equality of men and women; neither is afore or after the other. This spiritual equality will be realized without let or hindrance in the spiritual world which is to come. But in this present world of action between these equals, man and woman, man has a priority, and in the last resort authority belongs to him. As the world in which we live becomes more like the world to come, this qualification becomes less and less operative, just as the stronger races assert their power in diminishing degree over their spiritual equals, the weaker races. In times such as that in which St. Paul wrote the necessary qualification became a predominating influence, and in this matter, as in the case of slavery, St. Paul's teaching was conditioned by the existing circumstances of the world around him. He stooped to it that he might raise it. The statement then of what we believe to be the truth in regard to the human relations between men and women, as (we reverently say) in regard to the divine relations between the Persons within the Godhead, must needs take the form of a paradox. Difference of function between man and woman in the Church, as in the world, and the relative subordination of the woman in no way imply an inferiority of woman in regard to man.

Our firm conviction is that the precise form which St. Paul's disciplinary directions took was relative to the time and to the place which he actually had in mind, but that these directions embody an abiding principle. To transfer with slavish literalness the Apostle's injunctions to our own time and to all parts of our own world would be to renounce alike our inalienable responsibility of judgement and the liberty wherewith Christ has made us free. On the other hand it is our duty to endeavour clearly to discern the abiding law which underlay St. Paul's stringent temporary and local rules. We believe it to be this. Human nature being what it is, the Christian Church, whose duty and desire is to keep itself unspotted from the world, and to be like a home of brethren and sisters at unity with each other, must exercise unsleeping vigilance that in its regulations for worship in the congregation there lurk no occasion for evil or even for suspicion of evil; no occasion for confusion or strife; nothing which falls below the purest and strictest ideal of peace and seemliness and order. . . .

When we survey at any rate the recent history of some, if not all, parts of the Anglican Communion, we are obliged to confess that the Church has failed to treat women workers with generosity or even with justice. It is a platitude to say that some of the very best work of the Church has been done, with singular patience and conscientiousness, with singular vigour and ability, with singular devotion to our Lord, by women. But the women to whom we owe this great debt have received but scanty acknowledgement from the Church in the way either of actual salary or of recognition or of a responsible share in directing the activities or the policy of the Church either centrally or parochially.

It is now, we believe, generally, if not universally, recognized that the future must be different from the past. The education of women has advanced in a way which would have seemed incredible to our fathers. Witness the place which women take in the new and even in the ancient universities. Again in most parts of our Communion the Church is in a new environment of social life which it is impossible for us to neglect. . . .   And, further, within the Church we have seen an advance, great, though not commensurate with that in secular matters. . . .   Women also of mature judgement have spoken at mixed meetings of men and women on the difficult and delicate subject of sexual sin, its prevention and the rescue of its victims, with sympathy, with power, with restraint. These are facts; and we are convinced that, if the recognition of these facts is grudging and inadequate, at least two evil results will ensue. We run a grave risk of wasting a great power for spiritual good, which, as many are profoundly convinced, it is the will of God that we should use for His better service. We also run the grave risk of alienating from the Church, and even from Christianity, not a few of those able and high-minded women before whom, if they turn to social or educational work, there open out careers of great and increasing responsibility.

On the other hand there are reasons for caution. We dare not forget elementary facts of human nature. Women have the power of moving men. By effective speech on religious truths and experiences strong emotions are called into play. On strong emotions possible perils wait. And, especially in a generation which seems sometimes even contemptuously and recklessly to brush aside what a very few years ago were regarded as wise and indeed necessary restraints, the Church must be above suspicion and must not fear to be watchful. Again, there is a deep wisdom in the words of the New Testament which say of a faithful Christian woman "she shall be saved through her child-bearing." The Church, while fully acknowledging that some women are called to a life of celibacy, yet in these days of a falling birth-rate and of all that that sinister phenomenon implies, must not do anything which obscures or renders difficult woman's fulfilment of her characteristic function in human life. Again, looking at the whole position from another point of view, we realize how heavy a responsibility rests on the whole of our own Communion, and especially on its rulers, to avoid any action which might retard the growth of mutual recognition and regard between ourselves and other historic branches of the Catholic Church. Lastly, while a real advance as to the position of women is, we believe, not only advisable but even necessary, we feel that the Church owes a duty to all classes of its members, to those who are (as some may think) slow of movement as well as to those who are (as others may think) ambitious of revolutionary speed.

10. A. Maude Royden, *The Church and Woman* (London: James Clarke & Co., Ltd., 1924), pp. 231-33, 243-47.

Maude Royden did not think of herself as a theologian, but many of her published writings, including *Beauty in Religion* (1923), *The Friendship of God* (1924), and *I Believe in God* (1927), reflected theological sensitivities and judgments about the nature of Christian faith that were rooted in her experience as a woman. She was among many Christians in the suffrage movement who did not accept the common nineteenth-century notion that Christianity had raised the status of women above all previous religious or cultural perspectives. In *The Church and Woman* she declared flatly,

No one wishes to argue that men have been universally tyrannical, cruel, or inhuman to women. Such an argument would condemn itself by its own absurdity. All that is claimed is that, with a unanimity to which the few exceptions that exist only give a more striking character, women have everywhere and at all times been regarded as subordinate to men.[29]

That having been said, she found grounds for reform and for hope in the teachings of Jesus and in his relationships with women. But to right the wrongs committed by the Church against women and to restore the Church to its Christ-like state, much had to be done. The contributions to be made by women in this process would be considerable, she argued, and they would be seen in terms of theological reconstruction as well as in personal activity. Royden was one of the few who anticipated the kind of feminist theological reconstruction that would not be taken up for another half-century.

What contribution may be expected from women when they enter the sacred ministries of the Church? Is their coming in merely a matter of concern to themselves, or can we hope that the Church will be enriched, not only by their individual service, but by something common to their point of view which is not found in the point of view of men? Contrary to my own expectations when I took up definitely religious work, I believe that there is such a special contribution for women to make. It is true that there is no sex in the spirit: I do not believe that there is sex in the intellect. Yet both mind and spirit are affected by the experience of life. . . . [I]n their earnestness to proclaim the equality of men and women, it sometimes happens that feminists speak a little as though there were no special qualities in the experience of women which differentiate their point of view from that of men. Yet it would be strange indeed if the fact that they are incarnated in a body different from that of men had no effect upon their point of view. I believe that it has such an effect, and I think that that is all to the good. The contribution of women will enrich and diversify political, social, and ecclesiastical life for that very reason.

For example, the almost universal idea held of the inferiority of women to men, which is now largely disappearing, ought to disappear more quickly and more thoroughly when the Church recognizes their equality. It is impossible to deny that the effect created on the mind by the part played respectively by men and women in the life of the Church is inevitably to deepen the impression of the superiority of men over women. The fact that in any Church service the active and important parts are always played by men, and women are almost invariably (except in the Society of Friends and the Salvation Army) relegated to the passive duty of listeners, creates that impression at once. In almost every function of the Church women are seen to be at a discount. They are generally excluded from Anglican choirs, and, if their help is needed so badly with the singing as to be essential, they are expected to keep out of sight and not obtrude themselves upon the notice of the congregation. The simplest duties, such as taking up the collection, are considered too high for them. In a Church with ornate ritual a very large number of persons are engaged in the actual carrying out of the ceremonies. The oldest and the youngest members of the congregation may be enlisted, from the veteran sacristan or verger to the tiny boy who carries the incense boat. But all of these are males! The impression that women are unfit for any such service is continually repeated. . . .

Is it not significant that in the parable of which it has been said that it alone reveals to us the heart of the Christian religion, there is no advocate, no mediator, no victim at all? Between the Father and his defaulting son no reconciler is necessary. "Atonement" was needed indeed—no one can overestimate the greatness of that need—by humanity. The fact that *we* had so forgotten and misunderstood our God, demanded one who could show us what God really is, and reconcile us to God in his own person. But it is not God who requires this reconciler: it is not God who is alienated from us. We are not told at any point in the story that the father was angry or resentful against his erring child. All that we know is that "While he was yet a great way off, his father saw him, and was moved to compassion, and ran, and fell on his neck, and kissed him."

Once more it is necessary to reiterate the need of the world for such a conception of God as this. This sublime, amazing parable of his love has stood always in our gospels. Although but one evangelist has recorded it, there it stands. The world has not forgotten and cannot forget it. Yet in the light of the history of the doctrine of the Atonement alone, it is clear that the conception of God given to us in that parable has not sufficiently impressed the judgment of men. They have dwelt too long upon other aspects of his deity, and for the lack of this one—after all the greatest—their theology has suffered. It has been impoverished, it has been made rigid, it has lost poetry and beauty, it has lost even humanity, and, in losing that, has it not lost divinity?

No one can say exactly what contribution women will make to the theology of the future: only it is certain that they have a contribution to make. It will be broadly on the lines already suggested. It will be to emphasise the fact that God is Love, that he is our Father, that the world is our home and all men brothers. It will, in the radiant light of that revelation, soften the harsher aspects of God as the God of the battle-field and the Judge of the law-court.

Perhaps if I may dare to venture for a moment into the dangerous realms of prophecy—perhaps, even, there may enter into the minds of men some conception of the eternal motherhood in God. The baffled efforts of men to retain this conception are met in the Roman Catholic Church by the almost divine honours offered to our Blessed Lady. It is suggested by our Lord in words of infinite tenderness. He would, he said, as he yearned over the city of Jerusalem, have gathered her together "as a hen gathers her brood under her wings," though they would not. But men have not realized yet that motherhood as well as fatherhood is in God. This, too, has helped to render more harsh and austere their conception of the Deity. It was Julian of Norwich who first dared to speak of her "Mother God." Many women will dare so in the future, and men will learn something from their doing it.

It has been said by missionaries that no Christian will ever know all that Christ meant until all nations have received him. The West has brought its triumphant practical sense, its desire for victory, into its conception of the Christian faith. It needs yet the deeper spirituality of the East. It needs the wonderful capacity of the

Chinese to hold the spiritual and the practical together. It needs indeed the genius of every nation. . . . Shall we not require the help of both sexes? Would it not be strange indeed if only one sex had anything to bring to the better understanding of the teaching of Christ? It would be as strange and unnatural as though India were to be able to teach us nothing or China to contribute no wealth of her own to our conception of God and his Christ.

As long as women are shut out from preaching, and largely from teaching, theology will be deemed to be outside their province. It is true that they can even now study it, read it; they are even permitted to write it, although as yet they are rarely permitted to speak it. But it remains as a great pre-possession against them that theology is not for them, and our whole theological system has been built up almost entirely by the minds of men.

When the vocation to the ministry, whether of prophet or of priest, is expected of women as well as men, and by women as well as men, the whole situation will be changed. Women will begin to feel that they also have something to contribute to our theology. They will begin to contribute it. We shall begin to understand better him whom we worship.

"Upon this came his disciples, and they marvelled that he was speaking with a woman: yet no man said, What seekest thou? or, Why speakest thou with her? . . . So the woman left her water-pot, and went away into the city, and saith to the men, Come, see a man, which told me all things that ever I did: can this be the Christ? . . . And from that city many of the Samaritans believed on him because of the word of the woman."

NOTES

INTRODUCTION

[1] For some of these events, see Joyce Irwin, *Womanhood in Radical Protestantism, 1525-1675* (New York: The Edwin Mellen Press, 1979).

[2] See Gerda Lerner, "Placing Women in History: Definitions and Challenges," *Feminist Studies*, 3:1-2 (1975): 5-14.

[3] For a discussion of this in the American context, see Ann Douglas, *The Feminization of American Culture* (New York: Alfred A. Knopf, Inc., 1977).

CHAPTER ONE

[1] London: J. Roberts, 1723.

[2] Of the many examples of such argument, see *Man Superior to Woman*, Part II of *Beauty's Triumph* (London: J. Robinson, 1751); Thomas Gisbourne, *An Enquiry into the Duties of the Female Sex* (London: T. Cadell, 1797); and the Rev. Richard Polwhele, "The Unsex'd Females" (1798), in *Poems* (London: Rivingtons, 1810), pp. 36-44.

[3] *The Subjection of Women* (1869; Everyman ed., London: J. M. Dent & Sons, 1977), p. 258.

[4] See the discussions in Hilda L. Smith, *Reason's Disciples: Seventeenth-Century English Feminists* (Urbana: University of Illinois Press, 1982) and Katherine M. Rogers, *Feminism in Eighteenth-Century England* (Urbana: University of Illinois Press, 1982).

[5] *A Vindication of the Rights of Woman* (1792; Everyman ed., London: J. M. Dent & Sons, 1977), pp. 85, 57, and 164.

[6] Milton, *Paradise Lost*, ed. A. W. Verity (Cambridge: The University Press, 1921), Book IV, lines 288-99.

[7] *Man Superior to Woman*, p. 90. For medieval antecedents, see Eleanor Como McLaughlin, "Equality of Souls, Inequality of Sexes: Women in Medieval Theology," in *Religion and Sexism*, ed. Rosemary Radford Ruether (New York: Simon and Schuster, 1974), pp. 213-21.

[8] *Paradise Lost*, Book IV, lines 637-38.

[9] *Man Superior to Woman*, p. 77.

[10] *Early Quaker Writings, 1650-1700*, ed. Hugh Barbour and Arthur O. Roberts (Grand Rapids: Wm. B. Eerdmans Co., 1973), p. 502.

[11] *Ibid.*, p. 505.

[12] Sophia, *Woman's Superior Excellence over Man* (1740), in *Beauty's Triumph*, Part III, pp. 185-89.

[13] When Boswell reported that he had been to a Quaker meeting and heard a woman preach, Dr. Johnson replied, "Sir, a woman's preaching is like a dog's walking on its hinder legs. It is not done well; but you are surprised to find it done at all" [*The Life of Samuel Johnson*, 10 vols. (New York: Doubleday, Page and Co., 1922), II:255].

[14] See Ethyn Morgan Williams, "Women Preachers in the Civil War," *Journal of Modern History*, I (1929):561-69; and Keith Thomas, "Women and the Civil War Sects," *Past and Present*, 13 (1958): 42-62.

[15] *Malleus Maleficarum*, trans. with introduction by the Rev. Montague Summers (New York: Benjamin Blom, Inc., 1928), pp. 41-48; Keith Thomas, *Religion and the Decline of Magic* (1971; Harmondsworth: Penguin Books, 1973), chaps. 14-16.

[16] "A Paraphrase and Notes on St. Paul's First Epistle to the Corinthians," in *The Works of John Locke*, 10 vols. (London, 1812), VIII:150-51, 182.

17 B. Coole,"Some Brief Observations on the Paraphrase and Notes of the Judicious John Lock: Relating to the Women's Exercising Their Spiritual Gifts in the Church" (London, 1716), pp. 3-4, 18-19; William Rawes,"The Gospel Ministry of Women, Under the Christian Dispensation, Defended from Scripture, and from the Writings of John Locke, Josiah Martin, etc." (London: William Phillips, 1801).

18 Others include Anna Maria van Schurman of the Netherlands, whose works were translated into English; Bathsua Makin; and the anonymous author of *An Essay in Defence of the Female Sex* (London, 1696), a work often attributed to Mary Astell.

19 See *An Essay in Defence of the Female Sex*, pp. 11-21.

20 *A Serious Proposal to the Ladies, for the Advancement of Their True and Greatest Interest*, 3rd ed. (London, 1696), p. 15.

21 Lawrence Stone, *The Family, Sex and Marriage in England, 1500-1800* (New York: Harper & Row, 1977), pp. 356-58.

22 *Woman Triumphant*, p. 7.

23 *Woman Not Inferior to Man*, by Sophia, a Person of Quality (London, 1739), p. 56; also in *Beauty's Triumph*, Part I, p. 61.

24 *The Character and Conduct of the Female Sex* (London, 1776) p. 19.

25 *A Father's Legacy to his Daughters*, 2nd ed. (London, 1774), pp. 31-32.

26 Fordyce, *Character and Conduct*, p. 45; Gregory, *Father's Legacy*, pp. 11, 13.

27 *Vindication*, pp. 104, 109.

28 "Fordyce Delineated: A Satire, Occasioned by his *Sermons to Young Women*" (London, 1767).

29 Robert Barclay, *An Apology for the True Christian Divinity*, 13th ed. (1678; London, 1869), p. 200 (Proposition X).

30 *Some Account of the Life and Religious Labours of Sarah Grubb* (Dublin, 1792), p. 36.

[31] Stone, *Family*, p. 342, dates the poem at 1771. But the editor of Barbauld's works declares that the poems are presented in chronological order, insofar as that could be determined; in this edition it follows one for Priestley dated December 29, 1792 and is two before another dated 1795. Both the title and the first line suggest a close connection to Wollstonecraft's work.

[32] *The Works of Anna Laetitia Barbauld*, II:59.

[33] *Vindication*, pp. 59-60.

[34] Cited in James K. Hopkins, *A Woman to Deliver Her People: Joanna Southcott and English Millenarianism in an Era of Revolution* (Austin: University of Texas Press, 1982), p. 216.

[35] See Hillel Schwartz, *The French Prophets* (Berkeley: University of California Press, 1980).

[36] *The Strange Effects of Faith*, p. 60.

CHAPTER TWO

[1] Joseph Ritson, *The Romance of Primitive Methodism* (London: Primitive Methodist Publishing House, 1909), p. 141.

[2] Maldwyn Edwards, *Family Circle: A Study of the Epworth Household in Relation to John and Charles Wesley* (London: The Epworth Press, 1949), pp. 52-56. For the theological tradition which she represented, see John A. Newton, *Susanna Wesley and the Puritan Tradition in Methodism* (London: The Epworth Press, 1968).

[3] "A Plain Account of the People Called Methodists" (1748), in *The Works of John Wesley*, 14 vols. (1872; Grand Rapids: Zondervan, n.d.), VIII:249.

[4] Clifford W. Towlson, *Moravian and Methodist* (London: The Epworth Press, 1957), pp. 184-95.

[5] *The Letters of the Rev. John Wesley*, ed. John Telford, 8 vols. (London: The Epworth Press, 1931), I:272.

[6] *Ibid.*, pp. 260, 272.

7 As in *Ibid.*, p. 3 (September 21, 1739): "I heartily thank our brothers Westall, Oldfield, Cross, Haydon, and Wynne; and our sisters Deffel, Shafto, Oldfield, Thomas, Stephens, Mrs. Thomas, and Mrs. Deschamps."

8 "The Nature, Design, and General Rules of the United Societies" (1743), in *Works*, VIII:269-71.

9 "A Plain Account," pp. 258-59. For a fuller discussion of these topics, see Frank Baker, "The People Called Methodists. 3. Polity," in *A History of the Methodist Church in Great Britain*, ed. Rupert Davies and Gordon Rupp, 3 vols. (London: Epworth Press, 1965-), I:213-55.

10 For biographical details, see Stanley Ayling, *John Wesley* (Cleveland: Collins, 1979), chaps. 4, 10, 12. To one of his preachers he wrote in 1769, "You cannot be too wary in this respect" (*Letters*, V:133).

11 As in a letter of 1780: "I desire Mr. Peacock to put a final stop to the preaching of women in his circuit. If it were suffered, it would grow, and we know not where it would end" (*Letters*, VII:9).

12 *A Short History of Independent Methodism* (Warrington: Independent Methodist Book Room, 1905), p. 8.

13 See, for example, Richard Mant, *Puritanism Revived; or, Methodism as Old as the Great Rebellion* (London: Rivington, 1808), p. 38.

14 Wesley included it in his collection for *A Christian Library* and also published versions of it elsewhere. In one edition (1760) he wrote, "I am persuaded, it is not possible for me to write any thing so full, so strong, and so clear on this subject, as has been written near a hundred and fifty years ago, by a person of equal sense and piety" [*The Works of the Rev. John Wesley*, 10 vols. (New York, 1826), VI:162].

15 *Minutes of the Methodist Conferences*, 16 vols. (London: Wesleyan Conference Office, 1812-68), I:49.

16 *The Journal of the Rev. John Wesley*, ed. Nehemiah Curnock, 8 vols. (London: Epworth Press, 1915), V:102, 152.

17 J. Conder Nattrass, "Some Notes from the Oldest Register of the Great Yarmouth Circuit," *Proceedings of the Wesley Historical Society*, 3 (1902): 74.

[18] *Letters*, VIII:190.

[19] *Ibid.*, p. 229 (July 31, 1790).

[20] For a consideration of the relative importance of these sources, see Valentine Cunningham, *Everywhere Spoken Against: Dissent in the Victorian Novel* (Oxford: Clarendon Press, 1975), pp. 147-71.

[21] William Myles, *A Chronological History of the People Called Methodists*, 4th ed. (London, 1813), p. 291.

[22] Leslie F. Church, *More About the Early Methodist People* (London: The Epworth Press, 1949), p. 174.

[23] John T. Wilkinson, *Hugh Bourne, 1772-1852* (London: The Epworth Press, 1952), pp. 50-60.

[24] See Ritson, *Romance*, and W. M. Patterson, *Men of Fire, and Consecrated Women Also* (London: W. A. Hammond, 1911).

[25] Thomas Shaw, *The Bible Christians, 1815-1907* (London: The Epworth Press, 1965), pp. 30-31.

[26] John Barfoot, "Gleanings Concerning the Late Mrs. Sarah Bembridge," *The Primitive Methodist Magazine*, 1881, p. 163.

[27] *The Primitive Methodist Magazine*, 1857, p. 319.

[28] Lady Glenorchy of Scotland was another; see D. P. Thomson, *Lady Glenorchy and Her Churches* (Crieff, Scotland, 1967).

[29] Wesley was especially distrustful. On July 3, 1779, he noted in his journal, "I reached Grimsby, and found a little trial. In this, and many other parts of the kingdom, those striplings who call themselves Lady Huntingdon's preachers have greatly hindered the work of God. They have neither sense, courage, not grace to go and beat up the devil's quarters in any place where Christ has not been named; but wherever we have entered as by storm, and gathered a few souls, often at the peril of our lives, they creep in, and, by doubtful disputations, set everyone's sword against his brother. One of these has just crept into Grimsby, and is striving to divide the poor little flock; but I hope his labour will be in vain, and they will still hold 'the unity of the Spirit in the bond of peace'" (*Journal*, VI:241).

30 *Practical Piety* (1811), in *Works*, VIII:50-51, 12-13.

31 *Coelebs in Search of a Wife* (1809; New York, 1857), p. 226.

CHAPTER THREE

1 "The Condition of Women," *Blackwood's Edinburgh Magazine*, LXXXIII (1858):145.

2 E. S. Purcell, *Life of Cardinal Manning*, 2 vols. (New York: The Macmillan Co., 1898), II:653.

3 *Sir Thomas More; or, Colloquies on the Progress and Prospects of Society*, 2 vols. (London: John Murray, 1829), II:304.

4 Mrs. John Sandford, *Female Improvement*, 2 vols. (London, 1836); [Anne R. Dryden], *Can Woman Regenerate Society?* (London: John W. Parker, 1844). Dryden thought it possible, but only when woman regenerated herself by claiming the substance rather than the shadow of virtue, by utilizing her talents to the fullest, and by protesting against the double standard of morality.

5 M. M., "Women Teaching in the Church, etc.," *The Inquirer*, III (1840):437. See also Z., "Restrictions on Female Ministry," *Ibid.*, pp. 440-41; "Thoughts on the Ministry of Women," *Ibid.*, I (1838):84-89; and Alexander Tyrrell, "'Woman's Mission' and Pressure Group Politics in Britain (1825-60)," *Bulletin of the John Rylands Library*, 63 (Autumn, 1980):194-230.

6 Ann Jane, "The Responsibility of Mothers," *The British Mothers' Magazine*, II (March, 1846):50.

7 "Women's Work in Connection with the Church of England," in *Woman's Mission. A Series of Congress Papers on the Philanthropic Work of Women*, ed. The Baroness Burdett-Coutts (London: Sampson, Low, Marston, and Co., 1893), p. 121.

8 See Rev. J. B. Figgis, *Manliness, Womanliness, Godliness* (London: S. W. Partridge and Co., 1885).

9 *The Mental and Moral Dignity of Woman* (London: John Snow, 1842), p. 23.

[10] "Phoebe in London" (London: Rivingtons, 1877), p. 10.

[11] Christopher Wordsworth, "Christian Womanhood and Christian Sovereignty: A Sermon" (London: Rivingtons, 1884), pp. 21-22, 44.

[12] *The Subjection of Women*, p. 219.

[13] *Ibid.*, p. 236.

[14] *Ibid.*, p. 243.

[15] *Woman's Rights and Duties, Considered with Relation to Their Influence on Society and on Her Own Condition*, By a Woman, 2 vols. (London: John W. Parker, 1840), II: 322-23.

[16] [William Fulford], "Woman, Her Duties, Education, and Position," *The Oxford and Cambridge Magazine for 1856*, p. 472.

[17] "Women and Politics," *Macmillan's Magazine*, XX (1869):561.

[18] H. M. Swanwick, *The Future of the Women's Movement* (London: G. Bell and Sons, 1913), pp. 138, 27, 154.

[19] R. C. K. Ensor, *England, 1870-1914* (Oxford: The Clarendon Press, 1936), p. 150; David Owen, *English Philanthropy, 1660-1960* (Cambridge: Harvard University Press, 1964), pp. 395-401.

[20] *The British Mothers' Magazine*, III (1847):127.

[21] "The Education of Women," *Ibid.*, IV (1848):278.

[22] *Life of Frances Power Cobbe*, As told by Herself (London: Swan Sonnenschein & Co., 1904), p. 64.

[23] *Essays on the Pursuits of Women* (London: Emily Faithfull, 1863), p. 57.

CHAPTER FOUR

1 Josephine E. Butler, *Memoir of John Grey of Dilston* (Edinburgh: Edmonston and Douglas, 1869), pp. 326-28. "How is life sacrificed as to its most important ends, and given to vanity instead of to the service of God!," she exclaimed further. "What I plead for is, that those who are led by a necessity of duty, made up of choice, adaptation, and general circumstances, to desire a life of philanthropic usefulness, may have the means opened before them of adopting a profession, acquiring the skill and following out the practice of the particular line of service for which they are fitted" (p. 329).

2 For an early expression of this, see Southey, *Sir Thomas More*, II:318.

3 James Baldwin Brown, *Young Men and Maidens: A Pastoral for the Times* (London, 1871), p. 45. He went on:"The days are not far distant when the whole of our hospital work, and a large share of the visitation and relief of our poor, with the teaching of our troops of young children, will be handed over bodily to competent and cultivated women; who will feel that it is their distinguished vocation to serve the State in these spheres of its ministry, as it is the statesman's to serve it in council, and the soldier's in war. . . . Womanhood grows more Christlike than manhood when it bears the burden of this ministry" (pp. 46-47). But John Stuart Mill wondered whether the present condition of women enabled them to do what was needed: "She is not self-dependent; she is not taught self-dependence; her destiny is to receive everything from others, and why should what is good enough for her be bad for the poor?" (*The Subjection of Women*, p. 304).

4 For wider discussion of this problem, see Patricia Branca, "Image and Reality: The Myth of the Idle Victorian Woman," in *Clio's Consciousness Raised: New Perspectives on the History of Women*, eds. Mary S. Hartman and Lois Banner (New York: Harper & Row, 1974), pp. 179-91.

5 In"Cassandra," from Ray Strachey, *The Cause: A Short History of the Women's Movement in Great Britain* (London: G. Bell and Sons, 1928), p. 414.

6 John Boyd-Kinnear,"The Social Position of Women in the Present Age," in *Woman's Work and Woman's Culture*, ed. Josephine E. Butler (London: Macmillan and Co., 1869), p. 337.

7 She is one of ten included in the Religious Tract Society's publication, *Queen Victoria and Other Excellent Women* (London, 1904).

[8] *A Brief Sketch of the Life of the Late Miss Sarah Martin* (Yarmouth: C. Barber, 1844), pp. 119-20.

[9] Cited by Sir Edward Cook, *The Life of Florence Nightingale*, 2 vols. (1913; London: Macmillan, 1942), I:57.

[10] Florence Nightingale, *Notes on Nursing: What it is, and What it is Not* (New York: D. Appleton & Co., 1860), p. 136.

[11] See [A. R. C. Dallas], "Protestant Sisters of Charity. A Letter Addressed to the Lord Bishop of London" (London, 1826).

[12] See Peter F. Anson, *The Call of the Cloister*, rev. ed. (London: SPCK, 1964), Appendix I.

[13] *Conference of Bishops of the Anglican Communion* (London: SPCK, 1897), p. 19.

[14] A. B. M. Jameson, *Sisters of Charity and The Communion of Labor* (Boston, 1857), pp. 38-39; F. D. Maurice, "On Sisterhoods," *The Victoria Magazine*, I (1863):289-301; J. M. Ludlow, *Woman's Work in the Church* (London, 1865), p. 301.

[15] J. S. Howson, *Deaconesses; or, The Official Help of Women in Parochial Work and in Charitable Institutions* (London, 1862), p. 15.

[16] For discussion of this factor, see "Female Agency in the Church," *The London Quarterly Review*, XXV (October, 1865):167.

[17] B. Compton, "Deaconesses. A Sermon . . ." (London, 1868), p. 8.

[18] See *Church League for Women's Suffrage Monthly Paper*, October, 1916, p. 105.

[19] Brian Harrison, *Dictionary of British Temperance Biography* (Sheffield: The Society for the Study of Labour History, 1973), includes only eight women in a total of 387 names.

[20] Cited by J. M. J. Fletcher, *Mrs. Wightman of Shrewsbury* (London: Longmans, Green, and Co., 1906), p. 88.

21 *Ibid.*, p. 292.

22 [Robert H. Cheney], "The Missing Link and the London Poor," *The Quarterly Review*, 108 (1860):28.

23 F. R. Harvey, "What shall we do with OUR GIRLS?" (Andover, 1884), p. 8.

24 Le Plus Bas, *Woman's Rights and Woman's Wrongs* (London, 1865), pp. 32-37.

25 W. R. Greg, "Why are Women Redundant?" (1862), in *Literary and Social Judgments* (1868; Boston, 1873), pp. 274-308. Jessie Boucherett responded by suggesting that men should emigrate instead. This would create a vast excess of women over men; but because of the employment vacancies resulting from it, there would not be one superfluous woman! See "How to Provide for Superfluous Women," in *Woman's Work and Woman's Culture*, pp. 32-35.

26 Frances Power Cobbe, "What Shall We do with our Old Maids?", in *Essays*, pp. 58-101.

27 See Emily Faithfull, "The Unfit Employments in which Women are Engaged," *The Victoria Magazine*, 2 (1863):71: "The real question is not whether any particular kind of work has always been done by men, but whether there is in it anything intrinsically detrimental to distinctive womanhood, and on this point we must beware of mistaking custom for reason and prejudices for instinct."

28 *Woman's Work and Woman's Culture*, p. xxiii.

29 Mary E. Sumner, *An Earnest Appeal to Mothers* (London: James Nisbet & Co., 1886), p. 4.

30 James A. Walker, "Maude Petre (1863-1942): A Memorial Tribute," *The Hibbert Journal*, 41 (1942-43):345.

CHAPTER FIVE

[1] [Lady Elizabeth Eastlake], "The Englishwoman at School," *The Quarterly Review*, (July, 1878):40-41.

[2] Cited in Margaret J. Tuke, *A History of Bedford College for Women, 1849-1937* (London: Oxford University Press, 1939), p. 20.

[3] For a negative answer to all of these, see the sermon by J. W. Burgon, "To Educate Young Women Like Young Men, and With Young Men,–A Thing Inexpedient and Immodest" (Oxford, 1884).

[4] See the Rev. A. M'Caul, *The Ancient Interpretation of Leviticus XVIII:18, as Received in the Church for more than 1500 Years, a Sufficient Apology for Holding that, According to the Work of God, Marriage with a Deceased Wife's Sister is Lawful* (London, 1859).

[5] Lord Dalhousie's pamphlet, "Opinions of the Hebrew and Greek Professors of the European Universities on the Scriptural Aspect of the Question of Regarding the Legalization of Marriage with a Deceased Wife's Sister" (London, 1882), reported that of nearly fifty professors of Hebrew canvassed, only three (including Pusey of Oxford) maintained the appropriateness of the law on biblical grounds; the other two were Spanish professors, who appealed also to Catholic law.

[6] "Marriage with a Deceased Wife's Sister. Letters in Favor of a Repeal of the Law which Prohibits Marriage with the Sister of a Deceased Wife" (London, 1849), p. 6.

[7] Josephine E. Butler, *Personal Reminiscences of a Great Crusade* (London: H. Marshall & Son, 1896), p. 20.

[8] See *A Three-fold Cord; or, The United Testimonies of British Ladies, Ministers of the Gospel, and Medical Men, in favour of the Total and Immediate Repeal of the Contagious Diseases Acts Affecting the Women (not Cattle) of Great Britain and Ireland* (London: William Tweedle, 1870).

[9] [Josephine Butler], *The Constitution Violated. An Essay* (Edinburgh: Edmonston and Douglas, 1871).

[10] [Josephine E. Butler], *Sursum Corda; Annual Address to the Ladies' National Association* (Liverpool: T. Brakell, 1871), p. 12.

[11] See, for example, Hugh Price Hughes' appeal before the 1885 general election:"Let every Methodist elector refuse to vote for any man who defends these infamous acts. Let every Methodist also offer a relentless opposition to all unchaste candidates" (*The Methodist Times*, October 15, 1885, p. 68).

[12] Josephine E. Butler,"The Demand for Moral Members of Parliament," *The Methodist Times*, October 8, 1885, p. 665.

[13] *The Power of Womanhood; or, Mothers and Sons* (London: Wells, Gardner, Darton & Co., 1899), p. 182.

[14] "The Contagious Diseases Act. Shall the Contagious Diseases Act be Applied to the Civil Population?" (London, 1870), p. 4.

[15] See, for example, Francis W. Newman,"On State Provision for Vice, by Warranting Impunity" (1869), in *Miscellanies*, 3 vols. (London: Kegan Paul, Trench and Co., 1889), III:252-56.

[16] See Anthropos,"The Contagious Diseases Acts and the Contagious Diseases Prevention Bill" (London, 1872), pp. 28-30.

[17] See the report of the Lower House of the Convocation of Canterbury from the"Committee on the Alleged Increase of Prostitution and the Best Means for the Recovery of the Fallen" (1881), pp. 9-12.

[18] See Ann Robson,"The Significance of 'The Maiden Tribute of Modern Babylon,'" *Victorian Periodicals Newsletter*, 11 (June, 1978):51-57.

[19] *Commentaries on the Laws of England* (London, 1765), Book 1, Chap. XV, pp. 444-45.

[20] See Irving Browne,"Wife-Beating and Imprisonment," *The American Law Review*, 25 (1891):556-60.

[21] Cited by R. Emerson Dobash and Russell Dobash, *Violence Against Wives* (New York: The Free Press, 1979), p. 67 (Justice Coleridge citing Lord Mansfield).

[22] Browne,"Wife-Beating,", p. 568.

[23] *The Subjection of Women*, p. 262. Cobbe's letter was entitled by the editor,"Protection for English Christians."

24 "Wife-Torture in England," *The Contemporary Review*, 32 (1878):56, 63.

25 *Ibid.*, pp. 82ff. The 1878 Matrimonial Causes Act gave magistrates the authority to grant the last two items. For another discussion of suitable punishments for wife-beating, see Edward W. Cox, *The Principles of Punishment* (London, 1877), pp. 99-105.

26 The Rev. Wm. M. Cooper (pseud. for James G. Bertram), *Flagellation and the Flagellants* (1870; new ed., London, n.d.), pp. 396-97, records a news item from 1856 of an independent congregation established in Whitehaven by the Rev. George Bird on the principle that wife-beating was in accordance with the word of God.

27 "Wife-Torture in England," pp. 64-65.

28 Many studies of the process toward suffrage exist, including Roger Fulford, *Votes for Women* (London: Faber and Faber, 1957); Constance Rover, *Women's Suffrage and Party Politics in Britain, 1866-1914* (London: Routledge & Kegan Paul, 1967); and Martin Pugh, *Women's Suffrage in Britain, 1867-1928* (London: The Historical Association, 1980).

29 See "An Appeal Against Female Suffrage," *The Nineteenth Century*, XXV (1889):784-85.

30 Mrs. Bodichon, "Objections to the Enfranchisement of Women Considered" (London, 1866), pp. 2-5.

31 As an example, see Henry C. Raikes, "Women's Suffrage," *The National Review*, 4 (1884-85):631-41.

32 "An Appeal Against Female Suffrage," p. 781. Beatrice Potter Webb was one of the signers because, as she later wrote, "I had never myself suffered the disabilities assumed to arise from my sex" [*My Apprenticeship* (1926; London: Penguin Books, 1971), p. 354].

33 Sarah Steward, "Women and Women's Suffrage," *The National Review*, 5 (1855):722. See also Brian Harrison, *Separate Spheres: The Opposition to Women's Suffrage in Britain* (New York: Holmes & Meier, 1978).

34 This is the chief emphasis in Millicent Garrett Fawcett, "The Appeal Against Female Suffrage: A Reply," *The Nineteenth Century*, XXVI (1889):86-96.

35 Francis W. Newman, "Intellectual and Moral Tendencies of Female Suffrage" (1867), in *Miscellanies*, III:189-91; M. M. Dilke, "Female Suffrage: A Reply," *The Nineteenth Century*, XXVI (1889):98.

36 *The Times*, March 27, 1914, p. 13.

CHAPTER SIX

1 C. S. G., "Is it Right for a Woman to Preach in the Public Congregation? and What Says the Bible?" (Taunton, 1884), pp. 7-8.

2 *The Congregational Year Book* (London, 1918), pp. 557-63.

3 B. H. Streeter and Edith Picton-Turberville, *Woman and the Church* (London: T. Fisher Unwin, 1917), pp. 26-27.

4 For its contemporary use in the argument in favor of women in ministry, see *Yes to Women Priests*, ed. Hugh Montefiore (London: Mayhew-McCrimmon, 1978).

5 Streeter and Picton-Turberville, p. 104.

6 *The Challenge*, February 24, 1922, p. 237.

7 Streeter and Picton-Turberville, p. 107.

8 Charles E. Raven, *Women and Holy Orders: A Plea to the Church of England* (London: Hodder and Stoughton, 1928), p. 64.

9 Hatty Baker, *Women in the Ministry* (London: C. W. Daniel, 1911), p. 47.

10 See Elizabeth Isichei, *Victorian Quakers* (Oxford: Oxford University Press, 1970), pp. 94-95.

11 William Sturge, *Some Recollections of a Long Life* (Bristol, 1893), p. 41.

12 For other Quaker defenses early in the century, see Rawes, *The Gospel Ministry of Women*, and Henry Fry, *A Brief Account of the Lately-Intended Visit of Two Female Preachers* (London, 1810).

[13] Cited by David E. Swift, *Joseph John Gurney: Banker, Reformer, and Quaker* (Middletown: Wesleyan University Press, 1962), p. 210.

[14] See F. de L. Booth-Tucker, *The Life of Catherine Booth*, 2 vols. (New York: Fleming H. Revell Co., 1892), I:118-24, and Harold Begbie, *The Life of General William Booth*, 2 vols. (New York: Macmillan, 1920), I:245-50.

[15] William Booth was not fully convinced at first. He responded, "I would not stop a woman preaching on any account. I would not encourage one to begin. You should preach if you felt moved thereto: felt equal to the task. I would not stay *you* if I had power to do so. Altho' *I should not like it.* It is easy for you to say that my views are the result of prejudice; perhaps they are. I am for the world's *salvation*; I will quarrel with no means that promises help" (Begbie, I:236).

[16] Booth-Tucker, I:354.

[17] The 1860s saw the emergence of a number of other female revival preachers and generated a new debate about their appropriateness; for a discussion of this, see Olive Anderson, "Women Preachers in Mid-Victorian Britain: Some Reflexions on Feminism, Popular Religion and Social Change," *The Historical Journal*, XII (1969):467-84.

[18] As an example, see Bernard Shaw, *Major Barbara* (London, 1907).

[19] Margaret Lonsdale, "Platform Women," *The Nineteenth Century*, XV (1884):414-15.

[20] Alan Deacon and Michael Hill, "The Problem of 'Surplus Women' in the Nineteenth Century: Secular and Religious Alternatives," in *A Sociological Yearbook of Religion in Britain: 5*, ed. Michael Hill (London: SCM Press, 1972), pp. 87-102; Michael Hill, *The Religious Order* (London: Heinemann, 1973), pp. 276-78.

[21] *Annual Report*, The League of the Church Militant, 1928, p. 7.

[22] *Women of 1924 - International* (New York: Women's News Service, Inc., 1924), p. 328.

[23] The relationship between Royden, Shaw, and Shaw's wife is described in Royden's autobiography, *A Three-fold Cord* (New York: Macmillan, 1948).

[24] Newton calls her the first woman chosen "as a regular assistant in a great

city pulpit" [*Some Living Masters of the Pulpit* (New York: George H. Doran Co., 1923), pp. 123-24].

25 *I Believe in God* (New York: Harper & Brothers, 1927), p. 3.

26 *The Ministry of Women. A Report by a Committee Appointed by His Grace the Lord Archbishop of Canterbury* (London: SPCK, 1919), pp. 22-23.

27 See Raven, *Women and Holy Orders*; and *Women and Priesthood: A Memorandum with Appendices* (London: Longmans, Green, and Co., 1930).

28 *Report of the Lambeth Conference, 1930* (London: SPCK, 1930), p. 181. It also refused to recognize the Deaconess as identical in character and status with the Order of Deacon, preferring to affirm it as an Order *sui generis*.

29 *The Church and Woman* (London: James Clarke & Co., 1924), p. 19.

SUPPLEMENTAL BIBLIOGRAPHY

GENERAL

Branca, Patricia. *Women in Europe Since 1750*. New York: St. Martin's Press, 1978.

Bridenthal, Renate, and Koonz, Claudia, eds. *Becoming Visible: Women in European History*. Boston: Houghton Mifflin Co., 1977.

Brink, J. R., ed. *Female Scholars: A Tradition of Learned Women Before 1800*. St. Albans, Vt.: Eden Press Women's Publications, 1980.

Dictionary of National Biography. London: Oxford University Press, 1885- .

Kanner, Barbara, ed. *The Women of England: From Anglo-Saxon Times to the Present*. Hamden, Ct.: Archon Books, 1979.

Longford, Elizabeth. *Eminent Victorian Women*. New York: Alfred A. Knopf, 1981.

Stanton, Theodore, ed. *The Woman Question in Europe*. 1884; New York: Source Book Press, 1970.

Stenton, Doris M. *The English Woman in History*. New York: Macmillan, 1957.

Thompson, Roger. *Women in Stuart England and America*. London: Routledge & Kegan Paul, 1974.

CHAPTER ONE

Braithwaite, William C. *The Second Period of Quakerism.* Cambridge: Cambridge University Press, 1961.

Dallimore, Arnold A. *George Whitefield.* 2 vols. Edinburgh: Banner of Truth Trust, 1970-80.

Harrison, J. F. C. *The Second Coming: Popular Millenarianism, 1780-1850.* New Brunswick: Rutgers University Press, 1979.

Kinnaird, Joan K. "Mary Astell and the Conservative Contribution to Feminism." *Journal of British Studies,* XIX:1 (Fall, 1979): 53-75.

Leys, M. D. R. "The Rights of Women: An Eighteenth-Century Catholic Petition." *The Month,* N.S., 23 (1960): 83-88.

Lloyd, Arnold. *Quaker Social History, 1669-1738.* London: Longmans, Green & Co., 1950.

O'Malley, I. B. *Women in Subjection: A Study of the Lives of Englishwomen Before 1832.* London: Duckworth, 1933.

Perry, Ruth. "The Veil of Chastity: Mary Astell's Feminism." In *Studies in Eighteenth-Century Culture,* vol. 9, pp. 25-43. Edited by Roseann Runte. Madison: University of Wisconsin Press, 1979.

Reynolds, Myra. *The Learned Lady in England, 1650-1760.* Boston: Houghton Mifflin Co., 1920.

Rodgers, Betsy. *Georgian Chronicle: Mrs. Barbauld & Her Family.* London: Methuen & Co., 1949.

Smith, Florence M. *Mary Astell.* New York: Columbia University Press, 1916.

Walker, A. Keith. *William Law: His Life and Thought.* London: SPCK, 1973.

Williamson, Marilyn L. "Who's Afraid of Mrs. Barbauld? The Blue Stockings and Feminism." *International Journal of Women's Studies,* 3:1 (1980): 89-102.

CHAPTER TWO

Baker, Frank. "John Wesley and Sarah Crosby." *Proceedings of the Wesley Historical Society*, XXVII (1949): 76-82.

Bradley, Ian.   *The Call to Seriousness: The Evangelical Impact on the Victorians*. New York: Macmillan, 1976.

Brown, Earl Kent. "Women of the Word: Selected Leadership Roles of Women in Mr. Wesley's Methodism." In *Women in New Worlds*, pp. 69-87. Edited by Hilah F. Thomas and Rosemary Skinner Keller. Nashville: Abingdon, 1981.

Burder, Samuel. *Memoirs of Eminently Pious Women*. Philadelphia: J. J. Woodward, 1836.

Figgis, J. B., ed. *The Countess of Huntingdon and Her Connexion*. London: S. W. Partridge & Co., 1891.

Fitchett, W. H. *Wesley and His Century*. New York: Eaton & Mains, 1908.

Jones, M. G. *Hannah More*. Cambridge: Cambridge University Press, 1952.

McLeish, John. *Evangelical Religion and Popular Education: A Modern Interpretation*. London: Methuen & Co., 1969.

Meakin, Annette M. B. *Hannah More: A Biographical Study*. London: John Murray, 1919.

Simon, John S. *John Wesley and the Methodist Societies*. London: The Epworth Press, 1923.

Swift, Wesley F. "The Women Itinerant Preachers of Early Methodism." *Proceedings of the Wesley Historical Society*, XXVIII (1952): 89-94; XXIX (1953): 76-83.

CHAPTER THREE

Basch, Francoise. *Relative Creatures: Victorian Women in Society and the Novel.* New York: Schocken Books, 1975.

Brownell, David. "The Two Worlds of Charlotte Yonge." In *The Worlds of Victorian Fiction*, pp. 165-78. Edited by Jerome H. Buckley. Cambridge: Harvard University Press, 1975.

Dunbar, Janet. *Early Victorian Woman: Some Aspects of Her Life, 1837-1857.* London: George G. Harrap & Co., 1953.

Fee, Elizabeth. "The Sexual Politics of Victorian Sexual Anthropology." *Feminist Studies*, 1:3-4 (1973): 23-39.

Hellerstein, Erma O.; Hume, Leslie P.; and Offen, Karen M., eds. *Victorian Women: Documentary Account of Women's Lives in Nineteenth-Century England, France, and the United States.* Stanford: Stanford University Press, 1981.

Jay, Elisabeth. *The Religion of the Heart: Anglican Evangelicalism and the Nineteenth Century Novel.* Oxford: Clarendon Press, 1979.

Mare, Margaret, and Percival, Alicia C. *Victorian Best-seller: The World of Charlotte M. Yonge.* London: George G. Harrap & Co., 1948.

Rose, June. *Elizabeth Fry.* London: Macmillan, 1980.

Shanley, Mary Lyndon. "The History of the Family in Modern England." *Signs*, 4:4 (1979): 740-50.

Vicinus, Martha, ed. *A Widening Sphere: Changing Roles of Victorian Women.* Bloomington: Indiana University Press, 1977.

Vicinus, Martha, ed. *Suffer and Be Still: Women in the Victorian Age.* Bloomington: Indiana University Press, 1972.

CHAPTER FOUR

Allchin, A. M. *The Silent Rebellion.* London: SCM, 1958.

Boyd, Nancy. *Three Victorian Women Who Changed Their World.* New York: Oxford University Press, 1982.

Branca, Patricia. *Silent Sisterhood: Middle-class Women in the Victorian Home.* London: Croom Helm, 1975.

Davies, G. C. B. *Henry Phillpotts, Bishop of Exeter, 1778-1869.* London: SPCK, 1954.

Grierson, Janet. *Frances Ridley Havergal, Worcestershire Hymnwriter.* Worcester: The Havergal Society, 1979.

Harrison, Brian. "For Church, Queen, and Family: The Girls' Friendly Society, 1874-1920." *Past and Present,* 61 (November, 1973): 107-38.

Healy, Charles J., S. J. "Maude Petre: Her Life and Significance." *Recusant History,* XV:1 (1979): 23-42.

Heasman, Kathleen. *Evangelicals in Action: An Appraisal of Their Social Work in the Victorian Era.* London: Geoffrey Bles, 1962.

Hiley, Michael. *Victorian Working Women: Portraits from Life.* Boston: David R. Godine, 1979.

Manton, Jo. *Mary Carpenter and the Children of the Streets.* London: Heinemann, 1976.

Neff, Wanda F. *Victorian Working Women.* New York: Columbia University Press, 1929.

Pichanick, Valerie K. *Harriet Martineau: The Woman and Her Work, 1802-76.* Ann Arbor: University of Michigan Press, 1981.

Pinchbeck, Ivy. *Women Workers and the Industrial Revolution, 1750-1850.* New York: F. S. Crofts & Co., 1930.

Prochaska, F. K. *Women and Philanthropy in Nineteenth-Century England.* Oxford: Clarendon Press, 1980.

Showalter, Elaine. "Florence Nightingale's Feminist Complaint: Women, Religion and *Suggestions for Thought.*" *Signs,* 6:3 (1981): 395-412.

Williams, Thomas Jay. *Priscilla Lydia Sellon.* London: SPCK, 1965.

Woodham-Smith, Cecil. *Florence Nightingale, 1820-1910.* New York: McGraw-Hill, 1951.

Young, A. F. and Ashton, E. T. *British Social Work in the Nineteenth Century.* London: Routledge and Kegan Paul, 1956.

CHAPTER FIVE

Anderson, Nancy F. "The 'Marriage with a Deceased Wife's Sister Bill' Controversy: Incest Anxiety and the Defense of Family Purity in Victorian England." *Journal of British Studies,* XXI:2 (1982): 67-86.

Brittain, Vera. *The Women at Oxford: A Fragment of History.* London: George G. Harrap & Co., 1960.

Burstyn, Joan N. *Victorian Education and the Ideal of Womanhood.* London: Croom Helm, 1980.

Davies, Emily. *Thoughts on Some Questions Relating to Women, 1860-1908.* Cambridge: Bowes and Bowes, 1910.

Nield, Keith, ed. *Prostitution in the Victorian Age: Debates on the Issue from Nineteenth-Century Critical Journals.* Westmead, Hants.: Gregg, 1973.

Petrie, Glen. *A Singular Iniquity: The Campaigns of Josephine Butler.* London: Macmillan, 1971.

Rosen, Andrew. "Emily Davies and the Women's Movement, 1862-1867." *Journal of British Studies,* XIX:1 (1979): 101-21.

Smith, F. B. "Ethics and Disease in the Later Nineteenth Century: The

Contagious Diseases Acts." *Historical Studies,* 15 (October, 1971): 118-35.

Stephen, Barbara. *Emily Davies and Girton College.* London: Constable, 1927.

Walkowitz, Judith R. *Prostitution and Victorian Society: Women, Class, and the State.* Cambridge: Cambridge University Press, 1980.

Week, Jeffrey. *Sex, Politics and Society: The Regulation of Sexuality Since 1800.* London: Longman, 1981.

CHAPTER SIX

Bellamy, V. Nelle. "Participation of Women in the Public Life of the Church from Lambeth Conference 1867-1978." *Historical Magazine of the Protestant Episcopal Church,*LI:1 (March, 1982): 81-98

Bliss, Kathleen. *The Service and Status of Women in the Churches.* London: SCM Press, 1952.

Heeney, Brian. "The Beginnings of Church Feminism: Women and the Councils of the Church of England, 1897-1919." *Journal of Ecclesiastical History,* 33 (1982): 89-109.

Henson, Herbert Hensley. *Retrospect of an Unimportant Life.* London: Oxford University Press, 1943.

Kent, John. *Holding the Fort: Studies in Victorian Revivalism.* London: Epworth Press, 1978.

Royden, A. Maude. *Women at the World's Crossroads.* New York: The Woman's Press, 1923.

Stead, W. T. *Life of Mrs. Booth, the Founder of the Salvation Army.* New York: Fleming H. Revell Co., 1900.

Thomson, D. P., ed. *Women in the Pulpit: Sermons and Addresses by Representative Women Preachers.* London: James Clarke & Co., 1944.

INDEX

Alexander, C. F., 199
Astell, Mary, 14-21

Baker, Hatty, 272
Barbauld, Anna Laetitia, 47f.
Barclay, Robert, 40, 67
Barcroft, Wm., 233, 237-41
Barnett, Henrietta, 189
Bible Christians, 89f., 267
Blackstone, Wm., 241f.
Bodichon, Barbara, 194
Booth, Catherine, 277-83
Bosanquet, Mary (see Fletcher, Mary Bosanquet)
Boucherett, Jessie, 335
Bourne, Hugh, 89-93, 269
Bowdler, John, 54-60, 109
Brown, James Baldwin, 156-60
Bultitude, Elizabeth, 90
Bunting, Jabez, 88f.
Burgon, John W., 139-42
Butler, Josephine E., 161f., 193-99, 230-37, 283, 293

Cambridge, Alice, 87
Campbell, R. J., 255, 261-65
Charity Organisation Society, 189
Church League for Women's Suffrage, 256, 261, 265f., 309
Cobbe, Frances Power, 152-56, 193, 242-48, 272
Colles, W. M., 175f., 179-81
Coltman, Constance Todd, 270

Contagious Diseases Acts, 230-41
Creation motifs, 9-13, 111
Crosby, Fanny, 199
Crosby, Sarah, 66, 68f.

Davies, Emily, 214
Deaconess(es), 70, 162, 174-76, 181-85, 193, 272, 315-19
Deceased wife's sister bill, 222-30
Dickens, Charles, 241

Education, 7, 14, 122f., 133, 136, 211-21
Eliot, George, 80-87, 241
English Church Union, 293f.

Faithfull, Emily, 194
Ferard, Elizabeth, 182
Fletcher, C. J. H., 142-47
Fletcher, John, 73, 94
Fletcher, Mary Bosanquet, 66, 69, 72-76, 93, 277, 282
Fliedner, Theodor, 171, 175
Fordyce, James, 36-40, 47
Fox, George, 10, 40, 142
Fry, Elizabeth, 3, 116-21, 133, 165-68, 273, 277, 282

Gisbourne, Thomas, 36
Greg, W. R., 193
Gregory, John, 36f.
Grey, Margaretta, 161f., 164
Grey, Maria, G., 250f.
Grubb, Sarah Lynes, 41, 43-46